Deposit Accounts
A N D   S E R V I C E S

D1328868

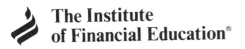

**The Institute
of Financial Education**®

Printed in the United States of America

Copyright © 1990 by The Institute of Financial Education

6 7 8 / 10 9 8

All rights reserved. No part of this publication may be reproduced, stored in a retrieval system or transmitted, in any form or by any means, electronic, mechanical, photocopying, recording or otherwise, without the written permission of the publisher.

The material in this publication was believed to be accurate at the time it was written. Due to the evolving nature of laws and regulations on this subject, The Institute of Financial Education makes no guarantee as to the accuracy or completeness of the information contained in this publication. The material in this book does not purport to be advice. If legal advice or other specialized services and knowledge are required, readers should seek a competent professional. Examples, including names and titles are purely fictitious and are not intended to represent actual financial institutions nor any real persons, living or dead.

ISBN 0-912857-53-6

Library of Congress Catalog Card Number: 89-85856

Requests for permission to make copies of any part of the work should be mailed to Permissions, The Institute of Financial Education, 111 East Wacker Drive, Chicago, IL 60601-4680.

C O N T E N T S

P R E F A C E

The term "deposit" is derived from Latin roots that mean "to put away." For customers of financial institutions, a deposit account is a means to put away funds for safekeeping. Customers entrust their funds to depository institutions so that they can meet their money management and investment goals. However, employees of financial institutions do not view deposits as funds that are "put away." These individuals accept the active responsibility for the care and maintenance of these funds. They are responsible for helping demonstrate that the customer's trust is justified.

To carry out their responsibilities, employees need to be knowledgeable about many aspects of opening these accounts. With that view in mind, the Institute has developed this revised edition of *Deposit Accounts and Services.* This text provides information that counselors can use to aid customers with the important decisions they must make when they open deposit accounts. In particular, the content of this text can help customers make three important decisions:

- What type of investment should this account be? A checking account? Savings account? Money market account? Certificate of deposit?

- What type of ownership is proper for these funds? Individual? Joint tenancy? Trust? Or, some other type?

- What related services can enhance the value of this account? An automated teller machine card? Overdraft protection? Mailed interest checks? Or, other services?

This text helps a counselor supply the information a customer needs to make these critical decisions. The first two chapters of this book lay the foundation for the study

of deposit accounts by introducing important characteristics of depositors, depository institutions and account
opening procedures. Then, Chapters 3 and 4 convey important features and benefits of deposit accounts as investments. Chapters 5 through 10 relate information
about account ownerships while Chapter 11 discusses
the wide range of services related to deposit accounts.
Throughout these chapters, the text recognizes and includes many important legislative, regulatory and judicial actions that have affected depository institutions.

Dale C. Bottom
President
The Institute of Financial Education
December, 1989

ACKNOWLEDGMENTS

Instructional Design

Catherine M. Izor — Project Manager/Writer
Christopher J. Ernst — Writer
Edward Rozalewicz — Writer
Ruby DauSchmidt — Word Processing Operator
Beverly Johnson — Word Processing Operator
Gaye Matravers — Word Processing Operator

Design and Production

Jean Lou Hess — Project Coordinator/Editor
Paula Cafferata — Designer
Janet Hill — Designer
Michael Tapia — Production Manager

This textbook was developed under the direction of Gail Rafter Meneley, Vice President, and John Schmidt, AIA, Vice President.

Institute textbooks are created under the guidance of two department directors: Naomi W. Peralta, Instructional Design, and Robert W. Brown, Design and Production.

A special thank you goes to the following individuals who contributed to the content of the manuscript:

Patrick Culhane, Arlington Heights, Illinois;
Roberta Driggett, Hales Corners, Wisconsin;
Kim B. Gates, Chicago, Illinois;
Lynn M. Gust, Milwaukee, Wisconsin;
Ruta Juska, Chicago, Illinois;
Michael B. Reddy, Chicago, Illinois;
Thomas R. Toman, Chicago, Illinois.

Figures

The Institute thanks the following organizations for permitting us to reprint their documents in this book:

SAF Systems and Forms, Inc., Chicago, Illinois; Thomas Cook, Princeton, New Jersey; Wisconsin Legal Blank Co., Inc., Milwaukee, Wisconsin.

Chapter Opening Photographs

The following organizations have granted permission for their documents and items to be displayed within the listed chapter opening photograph: Chapter 5: Equitable Bank, SSB, Hales Corners, Wisconsin. Chapter 8: George E. Cole Legal Forms. Chapter 9: Copied with permission, © Carlton Cards. Chapter 10: George E. Cole Legal Forms; **The Executor's Manual**, by Charles K. Plotnik and Stephen R. Leimberg, Doubleday & Co., Inc.: Garden City, New York, 1986. Chapter 11: ® Cash Station is a registered trademark of Cash Station, Inc., Reprinted with the permission of Citicorp Savings of Illinois; Thomas Cook, Princeton, New Jersey; VISA, the Three Bands Design and the Stylized C are registered service marks of Visa International and are reproduced with permission.

Deposit Accounts
AND SERVICES

CHAPTER

1

Depositors and Depository Institutions

KEY CONCEPTS

- Three stages in developing a personal investment plan;

- The relationship of risk and return, and its effect on an individual's investment goals;

- Three major factors that influence a depositor when choosing a depository institution;

- The role of *financial intermediaries* in the investment process;

- The importance of *diversification* in a personal investment program;

- Key characteristics of the four major types of depository institutions;

- Ownership and control of stock and mutual institutions;

- Stockholders' rights in a stock institution and members' rights in a mutual institution;

- The function of proxies in mutual and stock depository institutions.

John walked into First State Bank and asked the receptionist about opening a savings account. She directed him to Carol, a counselor in the new accounts department. Carol helped John open a regular savings account.

This type of scene takes place in thousands of financial institutions every working day. Deposit accounts are a widespread and heavily used service that depository institutions offer to customers. For many customers, opening a deposit account may be the first step in a lifelong investment plan.

This chapter explores the reasons people use deposit accounts and services, the process they follow in planning a personal investment program and the bases on which they choose a depository institution. It examines the four major types of depository institutions: savings associations, savings banks, commercial banks and credit unions. Finally, the chapter explains in greater detail the two forms of corporate ownership used by these institutions: stock and mutual.

DEPOSIT ACCOUNTS AND THE INDIVIDUAL

To understand how deposit accounts relate to the individual, counselors need to consider the accounts from the viewpoint of the consumer. When customers invest funds in deposit accounts, they may be doing so as part of an overall investment plan. First, consumers think through their financial situation. Their first priority, of course, is setting aside adequate funds for living expenses. But once they have covered this area, people may desire a personal investment plan that goes beyond their immediate needs.

The process of developing an investment plan typically has three stages:

- set investment goals;

- design an investment program;

- choose an investment provider.

Setting Investment Goals

As noted above, a first step in the investment process is to set goals. For example, an individual may have a short-term goal of accumulating savings for a vacation later in the year and a long-term goal of owning a home in 10 years. From time to time, the person may add new goals as he or she achieves or reevaluates existing ones.

Some consumers may have rather vague or overly broad goals such as a general desire to save money for the future. With such unfocused goals, they may have more difficulty making an investment plan. Counselors can help these customers make decisions about their investment plans by encouraging them to set specific goals.

As consumers refine their goals, they consider two factors: risk and return of investments. They desire both safety and maximum profit for their funds. Of course, they want to place their money in an immediately accessible, risk-free investment and receive the highest possible rate of return. However, such an investment does not exist. In the real world, depositors, as investors, must be willing to make some compromises.

Most experts believe risk and return of investments have an inverse relationship. A general concept of investing is that the higher the risk to the investor, the greater the potential return. The opposite is also true: lower risk probably results in a smaller profit. A deposit account in a financial institution is one of the safer investments. Therefore, investors should expect its potential return to be smaller than higher-risk investments.

Risk does not only mean that an individual may lose his or her investment dollars; it also indicates the possibility that the person may not get the desired rate of return. Since all investments carry some degree of risk, consumers must select goals that are compatible with the degree of risk they are willing to assume. For example, an individual who wishes to save for the downpayment on a house may find that a high-risk investment will produce yields that will help the downpayment accumulate fairly quickly. *If* all goes well, the time frame for achieving this goal can be five years. But if all does not go well, the downpayment can take several years longer to accumulate.

The individual may also consider a lower-risk investment that offers a lower yield but greater assurance of safety and guaranteed yield. With this investment, the downpayment may take six years. However, this person may decide that, with such an important goal, lowering the uncertainty about risk is more advisable than gambling on a higher-yield but higher-risk investment.

Low-risk options such as deposit accounts and homeownership appeal to large numbers of individuals. After these are in place, people often choose to acquire a variety of other assets to spread risk or to maximize return.

Designing a Sound Investment Program

Once they have established goals and weighed risks, individuals face the task of designing a general investment plan. This is difficult because, when laying plans for action today, investors must also keep an eye on the future. In this attempt, investors try to hedge against an assortment of contingencies.

Life and health insurance are investments that protect individuals against the contingency of premature death or costly medical expenses. Insurance thus protects against the chance of losing current income levels.

Retirement investments are another category of long-range financial protection that people include in investment programs. Typical retirement investments may include products such as annuities and Individual Retirement Accounts. Because they can supplement employer-provided pension and Social Security retirement benefits, they reduce the uncertainty about income for future years.

At the same time, an individual or family can begin to set aside a certain percentage of income in an insured deposit account and receive an attractive interest rate for future financial profit.

Homeownership is another basic step in a sound investment program for many individuals and families. In many instances, homeownership is a wise investment because:

- it provides a further means of saving through the potential for appreciation of the value of the real estate;

- it results in increased equity when the mortgage loan balance is reduced; and

- it may provide tax deductions.

At the same time they are making mortgage payments, investors can make regular additions to deposit accounts. As income increases and these savings grow, customers can invest a portion of these funds in higher-risk—but also higher-yielding—assets.

Depending on the state of the economy, stocks or bonds may be a logical next step in a sound investment program. An investment in industry in the form of high-quality stocks or high-grade bonds can sometimes be used as a hedge against the possibility of future inflation. However, experts point out that no one should buy stocks or other higher-risk assets unless he or she can adequately cover living expenses, has sufficient insurance coverage in force, and has already set aside funds in a deposit account to meet emergency and retirement needs.

Investing funds in a variety of financial products usually results in a *diversification* of assets. The objective of diversification is to yield a higher return on investments while decreasing risk. The individual usually invests a small portion of the assets in riskier investments and balances the portfolio with an assortment of low-risk investments.

Effective diversification is part of the process of meeting an investor's goals and needs. From investments, the investor can realize several types of income such as interest, dividends, rent and capital gains. Also, the individual can consider tax benefits and tax shelters for increasing income. The investment media selected and the economic sector from which they are derived should reflect the investor's objective of decreasing or controlling risk. Figure 1-1 illustrates how diversification of an investment portfolio can fit into an overall financial plan.

In the past, depository institutions offered only regular savings accounts to their savers. Today, depository institutions are better able to offer individuals more of the products and services necessary for a sound investment program. For example, mutual funds and various certificate of deposit accounts offer individuals more variety

Diversification as Part of an Investment Plan

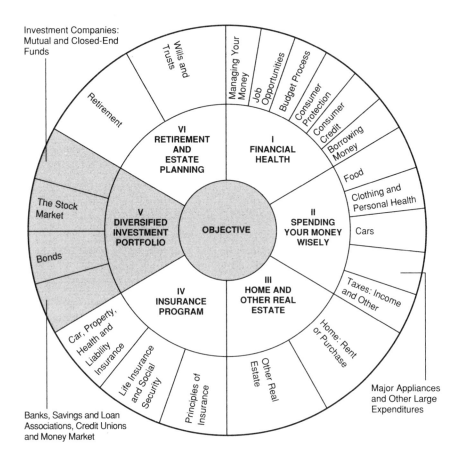

Stillman's schematic presentation of the six major areas of personal finance by Professor Richard J. Stillman. Taken from his book: *Guide to Personal Finance: A Lifetime Program of Money Management.* 5th Ed. Prentice-Hall, 1988. Reprinted with permission.

in their financial planning. Individuals are finding that they no longer need to do business simultaneously with a savings institution, a bank, a credit union, a mutual fund and a brokerage house in order to diversify their investment portfolios.

Choosing a Depository Institution

As with any investment decision, no two customers choose a specific depository institution for exactly the same reason. Many factors influence this choice. Surveys have shown that the three main factors influencing customer decisions are convenience, service and yield. Figure 1-2 breaks down these three main factors into more specific components. With this knowledge, institutions and counselors can better prepare to meet depositors' needs.

In this survey, customers rated several factors very highly. Convenience factors such as location and hours of operation strongly influenced a customer's choice of depository institution. For 74.2% of those surveyed, service factors such as employee courtesy and friendliness were of greatest importance in choosing, and staying with, a depository institution. Yield factors such as paying competitive rates on savings and charging competitive loan rates also ranked high among respondents.

The survey also asked people to describe their overall satisfaction with depository institutions. In response, the majority said they were very satisfied with their current depository institution. In contrast, 48.7% of depositors who were dissatisfied with any of the ranked factors had considered moving their business to another institution. This clearly shows that depositor loyalty to a particular institution can easily be affected by a proper mix of convenience, service and yield factors.

F I G U R E 1-2

Important Factors in Selecting a Depository Institution and Relative Satisfaction with Factors

Convenience Factors

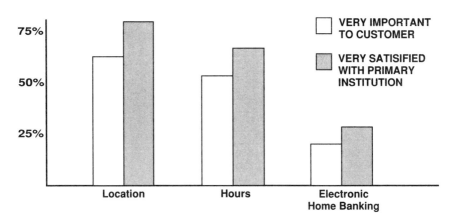

Service Factors

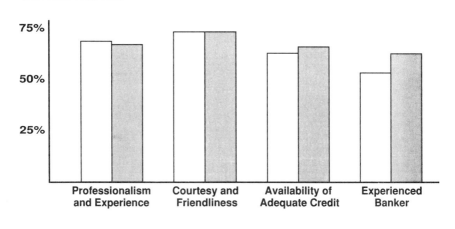

F I G U R E 1-2, Continued

Yield Factors

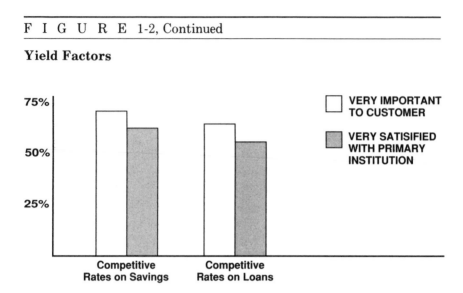

Source: *The Unidex Reports* (Atlanta: Unidex Corporation, January 1987).

Obviously, depository institutions differ in factors that customers consider important. But these institutions also differ in other ways. The remainder of this chapter reviews significant organizational similarities and differences among the four major types of depository institutions.

DEPOSITORY INSTITUTIONS AS FINANCIAL INTERMEDIARIES

A *financial intermediary* is an institution that accepts money from individuals and uses those funds to make loans and other investments in its own name. The institution acts as a go-between for customers with excess funds and customers that need to borrow funds. The process by which a depository institution accepts funds from depositors and channels funds to borrowers is called *intermediation*. Financial intermediaries are needed by many customers who lack the expertise, the time or the minimum assets needed for complex investment options. These depositors prefer the ease and safety of dealing with such institutions over investing directly in a variety of more complicated investments.

A movement away from the use of financial intermediaries is called disintermediation. *Disintermediation* occurs when investors take out the money they have placed in deposit accounts at financial institutions and invest it in open market securities such as government bonds, state and local government obligations, and, often, direct loans. Disintermediation is a concern for financial intermediaries. As depositors withdraw funds from a depository institution, the institution may have to change its operations. It may need to find additional sources of investment dollars or implement other strategies until the flow of funds regains a balance.

The four major types of depository institutions are commercial banks, savings associations, savings banks, and credit unions. The following section gives a brief overview of the purpose, deposit and lending activities, organizational structure, and asset size of each form. The investment portfolios of these institutions contain mainly prime securities and real estate assets. A comparison of the asset compositions is shown in Figure 1-3.

Savings Associations

Savings associations generally operate with a twofold purpose: to promote thrift and homeownership. The

---

F I G U R E 1-3

Asset Composition Compared

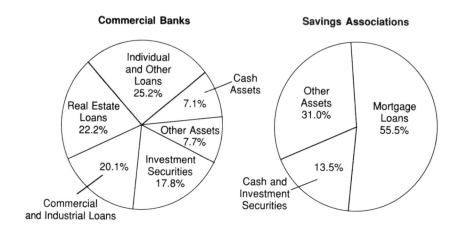

Commercial Banks

Individual and Other Loans 25.2%

Cash Assets 7.1%

Real Estate Loans 22.2%

Other Assets 7.7%

Investment Securities 17.8%

20.1%

Commercial and Industrial Loans

Savings Associations

Other Assets 31.0%

Mortgage Loans 55.5%

13.5%

Cash and Investment Securities

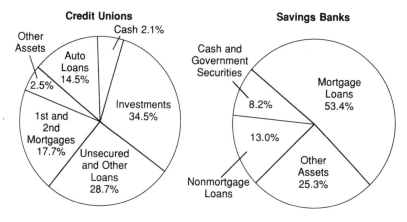

Credit Unions

Cash 2.1%

Other Assets

Auto Loans 14.5%

2.5%

Investments 34.5%

1st and 2nd Mortgages 17.7%

Unsecured and Other Loans 28.7%

Savings Banks

Cash and Government Securities

Mortgage Loans 53.4%

8.2%

13.0%

Other Assets 25.3%

Nonmortgage Loans

association accomplishes this purpose by taking in deposits from customers and investing the funds, primarily in mortgage loans to borrowers.

Deposits made at a savings association normally earn interest for the depositor and can be invested in a variety of ways. The interest paid can be considered a fee the association pays for the use of the depositor's funds. Interest earned on deposits also encourages the depositor to save money at the association. Deposit accounts at savings associations can include passbook savings, certificates of deposit, retirement accounts, NOW (checking) accounts and a variety of other options.

Savings associations promote homeownership through home mortgage financing. Over half the loans made by savings associations are for the purpose of financing the purchase of a home. Other lending activities of a savings association may include home equity loans, home improvement loans, auto loans, personal loans and a variety of other credit activities.

Savings associations have several other characteristics. As a corporation, a savings association may be either a mutual or a capital stock institution, and may be organized under state or federal charter. At the end of 1988, there were 1,123 federally chartered associations and 1,205 state-chartered associations. These associations held a total of $925.7 billion in assets and $675.7 billion in total deposits.

Depending on regional differences and preferences, savings associations are known by a variety of names, including savings and loans and homestead associations. Savings associations and savings banks (discussed in the next section) are generally referred to as *savings institutions* or *thrift institutions*.

Savings Banks

Savings banks were organized in the early 1800s to encourage thrift and provide a safe and profitable place for industrial workers to save. Unlike savings associations, savings banks at first had no commitment to finance housing and, in fact, invested heavily in bonds. Over the years, however, mortgage loans came to be considered a worthwhile investment of depositors' funds and currently amount to about 53% of total assets for savings banks. Deposit accounts and loans available at savings banks today are almost identical to those offered by savings associations.

Savings banks originally were allowed to operate only as state-chartered and mutually owned institutions; now they can convert to federal charter. A federally chartered savings bank can be either a mutual or a stock institution.

At the end of 1988, there were 1,113 savings banks in the United States with combined assets of $710 billion and total deposits of $518.3 billion.

Commercial Banks

The term "commercial" describes the operational purpose of a *commercial bank*: to facilitate and finance commerce and business. To accomplish this, commercial banks gear much of their deposit accounts and services to the business customer. Commercial banks may offer deposit accounts and loans to individuals, but these services often make up a small part of their business activities.

Deposit accounts offered at commercial banks can include demand deposit accounts (checking), NOW accounts, savings accounts, certificates of deposit, retirement plans and a variety of other business and personal accounts. Loans made by commercial banks can include loans to commerce and industry, real estate loans, individual loans and loans to other banks.

A commercial bank is a privately owned capital stock corporation that may be chartered under state law as a state bank or under federal law as a national bank. At the end of 1988, there were 13,114 commercial banks with combined assets of $3,030.8 billion and total deposits of $2,141.6 billion.

Credit Unions

A *credit union* is a mutually owned and operated depository institution that provides its members with deposit accounts and loans. First appearing in the United States in the early 1900s, credit unions were organized to promote thrift among members and to make loans to them from the accumulated savings.

Credit unions are distinguishable from other types of depository institutions by their "common bond" requirement for membership. In order to become a member and thereby take advantage of the services the credit union offers, a person must share a specified trait (common bond) with the other members. This common bond may be as specific as being an employee of the business firm that sponsors the credit union or as broad as being a resident of the geographical area the credit union serves.

Deposit accounts at credit unions are called *share accounts*, depositors are called *shareholders* and the return shareholders receive is called *dividends*. Regular share accounts are similar to regular savings accounts in that they usually require a small minimum balance, allow for frequent deposits and withdrawals, and pay dividends. Other deposit accounts and services available to credit union members can be share drafts (the equivalent of an interest-bearing checking account), share certificates and retirement accounts.

Most lending by credit unions takes the form of auto and personal loans to members. In recent years, credit unions have increased the amount of their loans for home mortgages; in 1988, this type of lending amounted to over 17% of total assets.

Credit unions may be organized under either a federal or state charter, and must be mutually owned and operated. At the end of 1988, there were 15,808 credit unions with $194.5 billion in combined assets and $174.8 billion in total deposits.

ORGANIZATION AND OWNERSHIP OF DEPOSITORY INSTITUTIONS

Depository institutions have specific corporate structures. To conduct business as a depository institution, the company must first obtain a charter. A *charter* is a legal authorization to conduct business and may be granted by either the state or federal government.

Depository institutions may be further categorized by their form of ownership. A savings institution may be either a mutual or a stock institution. Commercial banks cannot be mutually owned, while credit unions must be mutually owned. Although their structures differ, mutual and stock institutions offer many of the same deposit accounts and services.

This section examines depository institutions as corporations. It also explores some of the similarities and differences between mutual and stock institutions, as well as conversion of institutions from mutual to stock ownership.

The Depository Institution as a Corporation

By law, depository institutions are organized as corporations. A *corporation* is a group of persons who have legally organized into a business unit for a common purpose.

A corporation operates as a legal entity separate from the persons who organized and/or control it. This characteristic allows the corporation to act as an "artificial person." This means that it may buy, sell and hold property, as well as make contracts in its own name. Unlike the individual members of the organization, the corporation may continue to exist long after the original organizers are gone.

The Concept of Mutual Ownership

Mutuality refers to the equality of status and opportunity among members. In a mutual depository institution, all depositors and borrowers in the association are members of the institution. As members they are owners of the institution and have a voice in approving institution policies and electing the board of directors. A member with a $100 deposit account in a mutual institution has the same types of rights as a member with a $50,000 money market account or a borrower with a $75,000 outstanding mortgage balance.

The Concept of Stock Ownership

Stock institutions differ from mutual institutions because they can sell stock in the organization. When a corporation issues stock, it actually sells an ownership interest in itself. Stockholders, like members of a mutual corporation, have a say in approving institution policies and electing the board of directors. Depositors and borrowers in a stock institution are not owners and therefore have no say in the institution's operations, unless they also own stock in the institution.

Rights and Privileges of Members and Stockholders

Although a mutual institution and a stock institution may offer depositors essentially the same services, members of a mutual institution have rights and privileges different from those of stockholders in a stock institution.

Stockholders' Rights
Ownership of stock entitles the stockholder to a proportionate ownership in the undivided assets of the corporation and, often, other rights. These rights include the right to dividends, the right to vote and the right to subscribe to new offerings of stock.

Stockholders often have the right to the earnings of a corporation through the payment of dividends. However, the right to dividends is not a guarantee when purchasing stock. The board of directors of the corporation decides whether to pay a dividend based on, among other things, company profits.

Stockholders may also have a right to proportionate control of the company through voting power. Generally, the number of votes stockholders have depends on the number of shares they own. Voting usually occurs at the annual meeting of the shareholders and may include agenda items such as company policy changes, election or removal of directors, and amendment of the association bylaws.

Another stockholder right is the ability to purchase new offerings of stock from the company prior to the stocks being offered to the public. The right to purchase the new stock is directly proportionate to the amount of stock the individual currently owns. This right affords the stockholder the opportunity to maintain the same proportionate ownership interest in the company when it issues new stock.

Members' Rights

Members of a mutual institution have many of the same rights as stockholders in a stock institution. For example, a member of a mutual institution is entitled to attend the institution's annual meeting and cast votes for agenda items such as selection or removal of directors, approval of corporate policy, and amendment of the bylaws. Depending on the type of depository institution, members may be restricted to one-person, one-vote (credit unions), or have more votes, up to a limit, depending on their account balances (savings institutions). In addition, members may ask to inspect corporate books and records, as well as request and receive information regarding their own accounts.

One major difference in rights is that members of a mutual institution generally do not share in the immediate profits and losses of the institution as stockholders do. The rights and privileges of members and stockholders are compared in Figure 1-4.

F I G U R E 1-4

**Comparison of Stock and Mutual Institutions—
Members and Stockholder Rights and Privileges**

Stock Institution	Mutual Institution
Owned by stockholders	Owned by members (depositors and borrowers)
Profits and losses shared by stockholders	Depositors do not share in profits and losses
Stockholders vote on such items as institution board members and policies	Members vote on such items as institution board members and policies
Proxy granted by stockholders	Proxy granted by members (except for credit unions)

Proxy Regulations

A *proxy* is a written authorization that the member or shareholder grants to another person or committee to cast the individual's vote(s). Like corporations, both mutual and stock institutions must be concerned with the solicitation and administration of proxies. The only exception to this is credit unions. Federal credit union regulations prohibit members from voting by proxy. However, mail ballots are permitted in some cases.

As a practical matter, most members and stockholders of other depository institutions vote by proxy. In a mutual savings institution, many of the members are more interested in the investments the institution offers than exercising their voting rights as owners. A similar situation may exist with stockholders whose sole interest is the investment value of the stock.

A proxy normally is revocable by the issuer (the stockholder or member). This feature is important for a member who signs a proxy and later decides to attend the meeting and cast his or her vote in person.

A proxy may be continuous or limited in duration, depending on state law. In most states, proxies are continuous until canceled; in a few states, however, proxies may last no longer than 12 months, 24 months or some other specific time period. In either case, a proxy is no longer effective once the member or stockholder cancels it.

Proxy and the Mutual Savings Institution

Mutual savings institutions commonly solicit a revocable, continuous proxy at the time a deposit account is opened (see Figure 1-5). This is because the customer (member) is readily available to sign the card at that time. The counselor can give a short but complete explanation of the purpose of a proxy before the customer signs the proxy card. Institution policy will dictate how the counselor processes unsigned proxy cards.

Ten general rules of proxy administration apply when the institution accepts an executed proxy card:

- The signature on the proxy should appear exactly as the member's name appears on the institution's records.

- A joint tenancy account requiring all signatures for withdrawals requires a proxy signed by all joint tenants.

F I G U R E 1-5

Revocable Proxy

```
┌─────────────────────────────────────────────────────────────────────────┐
│                                                                           │
│   ┌──────────────────┐   _____      _____     │
│   (Social Security Number)         (Date)              (Account Number)    │
│                                                                           │
│            (Name of Member)                                               │
│   I appoint the members of the Board of Directors in office from time to time of │
│                                                                           │
│   as my proxy and authorize a majority of all such members in my absence at any meeting of members │
│   of said institution to cast any votes I would be entitled to cast if personally present, on any and all │
│   matters, from time to time, and from year to year, until this proxy is canceled by a writing delivered │
│   to said institution, said type of writing to include a subsequently issued proxy, and I authorize such │
│   a majority of said Directors (Trustees) to cast my vote or votes, or to designate a person or persons │
│   to cast my vote or votes, provided that such designation complies with applicable regulations issued │
│   by the Federal Home Loan Bank Board.                                    │
│                                                                           │
│   REVOCABLE PROXY          _____                    │
│   TO DIRECTORS                      (Signature)                           │
│   (TRUSTEES)               _____                    │
│                                     (Signature)                           │
│   14686 12/85                                                             │
│   406 BD                                        SAF Systems and Forms      │
└─────────────────────────────────────────────────────────────────────────┘
```

- A joint tenancy account permitting either joint tenant to act requires the signature of only one joint tenant on the proxy.

- Each joint tenancy account representing a different combination of joint owners constitutes a different membership, and, as such, the account holder may appoint a proxy to cast the maximum number of votes eligible for one member.

- A trustee or other fiduciary holding an account may perform the routine administrative act of executing a proxy for use at an annual or special meeting.

- A certified copy of the directors' resolution authorizing the corporate officer to sign the proxy should accompany a corporate proxy.

- In the case of conflicting proxies from the same account holder, the institution should accept the proxy with the latest execution date. In the absence of execution dates, most institutions consider postmarks.

- If proxies are lost or stolen, no known remedy applies other than to obtain new proxies.

- The institution should not solicit undated or post-dated proxies.

- No proxy should be part of any other document or instrument.

Proxy and the Stock Depository Institution

Depositors or borrowers in a stock institution are not affected by proxy regulations since they do not have the right to vote. Because of this, the depositor or borrower does not sign a proxy card when opening an account at a stock institution; the institution will solicit proxies from the stockholders.

Conversion from a Mutual to a Stock Savings Institution

In recent years, there has been a trend for mutual savings institutions to convert to stock ownership. Although an institution may do so for various reasons, the primary purpose is to raise capital through the sale of stock.

Federally chartered mutual savings institutions were first allowed to convert to stock institutions in 1974. Before then, all institutions operating with a federal charter were required to be mutual associations. Between 1975 and 1988, 827 institutions converted from mutual to stock ownership.

Increased capital from stock conversion can help institutions diversify their investment portfolios and invest in a greater variety of instruments. Among the investment areas practical for stock savings institutions are land development, mortgage banking and consumer finance.

Conversion to stock ownership, however, entails taking a risk. Once converted, the institution is accountable to its stockholders. The stockholders expect the institution to operate soundly and return a profit in the form of dividends or capital appreciation of the stock. If the institution is not profitable, its stock will have little or no market.

The members and board of directors of a mutual institution decide whether to convert the institution to a stock institution. This is an important decision because, after conversion, the depositors and borrowers will have no ownership rights unless they are stockholders. They will no longer have a voice in approving the policies and operations of the institution, although they will have the option to purchase stock and share in the success of the institution as stockholders.

The approval and the actual conversion are a lengthy process for an institution, and staff members become involved in several ways. In particular, they may help by responding to customer inquiries about the change.

SUMMARY

Prior to choosing a particular investment or depository institution, an individual usually establishes goals and objectives. These can be either general or specific, but achievable goals are most practical. While the depositor weighs many factors when choosing an investment, the main considerations typically are risk and return. The process of choosing a variety of investment options in order to minimize risk and maximize return is known as diversification.

Investors have many reasons for choosing one particular depository institution over another. Although the specific factors influencing an investor's choice of institution differ for each individual, the three basic factors are convenience, service and yield.

Depository institutions are called financial intermediaries; the process of accepting deposits and using the funds to make loans and other investments is called intermediation.

Four major categories of depository institution are savings associations, savings banks, commercial banks and credit unions. Although they differ in scope and customer-institution relationship, most feature government-sponsored insurance of accounts. Thus, funds in depositors' accounts are secure (within regulatory guidelines) regardless of the type of depository institution that holds them.

Depository institutions may be chartered by either the federal or state government. Some institutions may also be of either mutual or stock ownership. Depositors in mutual institutions, as members, are considered owners of the institution and thus have certain rights and privileges. Stock institutions are owned by the shareholders, and the depositors have no voting rights.

Opening Deposit Accounts

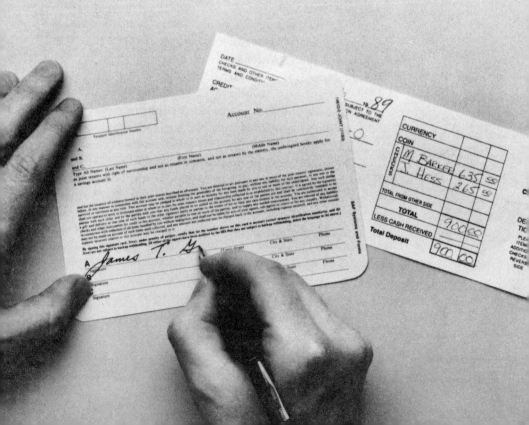

KEY CONCEPTS

- The role of the counselor when opening new accounts;

- Three decisions customers must make when opening deposit accounts;

- Components of the deposit account contract;

- Parties involved in the deposit account contract;

- Purpose of new-account documents and their standard components;

- Definitions of *power of attorney, stop payment order* and *suspension order;*

- Obtaining of tax identification numbers;

- Currency transaction reporting requirements;

- Restrictions and uses of check holds and account holds;

- Situations that require a new account contract.

A first impression is often a lasting one. The manner in which a counselor initially greets a customer, explains deposit accounts, asks questions and opens the account builds the foundation of the customer's business relationship with the financial institution. Because of this, friendliness, professionalism and technical competence are essential for counselors. They must be well informed about all of the products and services their institution offers and understand the nature of the deposit account contract.

This chapter explains the role of the counselor and describes how the counselor can aid customers' decision making. Then it discusses the parties involved in the deposit account contract and the documents the counselor works with when opening an account. Next, it describes how the counselor fulfills both institutional policies and legal responsibilities when he or she obtains and verifies customer information such as tax identification numbers, and processes transactions in accordance with requirements such as check-hold laws. Finally, it examines certain events that may require closing an existing deposit account and opening a new one.

THE ROLE OF THE COUNSELOR

For the purposes of this text, counselors are the representatives of financial institutions who help customers open new deposit accounts. These employees have various job titles at different institutions, such as customer service representative, new accounts counselor, savings counselor or financial services counselor, but they all hold an important position within their institution. They are responsible for providing customers with sufficient information to select the right type of account while at the same time protecting the financial institution's interests. To fulfill this dual responsibility, counselors must be competent in each of the following areas:

- providing professional customer service;

- aiding customers' decision making;

- counseling customers without practicing law.

Providing Professional Customer Service

Most customers value the quality of service at their financial institution. Various surveys have shown that much customer satisfaction is based on the quality of service customers receive and dissatisfaction may lead customers to take their business to another institution. In a survey of customers who had changed their primary financial institution, the largest group (25%) said they switched because they had changed residences. But the next largest group (21%) changed their primary financial institution due to poor service and employee errors.[1] These results show that the quality of customer service can indeed have a significant impact on an institution's ability to retain customers.

What defines professional customer service? What elements differentiate excellent service from poor service? According to a senior vice president at a southwestern bank, "What constitutes good quality service for one person may not be important to another. Not everyone wants it the same way. However, there are some basics that all service personnel must offer. These include product knowledge, courtesy, accuracy and speed of transaction.

Professionalism also ranks high in the perceived value of service. In many cases, friendliness and genuineness overcomes slowness or lack of great knowledge."[2]

Counselors can show their commitment to professional customer service in many ways. In particular, counselors can work to improve their skills in the four areas quoted above.

Product Knowledge

Counselors should develop their knowledge of investment products offered by their institution and by competitors. To learn about their own institution's products, they can study the institution's brochures and procedures. They can also ask questions of experienced employees who have worked with the institution's full range of investment products. To learn more about competitor's products, counselors can attend training programs, classes or seminars on investment topics. They can obtain brochures and advertisements from competitors and compare them to their own institution's products. By making comparisons, the counselor can determine the competitive advantages of their institution's products.

Courtesy

Whenever in contact with customers, counselors should demonstrate courtesy because an institution's success depends on attracting and keeping customers. A meeting between a counselor and a prospective customer is a business meeting and should be conducted as such. The counselor begins the meeting by welcoming the customer. An appropriate greeting, such as "Hello" or "Good morning" may be followed by an introduction such as "I'm Chuck Weaver. Please, have a seat," or "My name is Karen Templeton." The greeting and introduction should be businesslike, but not cold or overly formal. A pleasant voice, a friendly smile and perhaps a handshake can help put the customer at ease.

Once the customer is seated and comfortable, the counselor should give undivided attention to him or her. Counselors gain the best results by asking tactful questions, providing thorough explanations and answering questions patiently.

Accuracy

Accuracy is a third important quality of good customer service. Sound product knowledge is the source of correct information about services, but accuracy goes beyond full and complete knowledge of products. A counselor also must take the appropriate actions when opening accounts or initiating other services. Counselors can improve accuracy by double-checking their intended actions before carrying them out, such as verbally verifying customers' requests. They can also avoid procedural shortcuts, such as assuming certain documents can be completed after a customer has gone. Important information might be overlooked and be difficult to obtain later, and errors could result.

Speed

Customers value speed as long as accuracy and courtesy are not sacrificed. Counselors can develop speed in several ways. First, they can maintain organized desks and work areas where supplies are quickly available. They can develop work patterns that will enable them to handle routine situations smoothly. Learning their jobs thoroughly will also help improve speed because knowledgeable counselors seldom need to seek other employees' advice.

Aiding Customer Decision Making

Customers make several decisions when they open deposit accounts. In some cases, customers may have made these decisions before seeking out a counselor, but very often customers make such decisions while meeting with a counselor. During this meeting, the counselor can help the customer make the best decisions for his or her circumstances. For example, the counselor can describe savings options, such as various certificates of deposit, that will help the customer understand how the institution's services can meet his or her needs. Although the customer ultimately makes the decisions, the counselor can help ensure that these decisions are based on accurate and complete information.

When opening deposit accounts, customers typically make decisions about the following three items:

- investment type;

- account ownership;

- related services.

These three types of decisions are covered in the remaining chapters of this book.

Investment Type

One of the key decisions the depositor must make concerns the type of investment. Should he or she open a checking account, a regular savings account, a money market account or one of the other types of accounts the institution offers? Quite often, this is also the first decision that a customer considers.

This decision has become more difficult for customers due to an increase in the number of options. The variety of investment products has swelled to a bewildering array, and customers have more account information to consider before making an appropriate choice. Decisions become more difficult when people are faced with many options. In fact, one marketing consultant reports that customers are less satisfied with some aspects of service at financial institutions because of the increase in the number of complex products. As she says, "There are so many things to choose from, and there just isn't any good information available. Advice is a critical part of the service component and it may be that banks are not delivering."[3]

Counselors can help their institutions gain a competitive edge and improve customer service by providing clear information about their institutions' investment products. They can also learn their customers' investment goals and help them choose deposit accounts that will meet their objectives. Chapters 3 and 4 describe what counselors need to know to help customers make optimal investment decisions.

Account Ownership

The second decision customers make when opening deposit accounts concerns the type of account ownership. *Ownership* means holding a lawful claim or title to property. Cars and homes are common types of property which individuals own. Like these assets, deposit accounts can be owned by one or more persons.

Complete ownership of money or property consists of two elements:

- the legal title or ownership; and

- the right to use or benefit from the money or property. This is called *beneficial ownership* or the equitable interest.

These elements developed from two separate sources in Anglo-American law: common law and equity. While these two branches of law have now merged, the distinction between "legal" and "equitable" interests in property remains. Legal owners hold title to property. Equitable owners have the right to use or benefit from property. These two types of ownership were originally split between the king of England and his feudal lords.

Today, this split-ownership is most often the result of the creation of a trust or the making of a specifically enforceable contract. In these cases, the trustee or the seller may retain the "legal" title to the property in question, but they hold it solely for the benefit of the "equitable" title holder. They can be sued for violating their fiduciary duties to the holder of the beneficial interest in the property. Therefore, a person can be said to have "complete ownership" of property only when that person holds both the legal title and the beneficial interest in that property.

In addition to split ownership, more than one person can hold both the legal title and beneficial interest. For example, in joint tenancies, the account holder shares the elements of ownership with others.

The rights and responsibilities of both account owners and institutions are inherent in all forms of account ownership. The depositor's competency and the form of ownership he or she chooses, as well as various laws and regulations, legally determine the rights to control, protect and eventually dispose of deposit accounts.

Depositors can choose from a variety of ownership forms, each providing different rights and responsibilities to the owner. Counselors can help customers decide which forms of account ownership are best suited for their particular needs.

When choosing among ownership alternatives, customers must answer the following questions in order to make an appropriate choice. These questions relate to the beneficial ownership of the funds.

- *Who controls the funds?* With some forms of ownership, the owner controls the funds. In other forms, the owner has little or no control or possession of the money.

- *What is the eventual disposition of the funds?* The form of ownership determines the recipient of the funds in the event of the account holder's death, court-judged incompetency or, in the case of a business, dissolution.

An additional concern for customers is to obtain maximum protection for deposited funds through deposit insurance from federal insuring agencies. Maximum insurance protection is partially determined by ownership decisions when the account is opened. This text focuses on the legal foundations of account ownership. Insurance of accounts is covered in more detail in other publications such as *Insurance of Accounts*, published by The Institute of Financial Education.

Chapters 5 through 10 of this text cover the following forms of ownership:

- single ownership (including individual and corporation);

- joint tenancy;

- partnership;

- tenancy in common;

- tenancy by the entirety (recognized in some states);

- community property (recognized in some states);

- fiduciary;

- retirement plans.

Related Services

The third important decision customers make when opening deposit accounts is whether they need to initiate other, related services. These services perform functions similar to those of deposit accounts or are tied to a deposit account to enhance its value. Some customers have several financial planning goals in mind, and opening a deposit account will accomplish only one of them. In addition to an account, a customer may obtain an automated teller machine (ATM) card, apply for a credit card or get information on in-house brokerage services. A customer who opens a certificate of deposit may decide to have interest checks mailed. Other customers may not have planned to initiate additional services, but an alert counselor may find an opportunity to sell other services the institution offers.

Counselors need at least a basic knowledge of services related to deposit accounts to help customers make decisions about using these products. Chapter 11 includes information about related services that counselors can use to help customers make choices that match their investment and investment-related goals.

Counseling Customers Without Practicing Law

Counselors should only aid customers in their decision making; they should *not* make customers' decisions for them. One reason is that counselors can incur legal liability if their advice is construed as practicing law, because anyone who practices law must be licensed to do so. In addition, only natural persons may be authorized to practice law, and corporations are not natural persons. Since all financial institutions are chartered as corporations, they cannot practice law on behalf of others, either directly or indirectly.

However, opening a deposit account is not defined as practicing law. A deposit account is a legal contract between an account holder and an institution, but an attorney is not required to be involved for two reasons. First, negotiation and preparation of this contract are necessary for the institution to carry out its corporate purpose. Further, the parties to the contract are not required by law to conduct the transaction through an attorney. Therefore, opening an account is within the scope of the institution's authority and purpose and may be handled by any of its employees.

Avoiding the practice of law can be a troublesome area for counselors. Although counselors should be familiar with the law, they need to provide good service and sell products without overstepping the fine line between providing information and dispensing legal advice. *Providing information means stating facts about the institution's accounts and services; giving legal advice consists of offering opinions about correct customer actions.* If the counselor's words are construed as advice, the action may be illegal and possibly expose the institution to a lawsuit.

The problem of giving information without advice, for example, might occur when a parent wishes to give money to a child. After inquiring about the extent and nature of the proposed gift, the counselor can explain some of the options available to the parent. Some of these options might be an individual account, trust account (revocable or irrevocable), joint account or account arising under the Uniform Transfers to Minors Act (an account that is irrevocable until the child reaches the age of majority). After the counselor has fully explained these options, but refrained from recommending or endorsing any, the parent can choose the account most appropriate for his or her purpose.

As another example, consider this customer inquiry:

> I want to deposit my money in an account listing myself and my elderly mother as joint tenants. May I use my mother's social security number for tax purposes?

The following answer would be considered advice and could have legal repercussions:

> No, you have to give me your social security number, or else it will look like you are avoiding taxes.

In this case, the counselor has advised the customer on a matter related to income tax law. Consider the possible ramifications to the institution of recommending an improper tax identification number. Withholding and reporting regulations place a heavy burden on financial institutions to obtain accurate tax identification numbers. Inaccurate tax information could result in a penalty for the institution.

In addition, counselors must always keep in mind that state and federal laws (and all tax laws) are complicated and full of exceptions. Counselors do not have sufficient knowledge of any individual's entire estate to offer tax advice—another reason they are not allowed to practice law.

Here is a way to handle the above inquiry that gives only information:

I'm sorry, but I'm not in a position to give tax advice. The IRS provides guidelines for determining which social security number to use in the case of joint accounts. You also may want to talk with a tax consultant or attorney who is more familiar with your financial situation.

While the informational method helps the counselor to avoid practicing law, the counselor's manner can determine the success of this method in satisfying customers' needs. The informational method provides sufficient information for the customer to make a decision, but the counselor must use it in a helpful, friendly manner so that the customer will not feel as though he or she is being put off. The counselor's tone of voice should reflect a genuine concern even if giving specific advice is impossible. Although the counselor can provide factual information that will aid the customer's decision making, the counselor should stress that the *customer* must make the decision.

THE DEPOSIT ACCOUNT CONTRACT

After the customer has decided on the type of investment, the form of account ownership and related services, the next step is the actual opening of the deposit account. This step establishes the account contract and attaches certain contractual rights and responsibilities to each party. Counselors therefore need to understand the definition of a contract, the contractual nature of a deposit account and the parties involved in the deposit contract.

A *contract* is a binding agreement between two or more parties that is enforceable by law. It may be written or

oral and should thoroughly disclose all the terms and conditions of the transaction. This chapter deals only with
written contracts.

To create a contract that is legal, binding and valid,
the following five factors must exist:

- *The parties must be competent persons.* The parties to the deposit contract are the account owner
  (customer) and the financial institution.

- *The parties must mutually agree on the objective
  of the contract.* In a deposit contract, the two parties agree that title to the money deposited
  changes hands. The customer parts with the
  money and the institution accepts it, promising
  to deal with it in a specified manner.

- *The objective of the contract must be legal.* Depositing money is a perfectly legal objective.

- *Both parties must give and receive something of
  value for their promises.* This is also called mutuality of consideration. In a deposit contract, the
  customer and the financial institution possess
  mutuality of consideration. The customer receives
  security of his or her money and earns interest.
  The institution gains the opportunity to make
  profits by investing the customer's funds.

- *There must be the physical contract itself.* The
  terms and conditions of the deposit contract are
  in writing, although they may exist in several different documents.

The following sections explain the first and last factors
in detail.

Parties to the Contract

When a deposit account contract is established, two parties have reached a binding and legally enforceable agreement. One, the depositor, is usually a natural person. The other, the institution, is an artificial/corporate person.

Natural and Artificial Persons

A *natural person* is an individual as opposed to a business entity. Natural persons who are of sound mind (i.e., competent in the legal sense) have the right to enter into contracts with one or more other natural persons or artificial/corporate persons.

In contrast, a corporation is an artificial person. A corporation is a form of business organization that legally binds a group of individuals to act as a single entity to carry on one or more related enterprises and have the powers, rights and privileges of an individual. Under the law, an *artificial person* is created in the form of a corporation not to live and breathe but to act through its employees.

Depositor's Competency

The depositor's competency also affects the validity of the deposit contract. *Competence* is the quality or condition of being legally able to act in a particular way. *Incompetence* means that a person is under age or not of sound mind, and thus legally unable to act in certain ways. Individual states set the age at which a person is considered legally an adult, while a court of law determines mental competency. The subject of competency of minors is covered in more detail in Chapter 5.

Many state statutes protect financial institutions in dealing with the accounts of incompetents. Usually an institution is not held liable when honoring withdrawal requests from an incompetent person if it did not receive written notice that a court had declared that depositor incompetent.

The Uniform Commercial Code (UCC) also provides some, albeit incomplete, protection to financial institutions.[4] When an institution is ignorant of a depositor's incompetency, Section 4–405 of the UCC provides that "neither death nor incompetence of a customer revokes such authority to . . . pay (an item) . . . until the bank knows of the fact of death or of a court declaration of incompetency and has reasonable opportunity to act on it."

A question of competency may arise at any time. Many employees serve the same customers regularly and thus can recognize changes in their customers' behavior. Perhaps a depositor appears incapable of reason because of possible alcohol consumption or the side effects of certain prescription drugs, such as dizziness or fatigue. In such situations, employees who are concerned for their customers' well-being may be able to take some delaying action in dealing with a withdrawal request. Some institutions have policies that apply to these situations but others may not. Although there are no hard and fast rules or even practical guidelines for judging an individual's competence, employees still must handle the customer with tact and concern. The following two examples show possible courses of action.

First, consider an elderly person who makes a $400 cash withdrawal in the morning and later that day requests another large cash withdrawal. The customer seems confused and does not remember the earlier transaction. The concerned teller should help the customer recall the previous withdrawal and question or reaffirm the necessity of the second transaction.

As another example, suppose a customer who is apparently intoxicated requests a $2,000 cash withdrawal. The teller should ask for additional identification, such as a photo ID, and have the customer resign the withdrawal request in the teller's presence. If the customer is incapacitated to the point where the signature does not match the institution's records, the teller must refuse the withdrawal request. But what if the customer's signature and identification match the institution's records? In that case, a check may be more appropriate than a cash withdrawal. By issuing a check instead of cash, the employee allows the customer time to regain his or her senses before cashing it. If the intoxicated customer is obnoxious to other patrons, he or she may need to be escorted out by a security guard and invited to return when he or she can act more appropriately.

Sometimes a customer's signature changes radically due to an illness such as a recent heart attack or stroke. In these cases the customer's competency may not be an issue, but the employee may request a doctor's statement or other reasonable proof of hospitalization and a photo ID to verify the customer's identity. The employee should then have the customer resign the signature card.

Documentation of the Deposit Account Contract

What constitutes the written deposit account contract? A passbook or certificate? A signature card or other document bearing the customer's signature? Actually, the contract may include both of these as well as many other documents; no one document includes all the elements. The deposit account contract includes the state or federal laws under which the institution is incorporated and the rules and regulations implementing those laws. It also includes the corporate bylaws and institution charter issued by the supervising agency.

Of these many documents counselors are most concerned with the signature card (or similar document), rules of the account class and evidence of account. They may have to help create these documents and/or explain them to customers. Thus, counselors need a thorough understanding of these parts of the deposit account contract to explain or justify account rules.

Signature Card

One component of the deposit account contract typically is a signature card. A *signature card* is a form that establishes the parameters of account ownership and sets forth some of the basic account terms. The card is signed by all account owners at the time the account is opened.

Traditionally, customers complete a signature card for each new deposit account. Certain federal insuring agencies require that customers complete signature cards for some or all deposit accounts, or an agency may require that the customer's signature be obtained and kept on file on some other account document. Under these agencies' rules, an account may not be insured if a signature card (or similar document) has not been completed properly.

Whether or not an institution's insuring agency requires an actual signature card, many institutions still find using signature cards the best way to comply with certain other legal aspects of the account. For example, a completed signature card can help document legally the ownership intention of the parties involved.[5] It can also be used to identify customers by verifying their signatures on transactions. For purposes of this text, it is assumed that a signature card (or similar document) is executed for each new account.

Many institutions use different signature cards for each type of account offered. This prevents any slowdown in normal procedures when opening new accounts and helps minimize the risk of errors and omissions in the contract.

Other institutions use a universal, or general use, signature card. This helps reduce the number of new account forms that an institution needs to stock. A universal signature card contains the basic customer information and accommodates many forms of ownership; the counselor marks which portions apply to that particular deposit account (see Figure 2-1).

Many customers are willing to place their signatures on any standard card without questioning its content, perhaps because they have opened many accounts before and recognize the customary forms. However, a few customers may, out of conscientiousness or curiosity, request an explanation of the contents or purposes of a signature card. The counselor should be prepared to explain every item on the card. A superficial answer such as, "Oh, that's just a standard card that everyone has to sign when they open a new account," is inappropriate. First, it demeans the customer's intelligence. Second, it demonstrates a lack of technical competence and business acumen on the counselor's part.

Signature cards contain certain basic information regarding the account holder, the institution and the account. The following seven components are identified in Figure 2-2. They are key components in nearly every card, although some institutions may choose to include additional information.

- Item 1 states the form of ownership of the account, such as individual, joint tenancy and so on.

F I G U R E 2-1

Universal Signature Card, Side 1

| Tax I.D./Social Security No. | Date | Account Number | Account Type |

Account Name/Address/Phone

Ownership

_____ Individual
_____ Joint(Survivorship)
_____ Tenants in Common
_____ Payable on Death

_____ Uniform Transfer to Minor
_____ Partnership/Corporation/Organization
_____ Trust(Separate Agreements dated _____)

_____ No. of signatures required

  The signature(s) below signify that I (we) have applied for an account in Columbia Savings and the issuance of said account evidence. I (we) under penalties of perjury, certify (1) that the number shown above is my correct taxpayer identification number and (2) that I am not subject to backup withholding [If the Internal Revenue Service has notified any of the signers that they are subject to backup withholding, strike line (2) above].

  I (we) further acknowledge receipt of the current (1) rules of account class (2) rules and regulations and (3) fee schedule all of which may be subject to changes at our discretion.

x _____
 Signature   Title
x _____
 Signature   Title
x _____
 Signature   Title
x _____
 Signature   Title

POD Payee _____

POD Payee _____

POD Payee _____

Successor Custodian _____

Minor _____ Minor's Birthdate _____

Date of Birth _____ Date of Birth _____

Combined Statements Yes_____ No _____ UCS Yes_____ No _____

Card Type:

_____ Teller ID
_____ ATM Access
_____ GCC
_____ Super
_____ Classic

_____ One card-primary
_____ One card-secondary
_____ One card-both names
_____ Two cards-one each name
_____ Two cards-both names on both cards

F I G U R E 2-1, Continued

Universal Signature Card, Side 2

TERMS AND CONDITIONS

GENERAL: The following terms will govern this account unless otherwise agreed to in writing. "We," "our," or "us" means the depository institution and "you" means the accountholder(s). The account is subject to the Association's charter and bylaws, all applicable laws and rules of the United States and the State of Colorado, and any rules and regulations applicable to such account.

DEPOSIT/WITHDRAWALS: We may supply any endorsement for you on any check or other instrument tendered for the account and you hereby relieve us of any liability for collection of such items which are handled by us, further, we shall not be liable for the negligent acts of our agents, subagents, or others for any casualty. Withdrawals may not be made on account of such items until collected, and any amount not collected may be charged at any time to this account including expense incurred and any other outside expense incurred in connection with this account may be charged to it. We are not responsible for mail transactions until they are received by us.

ASSIGNMENT, TRANSFER AND PLEDGE: This account may be assigned, transferred or pledged only upon our written consent and any attempt to do so without such written consent shall not be binding on us. If you assign, transfer or pledge an account, you agree to supply us with documentation evidencing the transaction.

SET-OFF: By signing this form, you agree that we may at any time (without prior notice, except as prohibited by law) set-off the funds in this account against any debt owed to us now or in the future, by any of you having the right of withdrawal.

ACCOUNT OWNERSHIPS: The paragraphs below outline the various types of account ownership listed on the reverse side of this form. Only the paragraph corresponding to the particular type of account ownership selected will apply.

* Individual Ownership — This account is issued and owned solely by one person who does not intend to create any survivorship rights in any other person.

* Joint Tenants with Right of Survivorship — This account is issued in the name of two or more persons with the right of survivorship and not as tenants in common. It is understood and agreed that any one of you who shall first act shall have power to act in all matters related to this account. The withdrawal value of this account, the right to borrow upon the security of this account and other rights relating thereto may be paid, delivered or exercised in whole or in part by or to any one of you as joint tenants, whoever shall act first. Each person intends that upon their death the balance will belong to the survivor(s). The remaining joint tenants will own the balance of the account which will remain as joint tenants with right of survivorship until we are otherwise notified.

* Tenants in Common — This ownership is used for two or more persons each of whom owns a separate portion of the entire account. Unless noted on the face of this card, the Association will assume that each person deposited an equal amount. The signatures of all tenants in common is required for withdrawals on or cancellation of the account.

* Uniform Transfers to Minors — The person creating this account intends to make a transfer by irrevocable gift to a custodian for the benefit of a minor pursuant to Colorado Revised Statute 11-50-101, as amended. The terms and conditions relating to this account are governed by said statute.

* Trust (Separate Agreement) — The person creating this account type intends to create a trust arrangement the terms of which will be governed by a separate agreement. You hereby certify to us that you have the authority to create this account and you authorize us to rely upon your authority without further inquiry. At your discretion, you or any named co-trustee, may change beneficiaries or account types, withdraw funds from and cancel this account.

* Partnership/Corporation/Organization Account — This account ownership is issued in the name of a legal entity. The names set forth on the face hereof are the duly authorized officers/partners of the organization and specimens of their signatures are affixed on the face of this card. You hereby authorize us to act without further inquiry in accordance with a writing bearing the number of signatures set forth on the face of this card unless and until we have been notified otherwise in writing. You will supply us all necessary documentation concerning your authorization to open this account and invest funds with the Association and to accomplish any change of persons authorized to sign writings affecting this account.

* Individual or Joint Payable On Death Account — This account is established pursuant to Colorado Revised Statute 15-15-101 et. seq., as amended. Upon your death (or if joint, upon the death of the survivor of either accountholder) the proceeds of this account shall be delivered to the P.O.D. payee(s) as described on the face of this card, surviving, or to a survivor of them if one or more die before the accountholders. When more than one P.O.D. payee is designated, there shall be a right of survivorship between said P.O.D. payees for deaths occurring subsequent to your death(s) unless a pro rata share is otherwise indicated on the face of this card. If no P.O.D. payee(s) survives you, then the proceeds of this account shall be paid to your heirs (or if joint to the heirs of the survivor of you).

501 3/87

F I G U R E 2-2

Components of a Standard Signature Card

(1) (Form of account ownership)

(2) Owner's name

(3) Account number

(4) (Name of financial institution)

(5) Standard language
(see Figures 2-3a through 2-3e for detail)

(6) Owner's signature

(7) Date

- Item 2 contains the names of all account owners. For easier identification and greater accuracy, printing or typing of these names is preferred.

- Item 3 is the account number the counselor assigns to identify the account on the institution's books.

- Item 4 is the name of the financial institution.

- Item 5 is a paragraph containing standard contract language regarding ownership and administration of the account. Most of the sentences are

F I G U R E 2-3a

Sample Signature Card Language

> . . .*My signature is shown below and you may act without further inquiry in accordance with writings bearing such signature.* . . You may supply any endorsement for me on any check or other instrument tendered for this account and you are relieved of any liability re collection of such items which are handled by you without negligence and you shall not be liable for acts of your agents, subagents or others or for any casualty. . . Withdrawals may not be made on account of such items until collected, and any amount not collected may be charged back to this account, including expense incurred, and any other outside expense incurred re this account may be charged to it.

similar for all forms of ownership; others vary according to the specific form of ownership.

- Item 6 contains all the account owners' signatures.

- Item 7 is the date the account is opened.

Figures 2-3a through 2-3e illustrate standard language paragraphs of a detailed signature card. Although this language may vary on different institutions' cards, this type of information may be included. Each figure contains a short explanation of the highlighted information. *You* refers to the institution and all of its employees.

The first highlighted sentence (Figure 2-3a) indicates that the authorized signature(s) appears on the signature card and states that the institution assumes the signature is valid until it receives notice to the contrary. This sentence implies the institution's authorization to follow any

F I G U R E 2-3b

Signature Card Language (Continued)

. . .My signature is shown below and you may act without further inquiry in accordance with writings bearing such signature. . . *You may supply any endorsement for me on any check or other instrument tendered for this account* and you are relieved of any liability re collection of such items which are handled by you without negligence and you shall not be liable for the acts of your agents, subagents or others or for any casualty. . . Withdrawals may not be made on account of such items until collected, and any amount not collected may be charged back to this account, including expense incurred, and any other outside expense incurred re this account may be charged to it.

F I G U R E 2-3c

. . .My signature is shown below and you may act without further inquiry in accordance with writings bearing such signature. . . You may supply any endorsement for me on any check or other instrument tendered for this account and *you are relieved of any liability re collection of such items which are handled by you without negligence and you shall not be liable for the acts of your agents, subagents or others or for any casualty.* . . Withdrawals may not be made on account of such items until collected, and any amount not collected may be charged back to this account, including expense incurred, and any other outside expense incurred re this account may be charged to it.

instructions for account transactions as long as the instructions contain a valid signature.

The second sentence (Figure 2-3b) describes the method the institution can use to accept checks not signed by the account holder. (This assumes the account holder is also the payee.) If the check lacks the account

F I G U R E 2-3d

Signature Card Language (Continued)

...My signature is shown below and you may act without further inquiry in accordance with writings bearing such signature... You may supply any endorsement for me on any check or other instrument tendered for this account and you are relieved of any liability re collection of such items which are handled by you without negligence and you shall not be liable for the acts of your agents, subagents or others or for any casualty... **Withdrawals may not be made on account of such items until collected**, and any amount not collected may be charged back to this account, including expense incurred, and any other outside expense incurred re this account may be charged to it.

F I G U R E 2-3e

...My signature is shown below and you may act without further inquiry in accordance with writings bearing such signature... You may supply any endorsement for me on any check or other instrument tendered for this account and you are relieved of any liability re collection of such items which are handled by you without negligence and you shall not be liable for the acts of your agents, subagents or others or for any casualty... Withdrawals may not be made on account of such items until collected, *and any amount not collected may be charged back to this account, including expense incurred, and any other outside expense incurred re this account may be charged to it.*

holder's endorsement, the institution is authorized to provide some sort of endorsement or guarantee that the check is acceptable without the signature.

Figure 2-3c illustrates an exculpatory clause. An *exculpatory clause* relieves one party from liability in certain circumstances. In this case, the institution and its agents are relieved of all liability in the check collection process as long as they do not act negligently. For example, a customer may deposit a seemingly good check. If the check is returned unpaid because the maker placed a stop-payment order on it, the institution is not liable for the amount of the check.

In Figure 2-3d, the word *items* refers to checks or other negotiable instruments accepted for collection by the institution. This sentence also refers to checks that are passed from the account holder to the institution. In effect, this sentence stipulates that there must always be enough money in the account to cover the amount of checks that have not yet cleared the check collection process.

The last sentence (Figure 2-3e) protects the institution from having to pay any charges that occur as a result of accepting the customer's checks.

Rules of the Account Class

The *rules of the account class* (or simply *rules of the class*) describe other legal aspects of the account, such as duration, term, early withdrawal, computation of earnings and so on. Rules of the class are established by the institution's board of directors and form an integral part of the deposit contract. A comprehensive set of rules is established for each account classification, such as regular savings accounts, NOW accounts, money market deposit accounts and so on. Some rules (e.g., frequency of paying interest) may apply across the board to all account classifications, and some rules (e.g., minimum balance requirements) may be unique to certain classifications.

Counselors need to learn the rules of each type of account so they can give customers this information when opening accounts. Clear and complete communication is important to prevent misunderstandings with customers and to comply with various disclosure laws or regulations. Some federal regulatory agencies require or recommend that institutions disclose some or all of the following information in writing when an account is opened:

- the interest rate; compounding method; the basis, frequency, extent and limits of any variation in the rate;

- the dates or frequency at which earnings are distributed;

- the amount of the account and the date of its issuance;

- any provision converting the rate of return on the account to another rate of return, whenever any minimum balance requirement may cease to be met;

- any fees that may be imposed on the account;

- any provisions relating to redemption, call or repurchase;

- any account rules that limit the right of the customer to make additions to or withdrawals from the account;

- the minimum term and minimum balance requirement;

- any penalty or penalties for withdrawal prior to expiration of the term on term accounts, or failure to comply with any other rules of the account;

- any provisions relating to renewal or disposition of the funds when the term expires on term accounts;

- any provisions relating to earnings after expiration of the term or any renewal period.

These types of account rules are explained in Chapters 3 and 4.

Evidence of Account

The term *evidence of account* comes from a federal law governing savings institutions that says institutions may "issue passbooks, certificates, or other evidence of accounts."[6] Regulations for other depository institutions include references to certificates as "evidencing" the deposit of funds. Historically, evidence of account referred to the traditional passbook. During the 1960s, evidence was expanded to include certificates. Statement accounts, popularized in the 1970s, gave the term still broader meaning. Today, with the increasing popularity of electronic funds transfers and statement accounts, evidence may be a written agreement in almost any form.

Traditional passbooks and certificates are still in use, however, because many account holders prefer to have tangible evidence of their investment. However, these customers may not understand that such items are considered secondary evidence of account; they are actually no more than receipts or memoranda showing the ownership and dollar value of an account and are issued for information and convenience purposes. Federal and state regulations require that the primary evidence of each account holder's interest be shown on the institution's books as appropriate accounting entries. This should console the depositor who loses his or her passbook or certificate and fears that the funds are lost, too.

An important function of evidence of account is as a customer record of some terms and conditions of the deposit account contract. Such a written agreement also constitutes the institution's acknowledgement of the receipt of money subject to the conditions of the underlying account classification.

Regulation D of the Federal Reserve System also affects the language used in the evidence of account. Regulation D requires depository institutions to maintain reserves against their transaction accounts and nonpersonal time deposits (those not held by a natural person). Reserves must be held in the form of vault cash at the institution or non-interest-earning deposits at a Federal Reserve bank. Essentially, these reserve funds remain idle and do not contribute to the institution's profitability. Therefore, financial institutions seek to minimize the amount of their deposits that require reserves. To exempt their appropriate deposit accounts (primarily personal savings and certificate of deposit accounts) from the Regulation D reserve requirements, an institution must include one of the following statements on the evidence of account:

- Not transferable;

- Nontransferable;

- Not transferable as defined in 12 CFR Part 204;

- Not transferable except on the books of the depository institution;

- Not transferable except as collateral for a loan or as otherwise permitted by regulations of the Federal Reserve Board;

- Transferable only on the records of the institution;

- Transferable only with the permission of the institution.

An institution may also use any other statement that has the same legal effect. Such a statement prevents an account holder from assigning ownership to a third party without the knowledge of the depository institution.[7]

If a customer questions this language, the counselor should explain that the condition *nontransferable* has no effect on the customer's ability to transfer the funds to another account or change the account ownership. Also, it does not affect the customer's ability to pledge the account as collateral for a loan. The word *nontransferable* merely indicates the type of reserve requirement applied to this account.

SPECIAL RIGHTS OF ACCOUNT OWNERS

Account owners have two important rights that the previously described documents may not specifically define: the authority to grant a power of attorney and the right to execute a stop or suspension order. Some customers may never exercise these rights, but others find them very valuable.

Power of Attorney

For various reasons, an account owner may authorize someone else to make withdrawals from the account. To do this, the account owner grants a power of attorney. A *power of attorney* on a deposit account is a witnessed or acknowledged document that authorizes a person or persons to make withdrawals from another's account and states the official capacity of the person or persons named. In practice, the owner of the account, called the

F I G U R E 2-4

Power of Attorney

POWER OF ATTORNEY

With reference to Account No._____

in_____

The undersigned grantor(s) hereby appoint(s)

_____ and _____

whose signature or signatures appear at the left below, as Attorney in Fact for the undersigned to endorse any paper payable to the undersigned for payment into the above-
numbered account of the undersigned and make withdrawals from said account and
hereby authorizes said Institution to act with respect to said account upon said signature or signatures or either of them.

This _____ day of _____, 19____.

Signature(s) of grantor(s):

_____   _____

Signature(s) of Attorney in Fact:

(1)_____   _____
                                                (Address)

(2)_____   _____
                                                (Address)

14647-2 (1/78)   SAF Systems and Forms
400 POW

grantor, signs a document that authorizes the named person, called the *attorney in fact*, to act legally in place of
the owner under specified conditions and for specific purposes. The attorney in fact also signs the document. Figure 2-4 shows a power of attorney card.

A power of attorney does not affect any of the owner's
(grantor's) ownership rights. The owner retains the right

to revoke or change the power of attorney by advising the institution in writing. Upon the owner's death, the power of attorney ceases and the balance of the account is paid out in the same manner in which the specific form of ownership would be handled without a power of attorney.

Power of attorney is often associated with the individual form of ownership, but it may be used with other ownership forms. An individual, natural person and some owners of joint accounts are eligible to appoint an attorney in fact, but some forms of account ownership do not permit this appointment (see Chapter 7).

Counselors should explain to customers their rights to grant a power of attorney. Customers often do not realize that they have this right with certain forms of account ownership and may request inappropriate forms of ownership for the sake of convenience.

The power of attorney card used by financial institutions differs from the formal instrument known as a legal power of attorney. A legal power of attorney is a document that is usually prepared by the grantor's lawyer. The grantor's signature must be executed before a notary public. The attorney in fact may be granted authority to make any transactions in the grantor's absence and is not necessarily restricted to a specific account. Like a power of attorney, a legal power of attorney automatically ceases upon the grantor's death.

Some states have enacted *durable power of attorney* statutes.[8] These statutes restate and broaden the legal power of attorney by ensuring that third parties (e.g., financial institutions) will honor the agent's authority to make personal, financial and health care decisions for the principal at all times, including periods of disability. The law protects anyone from liability who relied in good faith on a copy of the power provided by the agent. The main emphasis of the durable power of attorney is that it survives the disability or incompetency of the principal, unless a court directs otherwise. Figure 2-5 shows an example of a durable power of attorney on a deposit account.

Stop Payment and Suspension Orders

Account owners possess the right to stop certain payments from being drawn on their accounts even if they gave previous authorization. A *stop payment order* is a written instruction from the customer requiring the financial institution to refuse payment of a specific draft or check. A *suspension or stop order* is a written instruction to stop or restrict all payments of withdrawals on a deposit account. Neither suspension nor stop payment orders may be imposed on an account by anyone other than an account owner, except by:

- a person specifically authorized by the owner in the signature card contract;

- a conservator, if the owner has been declared incompetent by a court; or

- a judge who orders the account impounded.

Courts of law have protected account owners' rights by not permitting other exceptions. For example, there have been cases in which attorneys were unable to place suspension orders on clients' accounts without court declarations of incompetency.[9]

Figure 2-6 shows a suspension order on a joint tenancy account. If one joint tenant signs this form, withdrawals

---

F I G U R E 2-5

Durable Power of Attorney, Side 1

FILE TITLE	ACCT #(s)	
DURABLE FAMILY POWER OF ATTORNEY	OTHER	T/C
SIGNATURE OF ATTORNEY		
IDENTIFICATION	GOOD UNTIL	
NAME OF ATTORNEY		
RES. ADDRESS - ATTY	BUS. ADDRESS - ATTY	
NAME OF INVESTOR	DATE	
MAIL ADDRESS - INVESTOR	BY	

SAV-908 6-87

---

will be honored only if all joint tenants sign the with-drawal slip. The card also has a cancellation section that requires all joint tenants' signatures.

Figure 2-7 is a sample stop payment order. Typically, the account owner first gives the institution an oral order over the telephone to stop payment. The oral order is effective for only 14 calendar days unless confirmed in writing within that period. A written order is effective for only six months unless renewed in writing. In either

F I G U R E 2-5, Continued

Durable Power of Attorney, Side 2

KNOW ALL MEN BY THESE PRESENTS: That I, _____

Do make, constitute and appoint the following family member (spouse, parent, child,

brother, sister, niece or nephew) _____ my true

and lawful attorney to withdraw from my savings/checking Account No(s). _____

which I now have in the Florida Federal Savings and Loan Association, any sum or sums of money up to and including the

full amount that may be in said account(s).

Said_____as my attorney-in-fact to have the same

withdrawal privileges from aforesaid account(s) as I now have in the future and to make said withdrawals in my place and stead,

and to transact any and all matters pertaining to these account(s). This durable family power of attorney to be in full force and

effect until such time as revocation of same in writing shall be filed by the undersigned investor with Florida Federal Savings

and Loan Association and receipt thereof acknowledged by said Association. This durable family power of attorney shall not

be affected by disability of the investor except as provided by statute.

Witness:_____ Signed:_____

                                                                         (Investor)

Witness my hand and seal this_____day of _____, 19_____

The Investor,_____personally appeared before me and

who first being duly sworn, deposes and says that (s)he executed the foregoing power of attorney for the uses and purposes

therein stated.

Date:_____ My Commission Expires:_____

STATE OF FLORIDA

COUNTY OF_____NOTARY PUBLIC_____

In conformity with this Power of Attorney, the following signature of my attorney-in-fact is to be recoginzed by Florida Federal

Savings and Loan Association.

Witness:_____ Signed:_____

                                                                       (Attorney-in-fact)

case, after six months a check is likely to be considered stale-dated or invalid if it has not been cashed.

Institutions may have recourse if errors or other special circumstances affect stop payments. Section 4–407 of the UCC provides a mechanism for institutions to recoup their losses if they inadvertently disregard stop payment orders. Also, institutions are protected when customers try to benefit themselves by placing unjustified stop payment orders.

F I G U R E 2-6

Stop Order on Joint Tenancy (Suspension Order)

STOP ORDER ON JOINT TENANCY ACCOUNT

TO: ACCOUNT NO._____

_____
(NAME OF INSTITUTION)

You are hereby instructed to suspend payment on Account No._____ and to permit withdrawals only on the signatures of all joint tenants until such time as this order has been cancelled in writing signed by all joints tenants and delivered to you.

DATE: _____   _____
                                                        Signature

CANCELLATION OF SUSPENSION ORDER

Please cancel the above order to suspend payment on Account No._____ and permit withdrawals on the signature of any one joint tenant.

_____   _____
         Signature   Signature

DATE OF RELEASE _____   _____
                                                        Signature

14657 STOP ORDER (7/84) SAF Systems and Forms

DEPOSIT ACCOUNT OPENING PROCEDURES

Institutions vary considerably in the procedures they use when opening deposit accounts. Some parts of the process, however, are dictated by regulations or practices

F I G U R E 2-7

Stop Payment Authorization

STOP PAYMENT AUTHORIZATION

Draft
Number _____ Dated _____ Amount $ _____

Payee _____

Reason _____ App'd By _____

_____

_____

If you should recover this draft please instruct us to cancel this order.

35101-5 (7/78)
NASPA-1

SAF Systems and Forms, Inc.

Account Number _____

Amount of Charge _____

Date _____ Time _____ AM/PM

Duplicate Issued? ☐ Yes ☐ No

This confirmation is our record of your Stop Payment order and represents our understanding of the order. ORAL Stop Payment orders are effective for 14 calendar days only. If you wish to stop payment, you must sign a written Stop Payment Order, copy of which is enclosed for your signature. A written Stop Payment Order signed by a depositor will not be effective after 6 MONTHS, but may be renewed in writing. (UCC 4-403)

The undersigned hereby agrees to hold the Institution harmless for all expenses and costs incurred by the Institution on account of refusing payment of said draft and agrees not to hold the Institution liable on account of payment contrary to this request if same occurs through inadvertence, accident or oversight.

_____
Signature of Account Holder

intended to prevent losses due to fraud or errors. Counselors are responsible for meeting these requirements while providing courteous customer service. At times, the counselor may need to explain the legal requirement for a certain procedure, such as a required disclosure, or tactfully clarify the reasons for a security procedure. A sound knowledge of the required procedures will enable the counselor to take appropriate actions confidently, correctly and courteously.

Obtain Customer Information

After the customer has decided on a type of investment and account ownership, the counselor obtains the basic information for opening the account. This information includes various types of personal data and a tax identification number.

Personal Information

The amount and type of personal information that a counselor obtains are determined primarily by the financial institution. This information frequently includes the following items, among others:

- names of all account owners;

- information about account beneficiaries, if appropriate;

- address, phone number and any other information needed to contact a customer;

- customer identification such as information from personal identification cards, birthdate, birthplace and mother's maiden name;

- amount and source of the deposit.

Tax Identification Number (TIN)

The Internal Revenue Service requires that institutions obtain a certified *tax identification number (TIN)* on all accounts. This is the number used to identify an individual or entity for federal income tax purposes. For most individuals, this is their Social Security number.

The form on which the customer provides the number must include the following information:

- name;

- address;

- tax identification number;

- customer's certification that the TIN is correct;

- customer's certification that he or she is not subject to backup withholding. *Backup withholding* refers to the IRS requirement that the institution withhold a portion of the interest from the customer due to certain circumstances, such as failing to provide a TIN in the past or underreporting interest or dividend income.

Some institutions have the customer fill out a separate form to obtain TIN information when opening a new account. Others find it more convenient to include the required language on a conventional new account form such as a signature card. Figure 2-8 shows a signature card that meets IRS requirements for TIN certification. If institutions do not use an Internal Revenue Service form (W-9) to collect this information, they still must provide the depositor with the substance of the W-9 instructions either separately or as part of the substitute

F I G U R E 2-8

TIN Certification

Taxpayer Identification Number			Account Number

(Last Name)	(First Name)	(Middle Name)

I hereby apply for a checking account in

and for issuance of evidence thereof. A specimen of my signature is shown below and you are hereby authorized to act without further inquiry in accordance with writings bearing such signature. I agree that you in receiving items for deposit or collection act only as depositor's collecting agent and assume no responsibility beyond due care; that all items are credited subject to final payment to you at your own office in cash or solvent credits; that you will use due diligence in the selection of collection agents, but will not be liable in case of their failure or negligence, or for losses in transit; that each correspondent so selected shall not be liable except for its own negligence; that you or collecting agents may send items, directly or indirectly, to any Institution including the drawer or payor, may accept check, draft or credit as conditional payment in lieu of cash, and shall not be liable for dishonor of checks or drafts or for reversal of credits so received in payment nor for losses thereon, that items and their proceeds may be handled by any Federal Reserve bank in accordance with applicable Federal Reserve rules, and by this you or any correspondent, in accordance with any common Institution usage, with any practice or procedure that a Federal Reserve bank may use or permit another Institution to use, or with any other lawful means. That you may charge back any item at any time before actual final payment, whether returned or not, and may also charge back any item drawn on the Institution, if, within your normal handling period for such item, it is determined by you that the item is not to be honored against the drawer's account; that in collecting bonds or coupons you may charge back amount of income tax, if any, and that this account is subject to all laws and regulations of the United States and of the State now or hereafter in force.

It is also agreed that when the balance in any month is not compensatory, a reasonable service charge may be made for activity, overdrafts, return or unpaid items, or other services. In addition, you reserve the right of setoff with respect to any funds due and owing on this account that have not been paid.

By signing this signature card, I(we), under penalty of perjury, certify that (a) the number shown on this card is my(our) correct taxpayer identification number(s), and (b) I(we) are not subject to backup withholding. [If either of the signers have been notified by the IRS that they are subject to backup withholding, delete the language in (b) above.]

Signature			Date

Street	City	State	Zip

(Optional Information) _____

Phone

27001:7 (11/83) CHECKING INDIVIDUAL

SAF Systems and Forms

---

form. Some institutions use a signature card that includes a TIN certification and provide the W-9 form to depositors solely to comply with the information requirement.

The IRS assesses severe penalties on institutions that fail to obtain tax identification numbers on accounts. For this reason, an institution may refuse to open an account if the customer does not provide a TIN. Additional information on TIN compliance procedures appears in other publications of The Institute of Financial Education and other sources.

Verify Customer Information

A counselor may need to verify certain information the customer provides when opening the account. The primary purpose of the verification is to prevent fraud or other illegal activities. The counselor should take extra caution when opening an account for a new customer because the chance for fraud is higher with unknown individuals. However, the counselor must balance the need for verification against the knowledge that most new customers are honest and could be offended if treated with suspicion.

Customer Identification

As a matter of policy, the counselor should request adequate identification from a new customer. Forms of identification that contain a photograph and signature are the most commonly accepted, but each institution establishes its own standards for acceptability. For example, many institutions accept all of the following items and others that meet their standards:

- unexpired driver's license;

- credit cards;

- employment identification;

- unexpired U.S. passport;

- unexpired armed forces identification.

The counselors should also inspect the identification documents for any alterations or characteristics that do not match the customer. For example, a photograph might have been switched or a description changed. An ID card that is smudged or excessively wrinkled might conceal alterations. The counselor should also ensure that the signature on an ID card matches the person's signature on new account documents.

Counselors fulfill an important responsibility when they follow their institution's rules for identifying customers. By accepting a customer's identification, the counselor establishes as far as possible that the document is genuine and matches the person presenting it. A person who intends to commit a fraud may try to establish a fraudulent identity, and the counselor's job is to prevent that from happening.

Credit Record

An institution may also require counselors to make phone calls or electronic system inquiries to obtain information on potential customers' past relationships with financial institutions. This is especially common when establishing a checking account. Such inquiries can alert an institution to an individual who has demonstrated illegal or abusive account practices such as frequent overdrafting. Such an effort is a small investment compared to the time and money required later to stop an account abuser.

Counselors make credit or check inquiries through information clearinghouses. These clearinghouses provide problem account information very quickly, usually within 20 or 30 seconds. Companies such as Telechek Services, Inc., and Chex Systems, Inc., maintain computerized files that contain information such as the names of people who have one or more bad checks outstanding at any institution and those who have had checking accounts closed for cause. When an account has been closed for cause, the institution rather than the account holder chose to close it. Normally, only checking and NOW accounts are closed for cause by an institution, due to consistent overdrafts or fraudulent activity, but each institution has its own policy.

Large Cash Deposits

If a customer deposits large sums of cash into a deposit account, counselors must follow special verification and reporting procedures. The Bank Secrecy Act requires that multiple, single-day cash deposits by a single individual or entity that total more than $10,000 be reported to the Treasury Department. When opening a deposit account in this situation, the counselor must verify and record the depositor's name and address as well as the identity documents, account number and tax identification number. The institution records this information on IRS Form 4789-Currency Transaction Report and files the report within 15 days of the transaction.

Process Transaction

Institutions differ in how they record new accounts on their computer systems. In some institutions, counselors post transactions through a computer terminal in their department. In others, tellers or other employees post transactions in a different area. All systems, however, have three basic elements:

- Check holds must meet funds availability legislative requirements.

- Account holds may be placed on the account.

- The customer should verify the deposit account documents.

Check Holds and Funds Availability

A *check hold* is an account record notation showing that a specific amount of money is being withheld temporarily from the balance available to the owner. Nearly all financial institutions place holds on uncollected funds as a matter of policy. *Uncollected funds* are funds that have been deposited in an account in the form of a check that has not yet cleared the check collection systems and been paid by the drawee bank.

In 1988, Congress passed the Expedited Funds Availability Act, and the Federal Reserve Board implemented the provisions through Regulation CC. This act gives customers faster access to funds from checks deposited into transaction accounts such as NOW accounts. It establishes schedules for maximum check holds and provides safeguards to minimize risk in situations such as new accounts.

In terms of funds availability, Regulation CC classifies deposits into three categories: low-risk, local checks and nonlocal checks. Low-risk deposits include:

- cash;

- electronic credits;

- U.S. Treasury checks;

- U.S. Postal Service money orders;

- Federal Reserve and Federal Home Loan Bank checks;

- state and local government checks;

- cashier's checks;

- certified checks;

- teller's checks;

- on-us checks.

Institutions generally must make funds from low-risk deposits available on the next business day, although certain conditions may apply to each of these deposit sources.

Local and nonlocal checks pose different requirements. A *local check* is a check written on a bank within the same Federal Reserve check processing region as the depository institution. A *nonlocal check* is a check written on a bank outside the Federal Reserve check processing region as the depository institution's. Regulation CC establishes both a temporary and a permanent schedule for maximum funds availability limits for local and nonlocal checks. The temporary schedule is intended to help institutions phase in the ultimate requirements on check holds and is as follows:

Temporary Schedule Effective 9/1/88 to 8/31/90

Check Type	Maximum Length of Hold
Local	3 days
Nonlocal	7 days

The permanent schedule takes effect as follows:

Permanent Schedule Effective 9/1/90

Check Type	Maximum Length of Hold
Local	2 days
Nonlocal	5 days

One exception to both schedules is that institutions must give next-day availability on the first $100 of local and nonlocal checks deposited.

Institutions can follow these schedules or implement shorter holds than those required. When making such decisions, institutions weigh operational difficulties against risk of losses. Whatever schedule an institution chooses, it must disclose it to the customers.

Counselors are concerned with another section of Regulation CC that imposes different rules for new account deposits. As stated earlier, the incidence of checking account fraud is higher with new customers. The regulation recognizes this higher risk by allowing different check-hold rules for the three classifications of deposits. On low-risk checks, including traveler's checks, the first $5,000 must be given next-day availability with the balance available in nine days. On local and nonlocal checks, the institution can place unlimited holds for the first 30 days after the customer establishes the account. As with the other check hold requirements, individual institutions can establish less restrictive rules if they wish.

Regulation CC requires that institutions give disclosures of funds availability policies to new account applicants *before* the transaction account is opened. See Figure 2-9 for an example. The following information must be included:

- availability policy summary;

- description of any categories of checks that receive delayed availability, such as checks deposited to new accounts;

- explanation on how to determine the category to which a particular check belongs, such as local and nonlocal checks;

- statement about the availability for each category of check;

- description of business days;

- statement about when a deposit is considered received;

- description of any of the safeguard exceptions that may be invoked;

- statement indicating when extended holds will generally expire;

- announcement that customers will receive notices if one of the exceptions is invoked;

- description of how customers can differentiate between proprietary and nonproprietary ATMs, and the applicable hold schedule if it varies.

Account Holds

When opening a deposit account, the counselor may need to place certain holds on the account. Both temporary and permanent holds may be placed on an account for monetary or informational purposes. Placing a hold on an uncollected check is an example of a monetary hold. A pledged account—an account that is used as security for a loan—also requires a monetary hold. An informational (nonmonetary) hold supplies information about the account to an employee processing a transaction. For example, the hold may signal that certain information should be requested from a customer. Or, another service may be linked to this account such as automatic transfer of interest to another account. Generally, an informational hold implies that some special care may be needed when handling transactions on the account.

F I G U R E 2-9

Funds Availability Disclosure

Funds Availability Policy of Talman Home Federal Savings and Loan Association of Illinois (Talman Home)

In some instances funds which you have deposited in your Talman account(s) may not be available for immediate withdrawal. The following information explains in detail the Funds Availability Policy of Talman Home Federal Savings and Loan Association. Please read the information carefully.

Determining when a deposit is made

The length of the delay is counted in business days from the day of your deposit. Every day is a business day except Saturdays, Sundays, and federal holidays. If you make a deposit in person to one of our employees, or at automated teller machines (ATMs) owned or operated by Talman Home before 12:00 noon, on a business day that we are open, we will consider that day to be the day of your deposit. However, if you make a deposit at one of our ATMs after 12:00 noon, or on a day we are not open, we will consider that the deposit was made on the next business day we are open.

Any deposit made through the mails (or in night depositories) will be considered deposited on the day the deposit is received by Talman Home (or the day it is removed from the night depository).

The length of the delay varies depending on the type of deposit and is explained below.

Same-day availability

Funds from the following deposits are available on the same day of your deposit.

Cash.

Wire transfers, including preauthorized credits, such as social security benefits and payroll payments.

Checks drawn on Talman Home (On-Us) that are payable to you.

Next-day availability

Funds from the following deposits are available on the first business day after the day of your deposit, if your checks or money orders deposited are payable to you.

U.S. Treasury checks.

State and local government checks.

Cashier's, certified, and teller's checks.

Federal Reserve Bank checks, Federal Home Loan Bank checks, and postal money orders.

Other check deposits

To find out when funds from other check deposits will be available, look at the first four digits of the routing number on the check:

Personal check

└── **Routing number**

Business check

└── **Routing number**

If the first four digits of the routing number (1234 in the examples above) are 0710, 0711, 0712, 0719, 2710, 2711, 2712, or 2719, then the check is a local check. Otherwise, the check is a nonlocal check. In some instances we will treat checks as local or nonlocal based upon the location of the bank by which the check is payable, not on the routing number on the bottom of the check. For example, if a credit union share draft is payable by a credit union that is located within Illinois or Indiana, the share draft will be treated as a local check, even if the draft is payable through a bank that is located outside of Illinois or Indiana as determined by the routing number on the check. Our policy is to make funds from these checks available as follows:

1. **Local checks.** The first $100 from a deposit of local checks will be available on the first business day after the day of your deposit. The remaining funds will be available on the second business day after the day of your deposit.

For example, if you deposit a local check of $700 on a Monday, $100 of the deposit is available on Tuesday. The remaining $600 is available on Wednesday.

2. **Nonlocal checks.** The first $100 from a deposit of nonlocal checks will be available on the first business day after the day of your deposit. The remaining funds will be available on the fifth business day after the day of your deposit.

For example, if you deposit a $700 nonlocal check on a Monday, $100 of the deposit is available on Tuesday. The remaining $600 is available on Monday of the following week.

If you deposit both categories of checks, $100 from the checks will be available on the first business day after the day of your deposit, not $100 from each category of checks.

F I G U R E 2-9, Continued

Automated Teller Machines

Deposits at our ATMs (Proprietary)

Funds from deposits that are made at our ATMs will be available in accordance with the same schedules described above.

ATMs owned and operated by other parties (Non-Proprietary)

Funds from any deposits (cash or checks) made at ATMs we do not own or operate will not be available until the fifth business day after the day of your deposit. This rule does not apply at ATMs that we do own or operate.

A list of our ATMs is enclosed.

Longer delays may apply

Funds you deposit by check may be delayed for a longer period under the following circumstances:

We believe a check you deposit will not be paid.

You deposit checks totaling more than $5,000 on any one day.

You redeposit a check that has been returned unpaid.

You have overdrawn your account repeatedly in the last six months.

There is an emergency, such as failure of communications or computer equipment.

We will notify you if we delay your ability to withdraw funds for any of these reasons, and we will tell you when the funds will be available. They will generally be available no later than seven business days after the day of your deposit for local checks and eleven business days after the day of your deposit for non-local checks.

Special rules for new accounts

If you are a new customer, the following special rules will apply during the first 30 days your account is open.

The first $5,000 from a deposit of U.S. Treasury checks will be available on the first business day after the day of your deposit. The excess over $5,000 will be available on the fifth business day after the day of your deposit. Funds from wire transfers into your account will be available on the first business day after the day we receive the transfer.

Funds from deposits of cash and the first $5,000 of a day's total deposits of cashier's, certified, teller's, travelers, and state and local government checks will be available on the first business day after the day of your deposit if the deposit meets certain conditions. For example, the checks must be payable to you. The excess over $5,000 will be available on the fifth business day after the day of your deposit. If you do not make the deposit in person to one of our employees, the first $5,000 will not be available until the second business day after the day of your deposit.

Funds from all other check deposits will be available on the fifth business day after the day of your deposit.

Summary of Availability Schedule

The following is a summary of the funds availability schedule. For more detailed information read the preceding Funds Availability Policy of Talman Home.

Type of Transaction	No. of Business Days After Which Funds Are Available to The Depositor. (5)	For Example: Funds Credited Monday Available for Withdrawal on:
Cash & Electronic Payment & On-Us Checks	0	Same Day
Treasury Checks; State & Local Government Checks; Certified & Teller Checks; Federal Reserve Bank Checks, FHLB Checks, U.S. Postal Money Orders (1)	1	Tuesday
Local Checks (2)	2	$100 on Tuesday Balance on Wednesday
Nonlocal Checks (3)	5	$100 on Tuesday Balance on Following Monday
Proprietary ATM Deposits (4)	2	Wednesday
Non-Proprietary ATM Deposits	5	Following Monday
Exceptions (6)	7 or 11	Following Wednesday or Tuesday
New Accounts	5	Following Monday

DEFINITIONS

(1) Deposits to account of payee of check (no second endorsements).

(2) $100 available next business day. Local check defined as checks with federal reserve routing numbers of 0710, 0711, 0712, 0719, 2710, 2711, 2712, 2719.

(3) $100 available next business day. Nonlocal check defined as not meeting the first two definitions.

(4) Proprietary ATM located at Talman locations. Deposits after 12:00 noon considered next business day.
Deposits of nonlocal checks are subject to the nonlocal availability time lines.

(5) "Business Day" means a calendar day other than a Saturday, Sunday or federal holiday.

(6) Exceptions will be disclosed to customer if applicable.

Account holds function in various ways. Some holds are designed to alert an employee every time a transaction occurs. Others are intended to alert an employee only if the customer attempts to withdraw funds or close the account. Still others require a supervisor's approval to continue processing the transaction. Informational holds occur for many reasons, including the following:

- *Payroll or government direct deposit.* An informational hold on this account can alert an employee closing an account that special arrangements must be made to discontinue the direct deposit.

- *Temporary signature card on file.* A hold on this account informs the employee to remind the customer to return the permanent signature card.

- *Decedent account.* A hold on this account can help prevent unauthorized transactions.

- *Lost evidence of account.* A hold on this account can alert an employee to a possibly stolen passbook or simply that other follow-up is needed if the lost evidence is found.

Verification by the Customer

The last step in opening an account is to ask the customer to verify the information printed on the documents. This information includes the customer's name and address, account ownership, type of investment, amount of deposit and any other conditions of the account. When the customer verifies this information, both the counselor and the customer can be assured of compliance with the customer's wishes.

SITUATIONS REQUIRING A NEW ACCOUNT CONTRACT

Once established, a deposit account can be governed by the same contract for many years. However, certain situations may require a new deposit account contract and a new account. Two such events occur when a customer loses the evidence of account and when the customer wishes to change the account ownership.

Lost Evidence of Account

Sometimes a customer loses the evidence of account such as a passbook or certificate. If the situation does not appear to have been caused by theft or fraud, the counselor flags the account with an account hold and follows the institution's procedure for lost accounts. Often the counselor obtains the signatures of all account holders on an affidavit for Lost Evidence of Account (see Figure 2-10). After a waiting period, which allows time to search for the lost evidence, the counselor issues a duplicate evidence of account. With this procedure, the customer continues to use the original account number. If the lost evidence of account is recovered, the counselor cancels the evidence in some manner and removes the account hold.

If it appears that the lost evidence was stolen, many institutions take more drastic and immediate measures. After completing the necessary paperwork, the counselor immediately closes the account and transfers the balance to a new account with a new account number, evidence of account and deposit account documentation. This process prevents fraudulent activity on the original account.

F I G U R E 2-10

Affidavit for Lost Evidence of Account, Side 1

State of _____

County of _____

} ss.

AFFIDAVIT FOR LOST EVIDENCE OF ACCOUNT
(ALL ACCOUNT OWNERS SHOULD SIGN)

Whereas_____

issued to the undersigned its savings account No._____, as shown by the books of the institution,

and whereas the account book, identification card, investment certificate or other evidence of said account has been lost or destroyed and the undersigned desires to obtain a duplicate, therefore.

The undersigned hereby make this affidavit to induce said institution to issue such duplicate evidence and makes oath that (1) said account was issued to the undersigned and is still owned by the undersigned (2) said account or evidence thereof has never been pledged or sold or transferred by the undersigned and is not subject to any kind of lien or claim of any other entity, (3) affiant further says that the evidence of the said account has been lost or destroyed and after diligent search cannot be located.

Wherefore, in consideration of the issuance of the duplicate evidence of the account, the undersigned hereby agrees to indemnify and hold the said institution harmless against any loss, damage, and expense on account of the issuance of such duplicate evidence, or on account of any claim of any other to or upon said account, and the undersigned further agrees that in the event of the discovery of said original evidence to promptly deliver the same to the institution.

This the _____ day of _____, 19____

_____   _____
Signature of Member   Signature of Member

(Over)

Change in Account Ownership

Counselors may take similar measures when a customer requests that the institution change the ownership of an existing account. The addition or deletion of a name without establishing a new deposit account contract could violate other account owners' rights or invalidate the existing form of ownership. Also, as explained in the section

F I G U R E 2-10, Continued

Affidavit for Lost Evidence of Account, Side 2

NOTARIZATION

Personally, _____appeared

before me this _____ day of _____

(SEAL)   19_____, who after being duly sworn made oath that the statements made in
              the affidavit for lost passbook or certificate on the reverse side are true.

_____
Notary Public

INDEMNITY BOND

For value received the undersigned hereby agrees to indemnify the institution named on the reverse side hereof
on account of any expense, loss or damage which may result from the issuance of duplicate evidence of the account
described on the reverse side hereof, or on account of any claim of any other to or upon said account.

This the _____ day of _____ 19 _____

_____   _____
Signature of Indemnifier   Signature of Indemnifier
14655-5—Affidavit for Lost Evidence of Account and Indemnity Bond
SC 442 A   3/75   SAF Systems and Forms

"Evidence of Account," a change of ownership is effective only when transferred on the institution's books.

The most effective way to prevent liability when adding or deleting names is by closing the old account and opening a new deposit account even if the form of ownership remains the same. For example, John and Jane Doe own an account in joint tenancy. Jane requests that her mother, Mary Smith, be added to the account as a third joint tenant. Even though ownership is still held in joint tenancy, a new deposit contract is required.

SUMMARY

Counselors in the deposit accounts area have responsibilities to both customers and the institution. They provide high-quality customer service and help customers make key decisions about the type of account to open. Counselors also help protect their institution from potentially risky situations by carefully following procedures and remaining within their role as counselor.

The deposit account contract sets out terms and conditions of responsibilities of both the institution and the customer. Each party agrees to the terms of the contract stipulated in documents such as a signature card, rules of the account class and evidence of account. Depositors also have special rights in the deposit account contract in terms of power of attorney and stop payment and suspension orders.

Procedures for opening deposit accounts vary among institutions, but all counselors help the institution meet legal requirements such as TIN compliance, large currency transaction reporting and check-hold laws. At times, counselors may need to close a deposit account and open a new one due to a change in the terms of the deposit account or some other event.

FOOTNOTES

[1]Laura Gross, "Elite Customers Move the Most, Account-Switching Study Shows," *American Banker* (October 5, 1987), p. 1.

[2]Leonard L. Berry, David R. Bennett and Carter W. Brown, *Service Quality: A Profit Strategy for Financial Institutions* (Homewood, Ill.: Dow Jones-Irwin, 1988), pp. 25–26.

[3]Laura Gross, "Service Earns 'Good' Consumer Rating," *American Banker* (September 29, 1987), p. 23.

[4]The Uniform Commercial Code relates to present commercial practices. It is compiled by the National Conference of Commissioners on Uniform State Laws and the American Law Institute.

[5]Case comment, "Signed Signature Card Held Essential for Existence of Joint Account," *Legal Bulletin* XLVIII (May 1982), pp. 103–104.

[6]See 12 USC 1464 (b)(1)(A)(ii).

[7]See 12 CFR § 204.9 for current reserve requirements.

[8]AL, AR, CA, DE, FL, GA, ID, IL, IN, KS, KY, LA, MA, MI, MN, MO, MT, NE, NV, NH, NJ, NC, ND, OK, PA, RI, SD, TN, TX, UT, VT, VA, WA, WV, WI, WY. Because this uniform law was developed somewhat recently, other states may have been added to this list after publication.

[9]*Lincoln National Bank* v. *Peoples Trust Bank*, 379 N.E. 2d 527.

Types of Investments: Regular Savings Accounts and Checking Accounts

KEY CONCEPTS

- Six characteristics of deposit accounts as investments;

- Comparisons of simple and compound interest, and tiered rate and blended rate structures;

- Typical features of regular savings accounts, regular checking accounts, NOW accounts and share draft accounts;

- Differences and similarities between checks and drafts;

- Elements of negotiable instruments and the basic parts of a check;

- How the check clearing process operates;

- Function of magnetic ink character recognition (MICR) encoding of checks;

- Standards for placement of endorsements on checks;

- How customers benefit from regular savings accounts and checking accounts.

W hen customers open deposit accounts, they must decide what types of investments the accounts will be. Generally, deposit accounts fall into one of four categories of investments: regular savings accounts, checking accounts, money market deposit accounts and certificates of deposit. Most customers decide which type of account to open on the basis of how they plan to use the account. Regular savings accounts and checking accounts respond mainly to the day-to-day money management needs of customers and form the basis of an overall financial plan. Money market deposit accounts and certificates of deposit help customers accomplish longer-range and higher-balance investment goals.

This chapter describes the basic characteristics of deposit accounts as investments. It explores two types of investments—regular savings accounts and checking accounts—and the typical features and customer benefits of each. The remaining two categories of deposit account investments will be examined in Chapter 4.

CHARACTERISTICS OF DEPOSIT ACCOUNTS AS INVESTMENTS

Certain features can typically be found in most types of deposit accounts:

- interest;

- minimum balance;

- accessibility;

- fees and/or charges;

- relationship banking policies;

- deposit insurance.

This section explores these characteristics in detail with emphasis on how each relates to deposit accounts.

Interest

Almost all types of deposit accounts available at depository institutions earn interest for the customer. In fact, the earning of interest may be one of the most important characteristics of deposit accounts from the customer's perspective. In a survey of depositors at savings institutions, respondents ranked interest rates as the second most important factor in choosing to maintain a deposit account at a particular financial institution.

Two factors that influence the actual return to the deposit account holder are the compounding of interest and the method of interest payment. Interest paid to a depositor generally is calculated as simple interest or compound interest. Possible methods of interest payment may include tiered or blended interest rates and a variety of interest distribution plans.

The wide variety of interest payment options available makes it more difficult for depositors to compare investment returns meaningfully. Thus, counselors need to be able to explain the various methods of interest payment available at their institutions.

Simple Interest

Simple interest is interest paid on the principal balance only. The depositor earns interest only on the amount held on deposit. For example, a customer who deposits

$100 to an account that pays 5% simple interest will earn
$5 interest for one year ($100 × .05 = $5).

Compound Interest

Compound interest is the interest that accrues when
earnings for a specified period are added to principal;
thus, interest for the following period is computed on the
principal plus accumulated interest. In other words, depositors earn interest on the amount they have deposited
plus interest on the interest they have earned. All other
things being equal, a compound interest account will earn
a greater return for the investor than will a simple interest
account paying the same rate of interest.

Effective yield, also called *annual yield*, is the actual
return expected on an investment after any compounding.
For example, a deposit account paying 5.5% compound
interest may have an effective yield of 5.73% if the interest remains in the account and is compounded.

Interest on deposit accounts at financial institutions
can be compounded continuously, daily, monthly, quarterly or annually. For example, if an account compounds
monthly, the interest for January is credited to the account on the last business day of the month (or February
1). During February, the interest earned during January
earns interest. The more frequently interest is compounded, the greater the return to the investor (see Figure
3-1). This phenomenon occurs because the interest
earned by the investment earns additional interest more
quickly.

Interest Rate Structures

Some depository institutions choose to pay different rates
on the same investment depending on the balance in the
account. They accomplish this through a system of tiered

F I G U R E 3-1

Effects of Compounding on Effective Yield
(Based on $10,000 Invested for One Year)

Annual Interest Rate	Compounding Frequency				
	Simple Interest	Semi-Annually	Quarterly	Monthly	Daily
5%	5.00% $ 500	5.06% $ 506	5.09% $ 509	5.12% $ 512	5.13% $ 513
6%	6.00% $ 600	6.09% $ 609	6.14% $ 614	6.17% $ 617	6.18% $ 618
7%	7.00% $ 700	7.12% $ 712	7.19% $ 719	7.23% $ 723	7.25% $ 725
8%	8.00% $ 800	8.16% $ 816	8.24% $ 824	8.30% $ 830	8.33% $ 833
9%	9.00% $ 900	9.20% $ 920	9.31% $ 931	9.38% $ 938	9.42% $ 942
10%	10.00% $1,000	10.25% $1,025	10.38% $1,038	10.47% $1,047	10.52% $1,052
11%	11.00% $1,100	11.30% $1,130	11.46% $1,146	11.57% $1,157	11.63% $1,163

Calculations based on a 365-day year; figures rounded to the nearest dollar.

rates or blended rates. Both tiered and blended rates reward customers for maintaining higher balances by paying a higher interest rate, but they have an important difference.

In a *tiered interest rate structure*, the entire account balance earns a higher rate once it reaches the designated level. For example, an institution with an interest rate tier set at $2,500 would pay the higher rate for the entire balance once the balance reaches or exceeds $2,500.

In a *blended interest rate* structure, only the balance above the designated amount earns the higher rate, while the balance below earns a lower rate. For example, an institution may offer to pay depositors 5.25% on checking account balances above $2,500 but only 3% on the portion of the balances below $2,500. In this case, a customer with $3,000 on deposit does not earn 5.25% on all of the checking account funds; instead, he or she earns a blended rate of between 3% and 5.25%.

Distribution of Earnings

The *earnings distribution date* is the date on which interest is credited to the account or otherwise made available to the account holder. Earnings on deposit accounts may be distributed monthly, quarterly, semiannually, annually or at maturity. The frequency of earnings distribution may affect the yield the depositor receives. Increased yield due to frequency of earnings distribution should not be confused with the compounding of interest discussed earlier.

Earnings distributed to deposit account holders may be either credited to the account, transferred to another account or sent to the depositor in the form of a check. Each method of distribution has advantages and disadvantages, depending on the depositor's needs.

Earnings are said to accrue when they are credited directly to the account where they were earned. One possible advantage to this method of distribution is that the earnings become principal when credited. This allows the account to earn additional interest on the increased principal balance. However, this method of earnings distribution is less advantageous if the account earns simple interest; in that case, the accrued earnings will not earn additional interest.

Earnings sent to the depositor in the form of a check or transferred to another account may also benefit the customer. Although the customer does not receive additional earnings on the original investment, he or she has the option to use the funds or deposit them elsewhere and earn additional funds.

Minimum Balance

A required investment minimum is another typical characteristic of deposit accounts. A depository institution frequently specifies a minimum deposit amount to open an account. Although there is no set standard, the minimum is likely to range from $50 to $100,000 depending on the investment.

Minimum balance requirements may benefit both institutions and depositors. In general, institutions find higher-balance accounts less costly to administer than low-balance accounts and thus provide more consolidated sources of funds for the institution to invest. The depositor often benefits from a larger deposit amount by earning a higher rate of interest.

An institution may establish policies to encourage customers to keep balances above the stated minimums. Examples of such policies are:

- imposing service charges when the account balance drops below the minimum;

- paying no interest or a lower rate of interest when the account falls below the minimum; and

- charging a penalty if the balance drops below the minimum.

Accessibility

Accessibility is how easily customers can obtain their funds. Many customers define accessibility in terms of liquidity and convenience. An important function of the counselor is to match the customer's accessibility needs with an appropriate deposit account.

Liquidity is the ability to convert an investment to cash without significant financial loss at a particular point in time. For example, a savings account is considered a liquid investment because the depositor can deposit and withdraw funds with relatively few restrictions. A depositor also knows that, in general, all deposited funds are returnable. An example of an illiquid investment is the purchase of a home. Homeowners who wish to sell their homes to raise cash have no guarantee of recouping their initial purchase prices. A homeowner may lose money on a sale if the market for homes is depressed or if property values have decreased.

Convenience refers to the ease with which depositors can access their funds. The convenience of a deposit account to a financial institution customer can be measured in many ways. Many customers appreciate the ease with which they can open deposit accounts. Some like the convenient locations of their institutions. Others appreciate the ease with which they can withdraw funds.

Fees and Charges

Some deposit accounts carry certain fees or charges. Among the common reasons institutions charge fees on deposit accounts are:

- to recover costs associated with offering the accounts;

- to earn a profit; and

- to encourage more profitable accounts.

Some deposit accounts may actually cost the institution more to administer than the financial rewards it receives from the deposits. For example, an account with a low balance but many transactions creates higher maintenance costs, which can exceed what the institution can earn by investing the balance. Some institutions charge fees and service charges on deposit accounts to make up for the high cost of administering the accounts. An example of this practice is a monthly service charge on a checking or NOW account, which helps offset the cost of offering the account to the customer.

Profit for the institution is another possible reason for charging a fee or service charge on a deposit account. Depository institutions are service providers, but they still must make a profit to remain in business.

Encouraging profitable accounts can also be a motive for imposing a fee or a service charge on deposit accounts. In general, accounts with small balances are more costly to maintain than those with higher balances. Because of this, some institutions charge a fee when the account balance falls below a predetermined amount. The purpose of such a fee is to encourage depositors to carry larger balances.

Relationship Banking Policies

In certain cases, depository institutions set policies that encourage relationship banking. *Relationship banking* is the selling of additional products and services that enhance the value of the initial account. For example, a customer who opens a high-balance certificate of deposit at a financial institution may qualify for a checking account with a low minimum balance and no monthly service charge.

Both the customer and the institution benefit through relationship banking policies. The customer profits from the added value of the additional product or service. For example, convenience and cost savings are added values for a customer whose regular savings account entitles him or her to a free checking account and low-cost traveler's checks, all from the same institution.

Institutions benefit through relationship banking from larger account balances and increased customer loyalty. Account balances may be larger because customers who have several accounts at an institution often maintain higher balances. Also, customers may develop increased loyalty to an institution if they use several services.

Deposit Insurance

Federal deposit insurance is another characteristic of many deposit accounts at financial institutions. Many customers choose to invest their funds at financial institutions because of the safety afforded by deposit insurance. Depositors gain peace of mind from knowing their money is secure.

The U.S. Congress has formed various agencies to guarantee the safety of funds deposited at depository institutions. Such funds are backed by the full faith and credit of the United States, up to prescribed limits. Institutions covered by federal deposit insurance are required to operate under strict guidelines to promote the safety of funds and are subject to periodic examinations by the insuring agency. The insuring agencies also require the institutions to display notice of the insuring agency for customers to see.

REGULAR SAVINGS ACCOUNTS

A *regular savings account* is a form of deposit account with no legal limits or requirements as to amount, duration, or times of additions or withdrawals. Credit unions call this type of deposit account a *share account*.

Regular savings accounts may be the oldest and best known type of deposit account. They appeal to a broad range of customers. In one consumer survey, 70% of the respondents said they had a regular savings account.[1]

Regular savings accounts come in either a passbook or statement record-keeping format. A passbook account takes its name from the small booklet in which the financial institution records such account transactions as deposits, withdrawals and interest postings. For a statement account, the institution records account transactions on a monthly or quarterly statement that it sends to the customer.

A variation of the regular savings account is a *club account*. With this type of account, the customer makes a certain number of periodic deposits over a specified time interval. At the end of this period, the institution usually closes the account and distributes the funds in a lump sum to the customer. The best known types of club account are Christmas or vacation club accounts. In the latter type, for example, the customer may deposit $10 a week for one year to save for a vacation trip.

Typical Features

Regular savings accounts generally have few restrictions or requirements. The minimum balance is often the lowest required for any type of deposit account at a particular institution. Some institutions allow as little as $1 to open an account; others have minimum requirements such as $50, $100 or higher. Many institutions impose no restrictions on deposits or withdrawals. Some charge no fees to maintain savings accounts, while others may charge a fee for low balances or a large number of transactions.

One important restriction with this category of deposit accounts is a regulated prohibition on check-writing privileges. Customers cannot write third-party checks against the account. However, customers can request payment of withdrawn funds in the form of a check.

An institution often pays a lower rate of interest on regular savings accounts than on most other types of deposit accounts. One reason is that balances in this type of account can fluctuate unpredictably. Therefore, institutions must be more cautious about making loans or other long-term investments with regular savings account funds. They must keep cash on hand to meet unexpected withdrawals. Also, these accounts may have low average balances and therefore carry higher account maintenance costs per deposit dollar than high-balance accounts. One such cost is maintaining the account on the institution's computer system.

Customer Benefits

Regular savings accounts are popular because they provide several benefits to customers. The primary attractions are that they are simple to understand and convenient to use. Because they have few restrictions, regular savings accounts are easy to open and funds are easily accessible. Also, they offer customers an easy record-keeping system; the customer can quickly determine the current balance and keep track of saving and spending activities.

When discussing this type of account with customers, the counselor can demonstrate how it can meet certain investment goals. For example, a regular savings account may be appropriate for a customer who wants a deposit account to help with emergencies or other unexpected financial needs. With the easy accessibility and minimal restrictions such an account offers, the customer can get to the funds whenever he or she needs them.

A regular savings account can also serve as a base for future financial plans. For example, Christopher, a recent college graduate, wants to start a savings and investment program. He explains to the counselor that he wants to start saving systematically by depositing a regular amount from each paycheck. He also intends to deposit any unexpected windfalls, such as occasional cash gifts from his grandparents. His aim is to build up his savings so that he can make other investments when he has accumulated a larger amount. The counselor can describe to Christopher how a regular savings account can meet his long-range financial goals. For example, with a regular savings account, Christopher can easily shift funds in and out of the account as he makes decisions on various investments.

Many customers view regular savings accounts as a haven for money needed in emergencies, as a vehicle for disciplined and regular cash accumulations, and as a way to set aside funds for a particular purpose, such as taking a vacation or buying a car. Many depositors regard regular savings accounts as the mainstay of their overall financial programs, because these accounts provide "the opportunity for small investments, the convenience of an emergency financial reserve, a persuasive credit reference, and a ready introduction to a loan source."[2]

CHECKING ACCOUNTS: NOW, SHARE DRAFT AND REGULAR CHECKING ACCOUNTS

NOW, share draft and regular checking accounts have an important characteristic in common: All are deposit accounts on which customers can write an unlimited number of third-party checks. These types of deposit accounts have some important differences, but customers often view them simply as variations on checking accounts. Therefore, counselors may need to help customers choose the most appropriate version for their needs.

Checks and Drafts

Depending on certain factors, either checks or drafts are drawn against NOW, share draft and regular checking accounts. A *draft* is an instrument on which one party orders another party to pay money to a third party. For example, John owes $10 to Ann and Ann owes $10 to Matt. Ann writes an order telling John to pay $10 to Matt and gives it to Matt. Matt presents the order to John, who pays Matt the money. A *check* is a type of draft;

the Uniform Commercial Code defines it as "a draft drawn on a bank and payable on demand."[3] Under this definition, checks are drawn on checking accounts at banks, while drafts are drawn on similar accounts at other financial institutions. For this reason, counselors occasionally see legal or procedural references to NOW account drafts or share drafts. However, the following discussion by a legal authority deemphasizes the differences between checks and drafts with respect to customer use.

> The Code distinguishes between a draft and a check... Both are simply negotiable instruments that order some third person to pay a sum of money. The "check" is characterized, among other things, by the fact that the third person is a "bank." The Code defines a "bank" very generally in 1-201(4) as "any person engaged in the business of banking." What, then, is "the business of banking"? And who is engaged in that "business"? The Code is silent on that. Both federal and local banking law usually are not. As a result, a thrift institution, e.g., a savings bank or savings and loan association, that may describe itself as a "bank" may not be a "bank," and thus an instrument drawn on that institution is not a "check" in the technical sense, but a "draft." The depositors in the thrift institution probably know little and care less about the technical nature of the instrument. For them, it looks like a "check" and, at least for their immediate purposes, works like a check, and that is check enough for them.[4] (In this same publication, the author refers to credit unions as another example of a typical financial intermediary.)

Despite the differences between checks and drafts, customers refer to both as checks and the accounts as checking accounts. For ease of reference, this chapter will use this terminology.

Negotiability

A check is considered a negotiable instrument. This means that it is transferable from one person to another in return for equivalent value so that the title passes to the payee. The UCC provides that for any written document to be a negotiable instrument, it must:

- be signed by the maker or drawer;

- contain an unconditional promise to pay a specified sum of money;

- be payable on demand or at a definite time; and

- be payable to order (that is, to someone) or to the bearer.[5]

Parts of a Check

Although each institution has its own check design, most check formats are standardized. Figure 3-2 shows the basic parts of a check:

- a place for the date;

- words of negotiability;

- a line for the stated payee;

- a place for the amount both in figures (line 4a) and in writing (line 4b);

- the name of the drawee institution (the institution in which the checking account is held);

- a line for the signature of the drawer (the owner of the account).

The Uniform Comm. Code does not specify that a under line be present on a doc.

F I G U R E 3-2

Parts of a Check

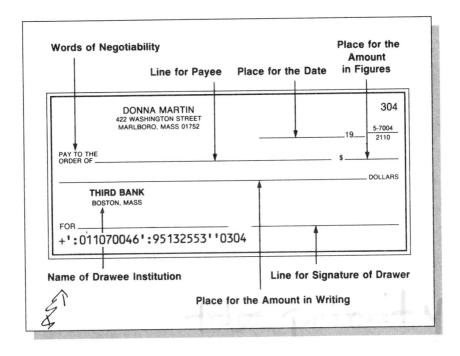

The Check-Clearing Process

Today's check-clearing system evolved from the need to efficiently settle checks drawn on one bank and presented for payment or credit at another. Commercial banks developed local *clearinghouses*—organizations to which member banks send their checks to be sorted and routed, and that debit and credit funds to the accounts of each member bank. Today, most major cities have a clearing-house whose member institutions are credited for checks drawn on other banks and debited for their own checks presented at other banks daily. In addition to local clear-inghouses, the Federal Reserve banks route checks on both a regional and nationwide basis. Checks generally clear promptly through the Federal Reserve System. This is important because laws restrict the amount of time funds from deposited checks can be considered unavail-able to depositors (see Chapter 2).

Magnetic Ink Character Recognition   *Magnetic ink character recognition (MICR)* facilitates the routing and identification of checks and drafts by electronically read-ing machine-readable characters printed in magnetic ink on the checks. The routing number of the drawee insti-tution, the customer's account number and the check se-rial number are printed in magnetic ink on the instrument itself. The check in Figure 3-2 shows this MICR encoding along the bottom edge.

Generally, the amount of the check is encoded as part of the proof-of-deposit process by the financial institution at which the check is first deposited. If this institution lacks the capability to MICR encode items, the first in-stitution in the check-clearing process with automated check-processing equipment encodes the amount for the institution.

Returned Checks and Endorsement Standards
Sometimes a check is returned unpaid. Reasons can in-clude that the drawer's deposit balance is lower than the amount of the check (known as "not sufficient funds," or NSF), or the check was made out or endorsed improperly. Whatever the reason, a check that is returned unpaid must be routed back through the same clearing process through which it came.

The need for prompt handling of returned items is the primary reason behind the endorsement standards enacted in Regulation CC. Prior to this regulation, returned or dishonored checks presented obstacles to efficient processing, because the endorsements were often faint, blurred, incomplete, misplaced or overlapping. Without clear endorsements, the returning institution had difficulty routing the check correctly and quickly. The endorsement standards in Regulation CC provide a system for clarifying endorsements and routing returned checks as expeditiously as possible. If an institution does not follow these standards and its noncompliance contributes to the delayed remittal of a returned check, it can be deemed responsible for obstructing the return-item process and perhaps liable for financial damages.

The endorsement standards cover several requirements. The most important one for counselors to remember is the proper placement of the endorsement on the check. When accepting checks from customers, the knowledgeable counselor can help ensure that the endorsements meet the required standards.

In order for the payer to identify an endorsement quickly, the endorsement should appear in a specific location on the back of the check. As Figure 3-3 shows, the back of a check is divided into three zones:

- payee zone;

- depositary bank zone;

- subsequent collecting bank zone.

The counselor should direct the customer to endorse the check within the 1.5-inch payee zone that starts at the trailing edge of the check. Then the financial institution accepting the check places its endorsement in the depositary bank zone. (Usually a teller or counselor stamps the institution's standard endorsement in this spot.) The depositary bank zone starts three inches from the leading

F I G U R E 3-3

Regulation CC Endorsement Placement Standards

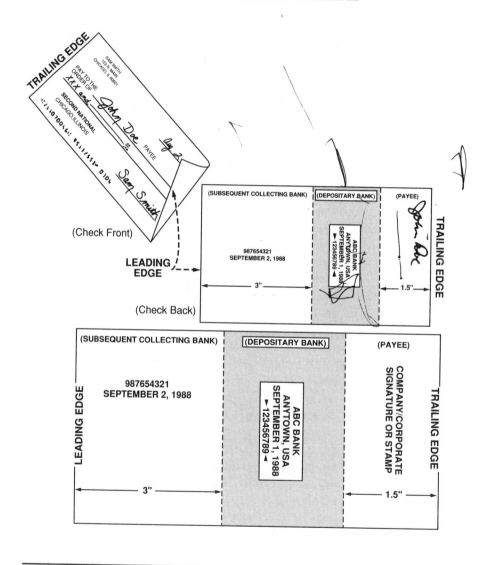

edge to 1.5 inches from the trailing edge. The third zone is the subsequent collecting bank zone and includes the section of the check three inches from the leading edge. The institution that handles the check following the depositary bank places its information in this area.

Regulation CC does not specify the size of the depositary bank zone other than that it is the space remaining between the 1.5-inch payee zone and the three-inch subsequent collecting bank zone. Obviously, the size of the depositary bank zone varies with the size of the check, and this can make exact placement of the endorsement more difficult for financial institution employees to determine (see Figure 3-3 for examples of two different-size checks).

To ease this problem, some institutions have suggested a rough standard for tellers to follow when stamping the institution's endorsement on checks. The 1.5-inch payee zone is roughly equal to the width of two fingers laid just next to the trailing edge of the check. By placing two fingers in this zone, tellers can quickly gauge the correct placement of the endorsement stamp.

Truncation/Check Safekeeping Depending on individual institution policy, cleared checks may or may not be returned to customers. If an institution returns checks to customers, it usually mails them with the monthly statement of account transactions. *Check truncation* is the process of microfilming customers' paid checks; the microfilm is the official record of the transaction. The customer's institution (or other designated clearing institution) retains the official record and does not return the canceled checks to the account holder. This system is also called *check safekeeping.*

Some institutions offer one system or the other, while some offer both. Check truncation usually is less costly for institutions, because it reduces the cost of mailing checking account statements. Also, institutions can reduce certain back office operations such as check filing. Thus, some institutions offer check truncation in combination with discounted fees, lower minimum balance requirements or higher interest rates.

Typical Features of Checking Accounts

Features of checking accounts vary considerably among financial institutions. The key features counselors need to know about their own institutions' accounts and those of competitors are:

- minimum balance and any fees charged if the account balance drops below the minimum;

- whether the account earns interest, the interest rate and on what basis the interest is calculated. For example, one institution may pay daily interest on the actual balance in the account each day, another may pay interest on the average balance in the account over one month, and still another may pay interest only on the lowest balance in the account during the month;

- fees charged such as per-check fees, monthly maintenance fees, NSF check fees, stop-payment fees, check printing fees, and account research or reconciliation fees; and

- whether use of other services (i.e., relationship banking) reduces account fees or improves other features.

In addition, many institutions offer at least two or more different types of checking accounts to attract customers with varying needs. For example, an institution might offer one type of account with a low minimum balance requirement in combination with a per-check or monthly maintenance fee, and another type with a high minimum balance and no per-check or monthly fee. By offering different plans, institutions try to meet the varying needs of customers while offsetting the cost of the checking accounts.

Regular Checking Accounts

Of the several features that set regular checking accounts apart from NOW accounts and share draft accounts, one feature is especially important. Regular checking accounts (or demand deposit accounts) are legally prohibited from paying interest.

In the past, the government placed restrictions on how some depository institutions could offer regular checking accounts. Savings institutions could only offer those non-interest bearing accounts to a narrow range of business customers.

These requirements changed with the enactment of the Financial Institutions Reform, Recovery and Enforcement Act of 1989. This law authorized federally chartered savings institutions to offer demand accounts to all customers.

NOW and Share Draft Accounts

The Depository Institutions Deregulation and Monetary Control Act of 1980 established NOW accounts and share draft accounts as two of its provisions. A *NOW account* is an account from which the account holder can withdraw funds by writing a negotiable order of withdrawal, called a *NOW draft*, payable to a third party. Unlike regular checking accounts, NOW accounts can legally earn interest. Both banks and savings institutions can offer NOW accounts. A *share draft account* is a similar type of account offered by federally insured credit unions that also earns interest. Credit union members can access account funds by writing share drafts.

Only certain categories of customers can open NOW accounts and share draft accounts. The funds in the account must be owned by:

- one or more individuals (or members at a credit union);

- an organization that is operated primarily for religious, philanthropic, charitable, educational, political, or other, similar purposes, and is not operated for profit; or

- a government unit.

In addition, regulators have permitted businesses that are operated as sole proprietorships to open NOW accounts. Examples would be a plumber or accountant who are self employed.

Customer Benefits

The primary benefits of a checking account concern the payment-making aspect. Checking accounts offer customers a highly convenient method for making payments at any time and place and in any amount their balances allow. Customers need not make a special trip to get checks from the offices of their financial institutions. Checking accounts also provide a secure method for making payments through the mail. It is risky to mail cash, and checks eliminate worry about items being lost in the mail; checks are replaceable, but cash is not. In addition, cancelled checks serve as receipts for funds the customer has given to other parties. Even if the customer's checks are truncated, he or she always has the security of being able to obtain copies when needed. Finally, with checking accounts that earn interest, customers can earn interest on balances that they must keep for transaction purposes anyway and otherwise would lie idle.

Counselors can help customers understand the various features of checking accounts and thus choose the best plans for their needs. They can help customers weigh the value of earning interest against requirements such as minimum balances and various fees. By establishing how customers plan to use their accounts, counselors can determine the size of the balances customers plan to maintain and how many checks they intend to use.

A survey of deposit account customers (see Figure 3-4) demonstrated the importance of savings and checking accounts to their basic financial planning and long-term relationships with their financial institutions. Customers were asked to identify the first type of account or service they held or received at a particular financial institution. A significant majority of respondents, particularly younger customers, named either a savings account or a checking account. These accounts help customers fulfill their primary financial needs and establish a money management relationship with a financial institution.

SUMMARY

When customers open deposit accounts, they must make decisions about the type of investment that will best meet their needs. Typical types of investments are regular savings accounts, checking accounts, money market deposit

F I G U R E 3-4

**First Account or Service Held or Received
at a Particular Financial Institution**

Age of Head of Household	Checking Account	Savings Account	Other Services
18 to 24	37.3%	56.0%	6.7%
25 to 34	47.6%	31.2%	21.2%
35 to 44	38.1%	31.4%	30.5%
45 to 54	27.4%	35.1%	37.5%
55 to 64	26.2%	30.2%	43.6%
65 and over	20.4%	31.4%	48.2%

accounts and certificates of deposit. This chapter describes the first two types.

Regular savings accounts impose few restrictions and have a broad appeal to consumers. They are simple to understand and use, and fulfill certain basic money management needs. Checking accounts are oriented toward making day-to-day payments easier and more secure. A primary difference between these two types of accounts is that checking accounts include check-writing privileges while regular savings accounts do not.

Both types of investments respond to important consumer financial needs. For the majority of customers, the first account opened at a financial institution is a regular savings account or a checking account.

FOOTNOTES

[1]"Banking: Part Two," *Consumer Reports* (August 1988), p. 495.

[2]George A. Christy and John C. Glendenin, *Introduction to Investments* (New York: McGraw-Hill, 1979), p. 518.

[3]Sec. 3-104(2).

[4]Thomas M. Quinn, *Quinn's UCC Forms and Practice: Volume 1/Articles 1-5* (Boston: Warren, Gorham & Lamont, 1987), pp. 3-126.

[5]Sec. 3-104(1).

CHAPTER 4

Types of Investments: Money Market Deposit Accounts and Certificates of Deposit

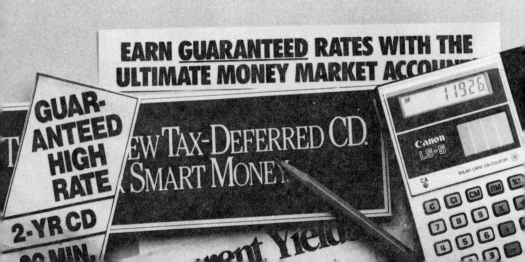

KEY CONCEPTS

- Typical features and customer benefits of money market deposit accounts;

- Typical features and customer benefits of certificates of deposit;

- Investment patterns associated with three customer age ranges;

- Important sources of investment information for customers.

Money market deposit accounts and certificates of deposit are two other major types of deposit accounts used as investments. These accounts complement regular savings and checking accounts in customers' financial plans. While regular savings and checking accounts are the core accounts that meet customers' daily transaction and savings needs, money market deposit accounts and certificates of deposit can be used to expand a customer's investment possibilities. These accounts are oriented toward larger investment balances and longer-term investment goals.

MONEY MARKET DEPOSIT ACCOUNTS

A *money market deposit account (MMDA)* is intended to compete with money market mutual funds. It has few legal restrictions other than some limitations on the monthly number of certain transactions. The features of MMDAs generally vary among financial institutions, but the majority of options are influenced by the economic and legislative history of this account.

Money market deposit accounts are a recent phenomenon relative to other types of deposit investments such as regular savings and checking accounts, but they have an interesting history. MMDAs were created in response to economic conditions that developed in the late 1970s. At that time, interest rates were rising precipitously, and mutual fund investment companies were luring millions of savers to their newly established money market mutual funds. *Money market mutual funds* pool investors' funds to purchase short-term, large-denomination securities offered by the U.S. Treasury, large corporations, commercial banks and certain government organizations. Money invested in money market mutual funds is not insured by an agency of the federal government. These funds allow check-writing privileges but may set a minimum check amount, such as $500 or $1,000. Their interest rate is competitive with those on other investments; however, it is not guaranteed and usually fluctuates. Due to the generally high interest rates available, these funds grew from zero in the mid-1970s to over $330 billion by the late 1980s.

The outflow of funds from deposit accounts at depository institutions into money market mutual funds adversely affected the balance of competition between depository institutions and investment companies. As a result, in 1982 Congress included a directive in the Garn-St Germain Depository Institutions Act, which established a "new deposit account [that] shall be directly equivalent to and competitive with money market mutual funds." The new money market deposit account was immediately popular with savers. Within eight weeks of its introduction, savers deposited $254 billion in MMDAs.

When the money market deposit account was first established, regulations included certain restrictions, such as a high minimum balance. Since that time, these restrictions have almost entirely disappeared. Today, the features of money market deposit accounts are highly competitive with those of other types of investments.

Typical Features

Typical features of MMDAs fall into the categories of account balances, transaction limitations and interest rates.

Account Balance

Institutions often set a relatively high minimum balance, such as $1,000 or $2,500, on money market deposit accounts. Accounts that offer exceptionally high rates of interest may require balances as high as $10,000 or even $25,000. Some institutions charge a monthly fee if the account balance drops below the established minimum.

Transaction Limitations

One legal restriction that remains on money market deposit accounts is a limitation on the monthly number of certain transactions. The purpose of this restriction is to qualify the funds as savings deposits and avoid imposition of higher reserve requirements for transaction accounts under Regulation D of the Federal Reserve (see Chapter 2 for an explanation of reserve requirements). Under this regulation, preauthorized or automatic transfers from an MMDA to another account of the depositor or to a third party are limited to six per calendar month (or four-week statement cycle). Three of these transfers may be made by checks drawn by the depositor to third parties. If fewer than three third-party checks are written in a given month, more than three preauthorized or automatic transfers may be allowed, up to a total of six. Telephone transfers and certain other debits from the account are also limited; however, some other types of debits are not restricted. Figure 4-1 summarizes the restrictions imposed by Regulation D.

To ensure compliance with transaction restrictions, institutions may refuse withdrawals that exceed the limitations or monitor accounts for excess withdrawals and contact customers when they occur. Some institutions charge a penalty for excess withdrawals.

F I G U R E 4-1

MMDA Monthly Transaction Limitations (Regulation D)

Limited Transactions (Up to Six)	Unlimited Transactions
• Preauthorized; automatic; or data transmission agreement, order or instruction to another account of the depositor at the same institution, to the institution itself or to a third party: No more than *three* of the six transfers may be made by: —check, draft or similar device drawn by the depositor to third parties —debit card transfers to third parties • Telephone transfers from MMDA to another account of the same depositor at the same institution	• Interaccount transfers in person or at an automated teller machine from MMDAs to accounts of the same account holder at the same institution • Transfers from MMDAs to repay loans and associated expenses at the same institution (except overdraft loans on depositor's demand account) • Cash or check withdrawals made in person, by mail, messenger, ATM or telephone (if paid by check to the depositor)

Interest Rate

Interest rates on MMDAs generally are high compared to those on other deposit accounts. Usually they are the highest for accounts that include check-writing privileges and compare favorably with rates on some certificates of deposit.

Money market accounts are likely to have tiered or blended rates of interest which benefit high-balance account holders. For example, the following two approaches demonstrate how institutions might use tiered rates. First, below a specified balance, the account may pay the institution's passbook rate or an even lower rate. At a higher balance, the account earns a higher rate. For example, an institution could pay the regular savings rate if the balance is below $2,500. If the balance is higher than $2,500, the account earns a market rate of interest.

Second, at some institutions, if the balance falls below the specified minimum, the account may earn no interest at all. For example, an institution could set a minimum balance of $1,000 to earn the rate on regular savings. If the balance falls below $1,000, the account earns no interest. If the account balance is above a higher, specified balance—say, at $5,000—the account usually earns a higher, market interest rate.

To remain competitive with money market mutual funds, rates on MMDAs fluctuate along with the rates offered on other nondeposit investments. Some financial institutions adjust the MMDA rate on a weekly or daily basis. This rate fluctuation contrasts with the relatively stable rates most institutions offer on regular savings and checking accounts. Although institutions may also adjust rates on these accounts, they seldom do so as frequently as they do on money market deposit accounts.

Customer Benefits

For many customers, the key benefit of MMDAs is high return combined with moderate accessibility of funds. For a customer who has more funds to invest than are needed for a passbook account, the money market deposit account is an excellent vehicle for earning a higher rate of interest. If the customer does not need the full range of accessibility (any amount, at any time, at any frequency and by any medium), the few restrictions on accessibility to a money market deposit account should present no problems.

For example, consider Sandra, who has a NOW account and a passbook account. She believes she is keeping an unnecessarily large balance in the passbook account and is considering transferring a portion of the funds to another investment. While talking to a counselor, she mentions that she has no long-range savings goals; at this stage in her life, she is not particularly concerned about retirement savings or buying a home. She does mention that she likes to travel, but because her job is demanding and her work load is not always predictable, she usually cannot make long-range vacation plans. Instead, she takes a few short trips each year with a few days' or weeks' notice and uses her passbook account funds for this purpose. The counselor describes a money market deposit account to Sandra because it will earn her a return higher than the passbook rate and still give her accessibility to her vacation funds.

CERTIFICATES OF DEPOSIT

A *certificate of deposit*, also called a *certificate* or *CD*, is a type of deposit account that typically has a fixed minimum term and requires a minimum initial deposit. At credit unions, these accounts are called share certificates. Certificates of deposit often earn the highest rates available on deposit accounts, but most institutions place significant restrictions on the accessibility of funds.

Typical Features

Generally, certificates have more features than the other types of deposit account investments. As with money market deposit accounts, these features fall into the categories of account balance, transaction limitations and interest rate.

Account Balance

Institutions usually require a high minimum balance, such as $500 or $1,000, to open a certificate. At one time the minimum balance was regulated at $1,000, and this precedent continues to influence current practice. However, some institutions may set a low minimum balance if they particularly wish to attract funds into these accounts.

Transaction Limitations

A key feature of certificates is that they have a set term, such as six months or one year, during which the funds are intended to remain in the account. The *maturity date* is the date on which the account holder may redeem the certificate for the principal balance plus interest. Based on this feature, institutions establish restrictions on deposits, renewals and withdrawals.

Deposits and Renewals   Most institutions place some restrictions on deposits to certificates. Many do not allow deposits to a certificate after the account is opened. Those institutions that do allow deposits may have restrictions on the amount or timing of additions. Also, the new deposits usually must remain in the account for the remainder of the term and may extend the term of the account for a full term from the date of the latest deposit.

Depending on the conditions of the investment contract, the institution may or may not renew the term of a certificate. With renewable certificates, the institution may offer to renew the account at the current rate available on a certificate of that term. If a certificate is renewable, the customer is allowed a *grace period* within which to either withdraw the funds or allow the certificate to renew for another term. The grace period generally is seven to 10 days following the maturity date. If the account is not renewable, the customer must make another investment with the funds. Some nonrenewable certificate contracts provide that if the customer does not withdraw the funds within the grace period, the funds will be transferred to a regular savings account.

Withdrawals　　Most institutions also place significant restrictions on withdrawals from certificates. These restrictions include no third-party check-writing privileges and penalties or limitations on withdrawals made before the maturity date.

Often institutions do not restrict withdrawals of interest earned by and credited to a certificate during the term. With an account that earns simple interest, this feature allows the customer to make another investment with funds that otherwise would lie idle. However, some institutions stipulate that if a certificate renews for another term, the interest earned in the first term is considered as principal during the next term and is subject to the usual restrictions on withdrawal from the principal.

Institutions usually discourage withdrawals from the principal balance of a certificate by assessing a penalty. A *penalty* is a charge imposed on the account holder for making a total or partial withdrawal from the certificate prior to its maturity date. The purpose of a penalty is to encourage customers to open certificates only for time periods during which they will not need to use the funds. Thus, if customer's financial needs change, the customer will still have immediate access to the funds but will have to pay the penalty.

The severity of the penalty depends on the terms of the certificate contract. Often the penalty involves a loss of some or all of the interest earned. Federal Reserve Regulation 204.2 requires minimum penalties of interest loss (to avoid payment of transaction account reserves), but institutions are allowed to assess more severe penalties. Some penalties involve larger amounts than the interest earned. Some institutions impose larger penalties for longer-term certificates. The certificate itself discloses the penalty terms and other important conditions of the contract. Figure 4-2 gives a sample of terms disclosed in a certificate.

Regulators for certain depository institutions require the waiver of early withdrawal penalties in specific situations. Mandatory penalty waivers apply:

- after the death of an account owner if any other owner of the account or the authorized representative of the decedent's estate requests the withdrawal; or

- after an account owner has been legally declared incompetent if the account was issued before the date of the determination and was not extended or renewed after that date.

Some institutions depart from tradition by offering no-penalty CDs (except for penalties that meet Federal Reserve regulation requirements). With these accounts, institutions allow penalty-free withdrawals at certain points during the term of the certificate, such as at one-year intervals on multiple-year certificates. The

F I G U R E 4-2

Sample Terms of Certificate of Deposit

	050-0001234
	Account Number
	FEB 28,89
	Date of Issuance
	$ 10,000.00
	Opening Balance
	FEB 28,90
	Initial Maturity Date

EQUITABLE SAVINGS
AND LOAN ASSOCIATION
NON NEGOTIABLE/NON TRANSFERABLE
FIXED RATE CERTIFICATE OF DEPOSIT
1 TO 4 YEAR TERM

I. Account Summary Section:

ACCOUNTHOLDER(S)   MR. ROBERT TELLER OR
MRS. SUZIE TELLER AS JOINT TENANTS
1234 ANYWHERE AVENUE
OTHERTOWN, WI

MINIMUM BALANCE	TERM	RATE	FREQUENCY OF COMPOUNDING
500.00	12 MONTHS	8.30%	DAILY
NO ADDITIONS PERMITTED	RENEWAL TERM — SEE SECTION IV		

Earnings distribution shall be at the end of each calendar quarter with the last distribution on the final maturity date.

II. General Section:
This certifies that the Accountholder holds a savings account with the Opening Balance and for the initial term expiring on the Initial Maturity Date shown hereon in Equitable Savings and Loan Association of Milwaukee, Wisconsin.

III. Earnings Section:
This account will receive earnings at the Rate of Earnings and with the Frequency of Compounding as above set forth. Such earnings shall be payable on the Earnings Distribution Dates above set forth, provided the balance in the account is not reduced below the Minimum Balance Requirement. If such balance is reduced below the Minimum Balance Requirement, the Rate of Earnings on the remaining balance shall thereafter be reduced to the rate then paid on regular savings accounts (also see Section V).

IV. Renewal Section:
This account shall be automatically renewed for a like term at the close of business on the Initial Maturity Date or on the maturity date of any renewal term unless (1) it is withdrawn within the 7-day period referred to in Section V hereof or (2) at least 15 days prior to any maturity date, the association gives written notice to the Accountholder that this account will not be renewed. In such latter event, upon maturity the account will be converted to a regular savings account and receive earnings at the rate then paid on regular savings accounts.
The rate of earnings for any renewal term shall be at the rate the Association is paying at that time on renewed accounts of this class.

V. Penalty Clause Section:
In the event of any withdrawal of principal from this account prior to a maturity date, the Accountholder shall forfeit an amount equal to six months of interest whether earned or not, on the amount withdrawn at the simple interest rate being paid on the amount, regardless of the length of time the funds withdrawn have remained in the account.
The penalty prescribed herein will not be imposed for withdrawal of principal following the death or adjudication of incompetence of any Accountholder.
Any withdrawal which reduces the account balance below the Minimum Balance Requirement, or any change in the term or Rate of Earnings prior to maturity, shall be considered as a withdrawal of the entire account balance and shall be subject to the penalty prescribed herein.
Earnings credited to the account during any term may be withdrawn at any time during such term without penalty. If the account is renewed at the same earnings rate, earnings during the preceding term as well as the current term may be withdrawn at any time without penalty during the Renewal Term. If the Renewal Term rate is different, earnings in the account at the commencement of the Renewal Term shall be deemed merged with the principal and only earnings for the Renewal Term may be withdrawn at any time without penalty during such term.
If the account or any portion thereof is withdrawn not more than 7 days after a maturity date, earnings shall be paid thereon at the Rate of Earnings above set forth to the date of withdrawal without reduction for any penalty.
To the extent necessary to comply with these requirements, deductions shall be made from the amount withdrawn or the remaining account balance.

EQUITABLE SAVINGS AND LOAN ASSOCIATION

By _____
Authorized Signature

competitive conditions of the local CD market may affect whether or not an institution offers this type of product.

Interest Rate

To offset the disincentives of their restrictions, certificates offer higher interest rates than do other deposit accounts. And customers have shown that rate is important in their selection of CD. In one survey, customers rated "best rates available" as the single most important reason for maintaining their most important CDs at specific institutions.[1]

In addition, institutions use various interest rate strategies to differentiate their certificates from competitors' products. Examples of these strategies include:

- *Higher rates for longer-term accounts.* An institution may offer certificate plans with different terms, such as six months, one year, two years, five years and 10 years, with progressively higher rates.

- *Higher rates for higher-minimum-balance accounts.* An institution may set a standard minimum balance for all certificates but offer an additional certificate that pays a higher rate with a markedly higher balance.

- *Higher rates for retirement plan accounts.* Because of their purpose, retirement funds are usually stable and can remain with an institution for many years if the customer is satisfied with the return on investment. Chapter 9 discusses these types of accounts.

- *Rates that rise at set intervals during the certif-*

icate term. Some institutions offer a long-term account whose interest rate rises at intervals such as every six months. Such an account is designed to attract customers who are hesitant about committing their funds to a long-term account when they believe market interest rates will rise during that period. For these accounts, institutions may guarantee a minimum rate of interest and a minimum rise in rate at each interval.

- *Variable rates that rise and fall with market rates.* During times of fluctuating interest rates, customers may be more inclined to keep funds in accounts that do not have term restrictions. To attract these depositors, institutions may establish certificates with variable interest rates that are indexed to an established economic indicator, such as rates on Treasury securities.

Figure 4-3 compares and contrasts the key features of MMDAs and CDs with those of regular savings and checking accounts.

Customer Benefits

In general, certificates are particularly appropriate for longer-term investment objectives, especially those associated with a particular time in the future. For example, a 10-year certificate would be a good choice for an individual who wishes to retire in 10 years and has saved a substantial sum for that purpose.

Furthermore, the range of terms various CDs offer can help customers manage maturities. Short-term CDs enable depositors to renew their accounts frequently—a potential advantage when interest rates are rising.

F I G U R E 4-3

Typical Features of Four Types of Deposit Accounts

	Regular Savings Account	Checking Account	Money Market Account	Certificate of Deposit
Minimum Balance	Low	Low to Mid-range	Mid-range to High	Mid-range to High
Interest Rate	Low	Low	High	High
Checkwriting	No	Yes	Yes (restricted)	No
Transaction Limitations	No	No	Yes	Yes
Term	No	No	No	Yes
Fees	Low	Variable	Variable	None, or low

Long-term certificates with a fixed interest rate let depositors obtain a sustained and predictable rate for many years without the capital fluctuations that ordinarily affect long-term investments. To take advantage of these different benefits, customers can open several certificates rather than commit all their funds to one account.

In addition, the high interest rate can be a critical feature for some customers. For an individual who is interested in the highest return and does not have an investment objective, but is still not concerned with accessibility, a certificate could be the best choice.

Renewal provisions are another important benefit. One survey asked certificate holders what they planned to do with the funds when the accounts matured. A significant number (43.2%) were unsure, but a large number (36.1%) planned to invest in another CD. For customers like these, renewal offers an easy way to reinvest.[2]

COUNSELING CUSTOMERS ON TYPE OF INVESTMENT

Individuals open deposit accounts to meet specific investment objectives. These objectives are unique to each customer and reflect that person's financial needs and plans for the future. However, many investments also reflect typical patterns that are connected to stages in a person's life (see Figure 4-4). As this chart shows, younger individuals may be most concerned about saving for emergency needs and upcoming large purchases, such as a car, furniture or a home. Middle-aged individuals place a significant emphasis on saving for retirement and sending children to college. Older people renew their concern for meeting unexpected expenses and want their investments to provide additional income.

Deposit accounts offer customers a wide choice of investments for meeting their objectives. The four primary types—regular savings accounts, checking accounts, money market deposit accounts and certificates of deposit—can be divided into a substantial number of subtypes that reflect the variety of features offered by individual institutions.

The variety of accounts available presents special problems for customers trying to gather information to make

F I G U R E 4-4

Most Important Reason for Saving or Investing Money

Age of Head of Household	Rainy Day/ Emergency	Retirement	Income	Future Purchase	College
18 to 24	40.9%	6.8%	16.5%	23.0%	12.9%
25 to 34	37.5%	20.0%	11.1%	15.2%	16.2%
35 to 44	30.8%	27.7%	9.9%	9.6%	21.8%
45 to 54	25.8%	46.1%	14.4%	4.4%	9.3%
55 to 64	25.7%	49.9%	18.2%	4.1%	2.0%
65 and over	43.2%	15.4%	34.2%	5.5%	1.5%
Total	34.5%	28.6%	20.3%	7.9%	8.7%

investment decisions. Customers find it time-consuming to research and sort through the myriad possibilities to find the accounts best suited to their needs. They read conflicting advertisements and hear differing advice from friends or experts.

Customers have rated the importance of these sources of information, and the results show a definite pattern. Counselors at financial institutions appear to have a significant effect on customer decision making (see Figure 4-5). Younger customers strongly depend on friends or relatives (possibly their parents) for advice, but after this stage they begin using other sources of information heavily. As they grow older, customers rate counselors as an increasingly important source of information on investing their money. Their respect for counselors continues to increase as they gain more experience with the assistance that counselors can provide.

As the survey in Figure 4-5 shows, counselors can increase their significance to customers by using brochures and articles from news media in their discussions with them. Written sources that support counselors' statements can substantially enhance counselors' effectiveness in promoting their institutions' products.

Counselors can help both customers and their institutions by learning all the features of their institutions' accounts and comparing them to features of key competitors' accounts. This strategy can help counselors more easily identify the competitive advantages of their institutions' products. As a result, counselors can respond intelligently to customers' questions and help them make comparisons.

Customers appreciate this type of assistance and may even choose to patronize particular institutions over competitors because of their counselors' professionalism. Customers may make these choices even if competitors offer

F I G U R E 4-5

Source of Information Rated Most Important

Age of Head of Household	Stock Broker	Savings Counselor	Adver- tisement	Friends, Relatives	News Media	Promotional Literature
18 to 24	4.0%	23.5%	3.1%	48.9%	6.6%	14.0%
25 to 34	7.2%	25.6%	2.8%	28.3%	19.2%	16.9%
35 to 44	6.8%	24.8%	5.0%	21.4%	26.0%	16.1%
45 to 54	10.2%	28.2%	5.3%	17.2%	21.6%	17.4%
55 to 64	11.3%	29.0%	9.6%	9.9%	23.6%	16.8%
65 and over	12.8%	34.3%	8.1%	10.7%	21.9%	12.2%
Total	9.9%	29.1%	6.5%	17.4%	21.9%	15.2%

a small advantage in a feature such as interest rate. They may feel that the personal attention and service they receive offset a small difference in investment return. Also, customers appreciate institutions that demonstrate that they want their business.

SUMMARY

Money market deposit accounts and certificates of deposit are two other primary types of deposit account investments. In contrast to regular savings and checking accounts, they are oriented toward higher-balance and growth-oriented investment goals of customers.

Money market deposit accounts became available in the early 1980s and quickly became popular with customers. Since then, most of the restrictions on these accounts that existed at their introduction have been eliminated, except for certain transaction limitations. MMDAs are particularly appropriate for customers who are interested in high interest rates combined with a moderate degree of accessibility.

Certificates of deposit have been a staple deposit account for decades. They are distinguished primarily by a requirement that the funds be kept on deposit for a predetermined period. Most institutions restrict transactions on certificates by imposing penalties for early withdrawals. Certificates generally offer the highest rates of interest among deposit accounts, especially for higher-balance and longer-term accounts.

Counselors are an important source of information on investments for customers. They can increase their effectiveness by developing their knowledge of customers' investment needs, their institutions' products and the products of competitors.

FOOTNOTES

[1]"CDs—Customer Demand, Rate Expectation and Intent on Maturity," *The Unidex Reports* (Atlanta: Unidex Corporation, May 1988), p. 3.

[2]Ibid., p. 4.

CHAPTER

5

Single Owner Accounts

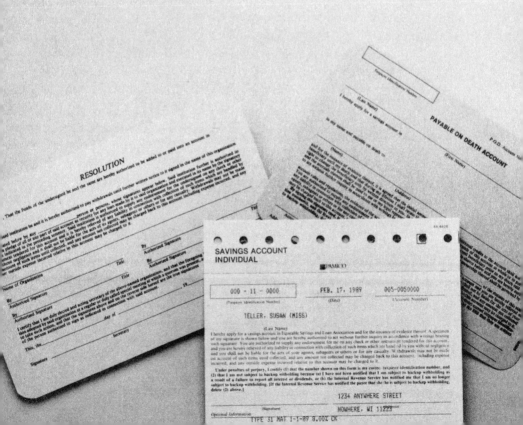

KEY CONCEPTS

- The rights of an individual account owner;

- Precautions to take before honoring withdrawal requests from single owner accounts;

- Legality of trade name accounts;

- Differences between ownership of a P.O.D. account and of a U.S. government savings bond;

- Twofold effect of state statutes concerning a minor's capacity to open a deposit account;

- Institutional liability in the handling of withdrawals from minors' deposit accounts;

- Role of a corporate resolution in a corporate deposit account contract;

- Changing the authorized signers on a corporate or voluntary association account;

- Differences and similarities between a corporate and a voluntary association account in terms of account ownership.

Single ownership means that one person or entity has complete ownership and control of the property. There are two forms of single ownership deposit accounts. One consists of individuals legally considered adults and minors; the other includes entities such as corporations and voluntary associations. This chapter describes each of these forms of single ownership, explains the rights and responsibilities of the parties involved, and suggests ways to avoid the potential difficulties associated with single ownership accounts. It also discusses the purposes of and proper ways to document and handle changes for each form of single ownership.

INDIVIDUALS

An *individual account* is the simplest form of deposit account single ownership because only one person retains complete ownership of the funds. No other form of account ownership can offer sole complete ownership. With other forms of ownership, in contrast, account holders are either authorized or choose to share one or both elements of complete ownership (i.e., legal title and beneficial interest).

Before opening any account, counselors should make sure their customers understand all ownership rights associated with the form of ownership they are requesting so that customers' intentions can be matched with the proper form of ownership. Often customers request an ownership form that is inappropriate for their situations because they are unaware that they can enjoy the same conveniences under individual ownership.

This section describes the rights of the individual account owner, the proper documentation for establishing individual ownership, the appropriate procedures for handling various situations and suggestions for avoiding difficulties.

Ownership, Control and Disposition

Employees should understand and communicate to customers the features of individual account ownership. These include the individual's ability to assign certain rights on the account to others, such as granting a power of attorney and pledging the account. Also, employees need to exercise certain withdrawal precautions and understand how individual ownership affects the disposition of deposited funds.

Assigning Rights to Others

Sometimes an individual account owner finds it inconvenient or too difficult to manage his or her deposit account personally due to lack of time, poor health or some other reason. He or she may want another person to transact his or her business on an account but not to share ownership. Without proper counseling, this person may request that the account be closed and then reopened in an inappropriate form that entails sharing complete ownership. In such a case, the better course of action may be to assign control rights on the account by granting a power of attorney. An attorney in fact may be named when the individual account is opened, using a signature card similar to the one shown in Figure 5-1. Or, an attorney in fact may be named at a later date. In such cases, a power of attorney card similar to the one shown in Chapter 2, Figure 2-4, may be used.

F I G U R E 5-1

Signature Card for Individual Account with Power of Attorney

```
┌──────────────────────────────────────────────────────────────────────────────────┐
│                                                                                    │
│   ┌─────┬─────┬─────┐                                                              │
│   │     │     │     │                                                              │
│   └─────┴─────┴─────┘                                                              │
│       Taxpayer Identification Number                                              │
│                                                 Account No. _____            │
│                                                                                    │
│   (Last name)                        (First Name)                                 │
│   I hereby apply for a savings account in                    (Middle Name)        │
│                                                                                    │
└──────────────────────────────────────────────────────────────────────────────────┘
```

and for the issuance of evidence thereof. A specimen of my signature is shown below and you are hereby authorized to act without further inquiry in accordance with writings bearing such signature. Any other person named in my handwriting and signing below is authorized to withdraw from this account. You are authorized to supply any endorsement for me on any check or other instrument tendered for this account and you are hereby relieved of any liability in connection with collection of such items which are handled by you without negligence and you shall not be liable for the acts of your agents, sub-agents or others or for any casualty. Withdrawals may not be made on account of such items until collected, and any amount not collected may be charged back to this account, including expense incurred, and any other outside expense incurred relative to this account may be charged to it.

By signing this signature card, I(we), under penalty of perjury, certify that (a) the number shown on this card is my(our) correct taxpayer identification number(s), and (b) I(we) are not subject to backup withholding. [If either of the signers have been notified by the IRS that they are subject to backup withholding, delete the language in (b) above.]

Signature

Address

Others Authorized to Sign: (Rule out if none desired when account is opened)

Name in Handwriting of Owner

Signature of Authorized Person

Name in Handwriting of Owner

Signature of Authorized Person

(form margin: 146035 INDIVIDUAL. P.O.A.(11/83))

(form margin: SAF Systems and Forms)

Another way for an individual account owner to assign rights is to pledge the account. To *pledge* is to deliver goods or personal property for use as security or collateral for borrowing additional money or backing a promise. If the depository institution offers loans that can be pledged with funds on deposit, depending on the type of account, the individual account owner may pledge the account.

The amount of the pledge will be unavailable for withdrawal. However, as the customer repays the loan, the amount pledged will be reduced and become available. Usually an individual cannot pledge his or her account from another institution to obtain a deposit account or other type of loan without first transferring that account to the lending institution.

Such deposit account loans can be advantageous to both the institution and the customer. The customer avoids any loss of earnings and at the same time obtains a loan at a lower cost than he or she might get elsewhere. The institution secures excellent collateral for repayment of the loan. Also, by offering this service, the institution strengthens its relationship with the customer.

Individuals have the right to save, spend, give away or share their monies in any legal way they desire. In contrast to a power of attorney, when customers want to share or give away ownership of the funds in their accounts, the most effective way to accomplish this is to change the account ownership form. A new account number and deposit account contract are assigned to the transferred funds. Employees must remember that such a change is effective only if it appears on the institution's records. An individual could not simply give a passbook to another person for the ownership to be changed.

Withdrawal Precautions

Employees may honor withdrawal requests from an individual account only on the authority of the owner or the owner's authorized agent. Consider the following situation. The husband of an individual account owner presents his wife's passbook and requests a withdrawal. The withdrawal slip does not contain the wife's signature. The teller, attempting to accommodate the customer, processes the withdrawal but makes the withdrawal check payable only to the wife. The husband then deposits the withdrawal check in a joint checking account without the wife's signature. Shortly thereafter, he writes a check for the balance of the checking account and leaves town with the money. The wife sues the financial institution. Can she collect?

Few courts would disagree that the institution that made the payout from the individual account would be liable for the unauthorized withdrawal. By honoring the husband's withdrawal request, the institution violated its deposit contract with the wife. The teller tried to protect the institution by making the check payable only to the wife. However, the employee should have been aware of the current depository institution practice of supplying missing endorsements on checks deposited to joint accounts. (See Chapters 2 and 6 for more information regarding the authority to supply missing endorsements.) Therefore, the teller should have known that a check payable only to the wife could easily be deposited in a joint account and then safely drawn upon by the husband.

For all types of individually owned deposit accounts—whether regular savings, money market deposit, certificate or checking—institutions establish procedures to verify if a person other than the owner has been authorized to make transactions or otherwise act on the account. They do this for two reasons:

- to ensure that a particular person is authorized to act on the account; and

- to ensure that the person acting, or attempting to act, is actually the individual authorized by the account owner.

To accomplish this, most institutions check that a properly completed power of attorney is on file and that the signature (or other identification method) matches the named attorney in fact.

Disposition of Funds

The eventual disposition of funds in an individual account is determined by the courts. Counselors can suggest that individual account owners have their lawyers draw up a will for them. With the existence of an up-to-date will, the courts will be able to expedite the disposition of the account.

Documentation

Counselors are responsible for properly documenting individual ownership. This responsibility is becoming more important due to the current trend among some financial institutions to have the employee who opens the account also enter the account information directly into the institution's computer files.

Deposit Contract

Figure 5-2 shows an example of a signature card for an individual account. The employee should enter all required information onto the card (or similar document). Before having the customer sign the document, the employees should ask the customer to verify that all the information is correct.

In addition to its contractual provisions, the account documentation ordinarily contains space for other information, such as the customer's home address and tele-

F I G U R E 5-2

Signature Card for Individual Account

14601 INDIVIDUAL (3/84)

Taxpayer Identification Number

Account No. _____

(Last Name)   _(First Name)_   _(Middle Name)_

I hereby apply for a savings account in

and for the issuance of evidence thereof. A specimen of my signature is shown below and you are hereby authorized to act without further inquiry in accordance with writings bearing such signature. You are authorized to supply any endorsement for me on any check or other instrument tendered for this account, and you are hereby relieved of any liability in connection with collection of such items which are handled by you without negligence and you shall not be liable for the acts of your agents, subagents or others or for any casualty. Withdrawals may not be made on account of such items until collected, and any amount not collected may be charged back to this account, including expense incurred, and any other outside expense incurred relative to this account may be charged to it.

Under penalties of perjury, I certify (1) that the number shown on this form is my correct taxpayer identification number, and (2) that I am not subject to backup withholding because (a) I have not been notified that I am subject to backup withholding as a result of a failure to report all interest or dividends, or (b) the Internal Revenue Service has notified me that I am no longer subject to backup withholding. [If the Internal Revenue Service has notified the payee that she/he is subject to backup withholding, delete (2) above.]

Account
Holder's
Signature _____

(Telephone Number)

Address _____

Introduced
by _____

Date_____

Optional Information, for identification purposes only

Where
Born _____

Date of
Birth _____

Mother's
Maiden
Name _____

© SAF Systems and Forms

phone number. This information is helpful for identifying the customer when he or she makes withdrawals. Another effective item of information for customer identification is the customer's mother's maiden name. Many financial institutions have found that this piece of information, more than any other, has helped identify customers in a variety of situations. For example, a customer stranded in a distant city might wire a financial institution for money. The institution can wire the money but instruct the telegraph service to pay it only if the customer supplies his or her mother's correct maiden name. This kind of information is also helpful to the tellers when paying withdrawals.

Preparing the Evidence of Account
In addition to the particulars identifying the type of deposit account (rate, term, maturity and initial deposit), the individual account owner's name is typed or embossed onto the evidence of account. The name should appear exactly as it does on the deposit contract. No other authorized signers appear on the evidence of account unless the account is being opened with a power of attorney and the institution's policy requires, or the individual requests, that the attorney in fact be so designated.

Variations of Individual Ownership

Two variations of individual ownership are trade name accounts and P.O.D. accounts. Trade name accounts are popular with individual proprietors while P.O.D. accounts have a limited demand.

Trade Name Accounts
Many individual proprietors open individual accounts for their businesses. Occasionally, an individual opens an account in an assumed name, or *trade name*, under which the business firm operates. Individual proprietors are allowed to do business under assumed names instead of their real names as long as their intentions are legal. The law requires an individual proprietor to register the

assumed name with the secretary of state so that the people with whom he or she deals will be able to identify the real owner of the business. By keeping this information on file, the state protects the public against possible fraud or deceit by the proprietor doing business under an assumed name. However, even if the account owner has failed to register his or her trade name with the state, the financial institution cannot refuse to honor a withdrawal request on the account. An assumed name is legal as long as the account owner has no illegal or fraudulent intentions.[1]

Institutions use signature cards similar to the one shown in Figure 5-2 when opening a trade name account. Only the trade name appears on the evidence of account. When opening trade name accounts, counselors should review the security procedures described in Chapter 2.

P.O.D. Accounts

P.O.D. means "payable on death." A P.O.D. account is an individual account in which the owner designates a recipient of the funds in the event of his or her death. P.O.D. accounts can have drawbacks because they resemble trust accounts and wills but lack the formal legal requirements of either. Thus, counselors must be sure to document P.O.D. accounts properly to prevent confusion with these other forms. An alternative to a P.O.D. account is a revocable trust account (see Chapter 8) in favor of a designated beneficiary, which will accomplish the same objective.

Some states have adopted legislation that specifically authorizes institutions to offer P.O.D. accounts.[2] Figure 5-3 illustrates a signature card developed for use in states where P.O.D.'s are authorized. The document provides a place to insert the number of the citation from the state

F I G U R E 5-3

Signature Card for Individual Payable on Death

Taxpayer Identification Number	P.O.D. Account No. _____

PAYABLE ON DEATH ACCOUNT

_____ (First Name) _____ (Middle Name)
(Last Name)

I hereby apply for a savings account in

in my name and payable on death to

_____ ,Beneficiary

_____ (Address)
(Name)

and for the issuance of evidence thereof, it is agreed that the initial amount credited, plus all additional credits to the account shall not vest in the beneficiary until my death and that during my lifetime I shall retain the right to withdraw the proceeds of this account in whole or in part and the right to change the beneficiary only by written direction to you. In the event of the death of said named beneficiary prior to my death said account and the accruals thereon shall be paid to me or my legal representatives. A specimen of my signature is shown below and you are hereby authorized to act without further inquiry in accordance with writings bearing such signature. This account and the ownership thereof shall be governed by your

account rules and regulations, the evidence of the account and the provisions of Section _____ of the statutes of this state. You are authorized to supply any endorsement for me on any check or other instrument tendered for this account and you are hereby relieved of any liability in connection with collection of such items which are handled by you without negligence and you shall not be liable for the acts of your agents, subagents or others or for any casualty. Withdrawals may not be made on account of such items until collected, and any amount not collected may be charged back to this account, including expense incurred, and any other outside expense incurred relative to this account may be charged to it.

By signing this signature card, I(we), under penalty of perjury, certify that (a) the number shown on this card is my(our) correct taxpayer identification number(s), and (b) I(we) are not subject to backup withholding. [If either of the signers have been notified by the IRS that they are subject to backup withholding, delete the language in (b) above.]

_____
Account Holder's Signature

Address _____Date _____

statute that authorizes institutions to offer the P.O.D. form of ownership.

Sometimes customers confuse the P.O.D. account with a U.S. government bond and mistakenly request a P.O.D. account. U.S. government savings bonds frequently indicate co-ownership or P.O.D. on their faces. However, government bonds payable on death to named individuals differ from P.O.D. deposit accounts because ownership of a government bond is a federal matter while ownership of a deposit account is determined by state law. Counselors should inform customers of this distinction. In these cases, the revocable trust form of ownership may be more appropriate for them.[3]

MINORS

Promoting thrift is one of the objectives of deposit accounts. Because habits learned early in life are the most enduring, financial institutions perform a service by focusing their efforts on young people. In addition, institutions can develop a relationship that lasts into a child's adult years. However, special considerations apply to accounts opened by minors.

First, who exactly is a minor? According to common law, a minor is a male or female under the age of 21 years. However, the age of *majority* may differ from that in the common law concept and may be set by the laws of each individual state. In all states, the age of majority is the same for both males and females. Most states set it at 18 and the remaining states at either 19 or 21.[4] Many states prescribe longer or shorter periods of minority in specific situations such as marriage prior to the age of majority. Generally, a *minor* is defined as any person who has not attained the age of majority as provided by state law.

This section focuses primarily on the contractual capacities of minors. In an effort to protect immature children, common law has given minors the power to disaffirm their contracts. While minors may make contracts with adults and hold adults to those contracts, common law permits them to disaffirm any of their contracts for other than necessities (goods the law considers necessary to life or health) with almost total impunity.

While minors do not acquire full legal capacity until they reach majority, most courts realize that children naturally develop an increasing capacity to do things as they approach the full age of majority. The power to add to and withdraw from a deposit account is considered as within a minor's capacity. As a general rule, minors in lawful possession of their own funds may place the funds with a depository institution and withdraw them freely. The institution is not responsible for determining or approving the purposes for withdrawals it pays to minors on their own demand. A parent who has not been appointed legal guardian of the minor's property has no authority over the minor's account. This rule also applies to funds placed with the institution in the minor's name, provided the parent does not actually retain title to the funds.

State Laws

State laws recognize the importance of teaching the habits of thrift to the young by specifying that a minor, when acting as a saver, is to be treated "as though he were of full age."

With respect to deposit accounts, most statutes concerning minors have a twofold effect:

- They place minors on the same basis as adults and deny them their usual rights of disaffirmance in dealings with depository institutions.

- They assure minors control over their deposit accounts free from any control by parents or guardians, if any. Thus, most states' statutes provide that minors may have binding deposit contracts with financial institutions.

Statutes that remove minors' disabilities with respect to deposit accounts fall into one of two types. The first type includes statutes in the majority of states and gives institutions complete freedom in opening and paying out minors' accounts. Usually these statutes spell out that minors of any age may become members of the institution and may establish, make additions to and make withdrawals from their accounts, including the earnings. At the same time, the statutes protect institutions by ensuring that releases signed by minors shall be "a valid and sufficient release and discharge of the institution."[5]

The second type includes statutes in the few remaining states and provides that accounts may be opened by, or in the name of, minors of any age and payments received from minors at any age. Minors are empowered to make binding withdrawals only after they reach an age specified in the statute.[6]

General Considerations Regarding Minors' Accounts

Sometimes parents who want their children to start saving for themselves establish deposit accounts in their children's names. However, they often choose a form of ownership other than individual ownership, and this may be inappropriate for their purposes. In most cases, if parents intend that their children maintain sole and complete ownership of the money, they should choose only the individual form of ownership.

If a child who is party to a deposit account is able to write, he or she should sign the deposit contract documents at the time the account is opened. In the case of younger children, the parent or guardian may sign the child's name, adding, for example, "by John Doe, father." Although the latter arrangement is binding, the child should sign the signature card as soon as he or she is able to write. Also, it is a good idea to remind both the parent and the child to have the child resign the signature card as the child matures and his or her handwriting changes.

CORPORATIONS

A corporation is a form of business organization that legally binds a group of individuals to act as one entity while carrying on one or more related enterprises. It has the powers, rights and privileges of an individual. The corporation as an entity continues to exist regardless of changes in its membership or ownership.

Characteristics of Corporate Ownership

Corporations are artificial persons that receive their powers from their charters and bylaws. A corporation's board of directors authorizes and empowers certain officers to act on its behalf. As time passes, a corporation's employees, officers, board of directors and objectives may change; however, a successful corporation remains an ongoing entity that changes to keep up with the times.

Corporate accounts are very appealing to financial institutions for several reasons:

- A corporation tends to make relatively large deposits and maintain a long-term relationship with the institution.

- Often a corporation maintains several accounts and uses other services.

- As a corporation grows, its need for additional financial services also expands.

- The corporation's employees and customers may also establish deposit accounts with the institution.

Corporate Resolution

When a corporation deposits funds with a financial institution, its board issues a *corporate resolution* that authorizes the account and empowers certain officers to handle the account funds on behalf of the corporation. The corporate resolution may be preprinted in the standard corporation account documents and is certified with the corporate seal. It names the officers who are authorized to handle the account, along with their corporate titles. These are the only individuals permitted to make transactions or changes concerning the account. They are also the ones who sign the deposit contract. If a change in the authorized officers occurs, the corporation issues a new corporate resolution and deposit contract document.

Without a corporate resolution, a financial institution would not know which officers were allowed to handle corporate funds or whether two or more signatures were required for an authorized withdrawal. In a 1979 case, a New York bank was held liable for permitting a corporation president to open a corporate account and make withdrawals from it without a corporate resolution.[7] Obtaining a corporate resolution therefore is a precautionary procedure that is an important responsibility of a counselor.

Updating and Enforcing Corporate Deposit Account Provisions

Corporate resolutions and deposit contracts must be kept current. Obtaining the corporate resolution and keeping it on file is only one part of the financial institution's total responsibility to its corporate account holder. The authority specifically granted to the institution in the resolution must be followed to the letter. If the corporation that owns the account wants to make any change in that authority, it should do so by adopting another resolution. It is the corporation's, not the financial institution's, responsibility to ensure that the corporate resolution on file with the institution is kept up to date.

For example, the counselor should advise the corporation's authorized agent who is opening the account that he or she should promptly report to the institution any change of officers or persons authorized to withdraw from the account. Whenever a change in authorized individuals occurs, the corporate officers should execute a new corporate resolution and deposit contract documents. If they fail to give proper notification, the institution will continue to honor only the authorized individuals listed in its records.

Another important responsibility of institution employees is to follow special procedures relevant to corporate ownership of deposited funds. For example, alert employees can stop corporate officers who attempt to convert corporate funds to their personal accounts. A corporate officer who is authorized to make additions to and withdrawals from the corporation's account might endorse a check that is payable only to the corporation (issued either by an outside party or by the institution when paying a withdrawal) and request that the amount be credited to his or her personal account. But the institution is not authorized to credit a personal account with the amount of a check payable only to the corporation. If the institution knowingly honors this request, it can be held liable by the corporation for assisting in the "conversion" of corporate funds to an officer's personal account.[8] The institution should apply the same rule to the officers of municipalities and other public corporations.

Documentation

In addition to obtaining the corporate resolution, the counselor is responsible for properly completing the deposit contract and any evidence of account for the corporate depositor.

Deposit Contract

An example of a corporate and voluntary association signature card and a typical corporate resolution it would contain is shown in Figure 5-4. In this example, the counselor would ensure that several critical pieces of information are entered on the form:

- the number of authorized individuals required to transact business;

- the name of the corporation;

- the signatures and titles of the authorized individuals;

- the signature of the secretary certifying the resolution;

- the impress of the corporate seal on the form.

In some situations, the corporate officers may indicate that they will be opening a number of accounts and ask whether they can use a master deposit contract. For example, an insurance company that is investing in a separate account for each of its annuity policyholders could use a master deposit contract. A master deposit contract pertains to several accounts, each held in the exact same ownership. It eliminates the necessity to obtain the authorized corporate officers' signatures on deposit contracts for subsequent new accounts. Whenever corporate officers ask about using a master deposit contract, the counselor should check with his or her supervisor or manager, who will check the officers' authorization and consult with the institution's attorney to determine the feasibility of using a master deposit contract.

Preparing the Evidence of Account
The counselor needs to type or imprint only the name of the corporation onto the passbook, certificate or other evidence of the account. The authorized officers' names appear only on the deposit contract and the corporate resolution. When changes occur within the corporation, only the deposit contract documents and corporate resolution need to be changed, not the evidence of account.

VOLUNTARY ASSOCIATIONS

A *voluntary association* is a body of persons acting together without a charter, but upon the methods and forms used by incorporated bodies, in pursuit of some common enterprise. Examples of voluntary associations

F I G U R E 5-4

Signature Card for Corporation/ Voluntary Association, Side 1

can be bar associations, women's and men's clubs, bowling leagues, investment groups, lodges, churches, unions, societies, and educational and charitable groups. A voluntary association is classified as a single owner account because the ownership is in the name of the entity rather than in the names of the individuals acting on its behalf.

F I G U R E 5-4, Continued

Signature Card for Corporation/ Voluntary Association, Side 2

RESOLUTION

RESOLVED, That the funds of the undersigned be and the same are hereby authorized to be added to or paid into an account in

and that said institution be and it is hereby authorized to pay withdrawals until further written notice to it signed in the name of this organization as indicated below by any _____person or persons, whose signatures appear below. Said institution further is authorized to accept a pledge of all or any part of said account as security for any loan made by it to said organization and executed in its name by the signatory parties indicated in the preceding sentence. Said institution is authorized to supply any endorsement for the undersigned on any check or other instrument tendered for this account and it is hereby relieved of any liability in connection with collection of such items which are handled by it without negligence and it shall not be liable for the acts of its agents, subagents or others or for any casualty. Withdrawals may not be made on account of such items until collected, and any amount not collected may be charged back to this account including expense incurred, and any other outside expense incurred relative to this account may be charged to it.

Name of Organization

By _____		By _____	
Authorized Signature	*Title*	Authorized Signature	*Title*
By _____		By _____	
Authorized Signature	*Title*	Authorized Signature	*Title*

I certify that I am duly elected and acting secretary of the above-named organization, and that the foregoing is a true and correct copy of a resolution adopted by said organization at a regular or duly called special meeting at which a quorum was present, and that said organization is authorized to take such action, and that the signatures above and on the reverse side hereof are the true signatures of the person authorized to sign as indicated in connection with said account.

This, the_____day of _____, 19_____   (Corporate Seal)

Signature _____
                              Secretary

Characteristics of Voluntary Associations

A voluntary association differs from a corporation in that a corporation owes its existence to legislation and a charter granted under state or federal authority, while a voluntary association is created through the execution of a private contract agreed to by the persons who wish to become associated. The terms of the contract usually are embodied in "articles of association" or in a "constitution" with the adopted bylaws. Informal associations may also be created by oral contract. As long as they do not violate public policy or law, members of a voluntary association may include in their contract any provisions on which they agree. Of course, just as a contract made for an illegal purpose would be void, a voluntary association formed for illegal purposes would be invalid because it is based on a contract.

Unlike corporations, unincorporated or voluntary associations are not considered "legal persons" apart from the individuals who comprise them. The statutes of many states contain special provisions allowing voluntary associations to be sued through their president or treasurer. If all legal technicalities are closely observed, a suit brought against a voluntary association in one of these states can be successful in holding the various members liable and in encumbering any property belonging to the group.[9]

Many voluntary association accounts benefit financial institutions in the same way that corporate accounts do. Both entities may maintain large balances, have substantial transaction amounts, and periodically require other services and products the institution provides.

Documentation

In the case of a voluntary association that is organized formally under a constitution and according to bylaws and is functioning actively, depository institution employees may accept and handle the association's account in the same way they do corporate accounts. The documentation for the voluntary association account is similar to that for the corporate account in most respects.

Deposit Contract

The counselor should obtain a proper resolution authorizing the voluntary association account and naming the person or persons authorized to make additions and withdrawals. This resolution is often preprinted on the deposit contract (see Figure 5-4). Notice that the same deposit contract can be used for both corporate and voluntary association deposit accounts.

Difficulties may arise if an informal group that lacks a written constitution and bylaws requests a voluntary association ownership. Certain provisions, such as how many authorized individuals will be named or how many authorized signatures should be required for withdrawals, may be questionable. An example would be a group of people trying to organize a high school reunion. Usually such a group would consist of volunteers who plan the event, contact alumni and collect monies from those wishing to attend. The group may request a voluntary association account, not knowing which form of ownership would be most appropriate. Some financial institutions will not accept the voluntary association form of ownership without completion of a resolution. However, counselors still may accept the funds for deposit under a different form of ownership, such as a revocable trust account (see Chapter 8). The account can be opened in the name of the individual presenting the funds as trustee or custodian for the group, with withdrawals to be paid to this individual in his or her fiduciary capacity.

Preparing the Evidence of Account

The passbook, certificate or any other evidence of account for voluntary associations is prepared in the same way as that for a corporation account. Only the name of the entity is typed or imprinted on the evidence of account, since the names of the people authorized to handle the account may change. As with corporate accounts, changes in authority can be implemented by completing another resolution and deposit contract.

SUMMARY

Single owner accounts consist of two forms of ownership: individual and corporate or voluntary association. Both natural and artificial persons may have deposit accounts in a single ownership form.

Clear communication between depository institution employees and customers is essential during the opening and subsequent administration of a single ownership account. A customer should understand all rights associated with individual account ownership, including the rights to grant a power of attorney and to pledge the account. When customers understand all matters relating to individual ownership, they will know whether their ownership needs can be met and fewer difficulties will be likely to arise.

State laws permit and even encourage minors to open their own deposit accounts. The statutes have a twofold effect:

- to protect the institution by denying the minor's rights of disaffirmance; and

- to ensure the minor's sole control of the account.

Financial institution employees must be careful to document individual, corporate and voluntary association ownership accounts correctly. The individual account deposit contract should be used exclusively for its purpose. Resolutions are necessary for corporate and voluntary association accounts and must be followed precisely. If a counselor is alert when an account is opened, he or she can avoid problems later and can promote cordial relations between the customer and the financial institution.

FOOTNOTES

[1] See 65 *Corpus Juris Secundum* 25; see also *Hayes* v. *Providence Citizens' Bank & Trust Co.*, 290 S.W. 1028.

[2] AL, AZ, CA, CT, GA, IL, IA, KS, LA, MA, MN, MS, MO, MT, NE, NV, NJ, NM, OH, OK, PA, TN, WA, WI and WY have statutes specifically authorizing P.O.D. accounts.

[3] For further information on P.O.D. accounts, see "P.O.D. Accounts Held Invalid as Attempted Will," *Legal Bulletin*, XXIX (May 1962), pp. 111–113; "P.O.D. Instruments Invalid as Attempted Testamentary Dispositions (Two Cases)," *Legal Bulletin*, XXXII (September 1966), pp. 288–291; "P.O.D. Account Not a Will, Escrow, Gift, Trust, or Anything but Nugatory," *Legal Bulletin*, XLI (July 1975), pp. 183–188. See also *Northwestern National Bank* v. *Daniel*, 127 N.W. 2d 714, and *In re Atkinson's Estate*, 175 N.E. 2d 548.

[4] The age of majority in Pennsylvania is 21; in Alabama, Nebraska and Wyoming 19; and in all other states 18. "Age of majority" generally means the age at which an individual has legal control over his or her own actions and business, e.g., ability to contract. In many states, however, the age of majority is arrived at upon marriage even where the minimum legal marrying age is lower than the prescribed age of majority.

[5] Every state except LA, ME, NE, NJ, RI, WA, WV and WI has laws that overcome a depositor's minority status with binding releases.

[6] The following description lists the states that have statutes empowering minors to make binding withdrawals only after they reach an age specified in the statute. No statute is found in Maine at all; Nebraska, New Jersey, New Mexico, Rhode Island and Washington treat minors as adults but have no "release" or "discharge" language in their statutes; Louisiana allows bind-

ing withdrawals for minors over age 10, with no release language; Nevada and West Virginia release the institution if the minor is over 14. Finally, in Wisconsin, the board of directors of an institution has the discretionary power to allow a withdrawal of a minor age 14 and over.

[7]See *New York Metro Corp.* v. *Chase Manhattan Bank*, 423 N.Y.S. 2d 423, and "Association Liable for Unauthorized Payout of Corporation Account," *Legal Bulletin*, XXX (May 1964), pp. 165–168.

[8]See *Brede* v. *Jefferson Bank*, 345 S.W. 2d 156, and "Corporation Check Placed in Officer's Personal Account," *Legal Bulletin*, XXVII (September 1961), pp. 241–244.

[9]For further information on voluntary association accounts, see Jean G. Harth, "Legal Nature of Voluntary Associations," *Legal Bulletin*, XXX (March 1964), pp. 71–88.

CHAPTER

Joint Tenancy

JOINT TENANTS WITH RIGHT OF SURVIVORSHIP AND NOT AS TENANTS IN COMMON.

- The four unities necessary for creating a valid joint tenancy and how a counselor determines whether each is present when opening a joint tenancy account;

- Differences between joint tenancy deposit contracts that require only one joint tenant's signature and those that require all joint tenants' signatures;

- Responsibilities of joint tenants in imposing and removing suspension orders or lost account holds;

- Right of survivorship and its importance in joint tenancy;

- The three parties involved in a joint tenancy deposit contract;

- The gift language in a joint tenancy deposit contract;

- Why the word *and* instead of the word *or* may be preferred between the names of joint tenants on evidences of account;

- Three actions that may automatically sever a joint tenancy among account owners and how one of these actions may be permitted;

- How accounts-in-two-names statutes protect a financial institution and situations in which they would not.

Joint tenancy ownership is one of the most popular forms of multiple ownership of deposit accounts. Unlike in individual ownership, in joint tenancy, complete ownership is shared equally among two or more individuals. At first glance, joint tenancy appears to be a convenient and simple form of ownership. However, customers sometimes overlook the requirements for establishing a valid joint tenancy. Also, customers may not know all of their rights as joint tenants or be aware of several actions that can automatically terminate a joint tenancy or convert it to a different form of ownership.

Counselors and other employees who work with deposit accounts need a thorough understanding of all facets of the joint tenancy form of ownership so that they can inform their customers about the rights and responsibilities of joint tenants. Financial institutions value this knowledge because it helps counselors avoid informing customers about inappropriate forms of ownership.

This chapter describes how counselors can properly document joint tenancy ownership and explains the language in a joint tenancy deposit contract. It also discusses how a joint tenancy can be severed and changed and how accounts-in-two-names statutes protect financial institutions.

CHARACTERISTICS OF JOINT TENANCY

Joint tenancy is a form of ownership by two or more parties who share equal rights in and control of property, with the survivor or survivors continuing to hold all such rights on the death of one or more of the tenants. No matter how many joint tenants own an account or other piece of property, each tenant owns an undivided interest.

For example, if three joint tenants own an account, it is not possible to assign one-third of the account to each owner. The account is considered as a whole entity rather than the sum of several parts.

Ownership, Control and Disposition

When all the essential elements of a joint tenancy are present, each tenant in the account has certain rights, the most important of which are withdrawal rights and the right of survivorship. Each joint tenant possesses withdrawal rights as explained in the deposit contract. Some deposit contracts permit withdrawals with any one joint tenant's signature; others require all joint tenants' signatures. Another right of joint tenants is the right of survivorship, which determines the disposition of a joint tenancy account. General ownership rights, such as power of attorney, also apply to each joint tenant (see Chapter 2).

Because a joint tenancy account has more than one owner, the institution's employees must be careful when handling these accounts. For example, some joint tenant owners' rights may be exercised with only one signature, while all joint tenants' signatures may be required to cancel an action.

The Four Unities
In all 50 states, the only completely effective way to create a joint tenancy account with right of survivorship is to adhere to the four unities of joint tenancy:

- time;
- title;

- interest;

- possession.[1]

The absence of any of these elements when a joint tenancy deposit account is opened may indicate that the customer's true intention or need is to establish a different form of ownership. Careful yet tactful questioning by a counselor can help determine whether the customer understands these characteristics of a joint tenancy.

Time The *unity of time* requirement means that all joint tenants must attain ownership at the same time. This sounds like a simple requirement to meet, but it is often overlooked. For example, assume Joe and Larry are joint tenants of an existing deposit account. They decide they want to make Chris a joint owner, so the counselor adds Chris' name to the account. But this joint tenancy account could be declared invalid, because the unity of time is missing; that is, Joe, Larry and Chris did not all become owners at the same time. Therefore, one of the joint tenants could refute the validity of the joint tenancy at some future date.

As another example, assume Joe requests that Chris' name be added to Joe and Larry's joint statement account. The counselor does so but never requests Larry to sign a new signature card, or similar document, for the account. In fact, Larry is completely unaware that Chris' name has been added. Shortly thereafter, Joe dies in an automobile accident. Then Larry receives the monthly statement and learns that Chris' name had been added to the account. Larry could subsequently refute the validity of the joint tenancy with Chris.

In either of the above cases, the most effective way to achieve the unity of time would have been to close Joe and Larry's original joint account and transfer the bal-

ance to a new joint account in the names of Joe, Larry
and Chris. Although the old and new accounts are both
held in joint tenancy, the counselor should not alter the
original signature card, or similar account document, to
accommodate another name. Whenever a joint tenant is
removed from or added to an account, new deposit contract documentation is required to maintain the unity of
time.

Title Title is the ownership right to property, including
the right to possession. To achieve *unity of title*, each
tenant must receive title by the same conveyance. *Conveyance* is the means by which the tenants acquire title,
usually by a deed, will, cash, check or transfer from another account.

Usually the unities of time and title are present simultaneously, and individuals may find it difficult to distinguish between the two elements. If two or more parties
acquire ownership by means of the same conveyance, they
acquire title at the same time. Refer again to the example
of Joe, Larry and Chris. If a new account had been opened
naming Joe, Larry and Chris as joint tenants, the three
owners would have acquired title through the same transfer—Joe and Larry conveyed title of the funds to Joe,
Larry and Chris.

Interest The *unity of interest* requirement means that
each tenant must have the same legal claim and estate
in the account. This includes all the ownership rights to
the account. Each tenant equally may use his or her right
of ownership to make any transactions allowable according to the rules of the account class.

If the unity of interest concept is applied to the example
of Joe, Larry and Chris as owners of a new account, any

one of them could exercise his ownership rights to the funds on deposit. Unless the deposit contract requires all signatures for withdrawals, either Joe, Larry or Chris may act on his own without the permission of the others.

Possession   The *unity of possession* requirement means that each tenant owns an undivided share of the whole estate rather than an equal fractional portion. Therefore, when a joint tenant dies, the remaining tenant or tenants do not inherit the property, because they already own it.

Now consider the example of Sam, Mary and Carol. Assume that Sam, Mary and Carol each picked a winning number in their state's three-digit lottery game. Each won $30,000, and they decided to establish a joint tenancy deposit account with the combined total of $90,000. The unity of possession requirement means that they must have agreed that any one of them could withdraw any portion of the entire account. It is not possible to assign one-third of the account to each party. The account is considered a whole entity rather than the sum of several parts.

Withdrawal Rights
The right of withdrawal allows each joint tenant equal access to the funds on deposit. When counselors open joint accounts, they let the owners decide whether the withdrawals will require the signature of any of the joint tenants or the signatures of all joint tenants. If the owners desire that all signatures be required for withdrawals, the counselor should explain that this condition applies to all other matters relating to the account as well, except, of course, for cash deposits. Figures 6-1 and 6-2 show the signature card used in each case.

F I G U R E 6-1

Signature Card for Joint Tenancy—
Any One Signature

Financial institution employees, especially tellers, must be extremely careful when processing transactions for customers with joint accounts that require all signatures. They should keep in mind the following rule: Any time a check is cashed against an account that requires all signatures, the check must be endorsed by all the joint tenants, regardless of to whom it is made payable. This

F I G U R E 6-2

Signature Card for Joint Tenancy—
All Signatures Required

precaution is necessary if the check is returned unpaid. By honoring a bad check that had been cashed without obtaining all tenants' signatures, the institution would be unable to deduct that amount from the account.

Even though two or more people have access to the funds in a joint account, a power of attorney sometimes is convenient. The deposit contract chosen when the account is opened determines whether any one tenant's signature or all tenants' signatures are needed to grant a power of attorney. For example, assume Mary and Jane have a joint account in which either one's signature is sufficient for making withdrawals. They are planning a three-week vacation and intend to leave on October 20. Mary remembers that the rent is due on the first of every month and names her father as attorney in fact. Since only Mary's signature is needed to grant this authority, Mary's father can now withdraw funds from the account to pay the November rent.

Other Signature Authorizations

Stop payment orders also require a signed authorization. The number of signatures needed on a written stop payment order depends on whether any one or all signatures are required for other account transactions. Any one tenant may place a verbal stop payment order. The verbal order remains effective until the written order is signed, which must occur within 14 days. Institutions inform customers that, because a verbal stop payment order is only temporary, it is urgent that the customer sign a written stop order.

While a stop payment order affects checks and NOW drafts, a suspension order (illustrated in Chapter 2, Figure 2-6) halts all withdrawals from the account until all the tenants sign a release. Any one tenant or a court order may impose a suspension order. Employees release a written suspension order only when all tenants have signed to cancel it. This procedure prevents any one tenant from restricting the withdrawal rights of the other tenant(s) without equally restricting his or her own withdrawal rights. The unities of interest and possession require this equality. Employees should make this clear to any tenant wishing to place a suspension order on a joint account.

Occasionally—say, after a quarrel—a husband or wife may phone the institution where the couple has a joint account and request that a suspension order be placed on the account. As a matter of public relations, most institutions have adopted a policy of recognizing such verbal instructions provided they receive written confirmation within a prescribed period (such as one or two days) following the call. If the institution does not receive the written confirmation during the specified time period, it may assume that the person has decided not to place a formal suspension order. The institution should then release the suspension order.

If the owners of a joint account wish to change the status of the account permanently from any one signature to all signatures required, the most effective way for the counselor to adhere to the four unities is to transfer the account balance to a new account number and use the all signatures required contract (see Figures 6-2 and 6-3).

Sometimes, a customer telephones the institution to claim that he or she lost the passbook or other evidence of account and wants all action on the account suspended. In accordance with many institutions' policy of honoring verbal suspension orders, the employee receiving the call may accept such verbal instructions. However, all joint tenants' signatures are required on a lost account affidavit to ensure that the evidence of account was really lost and is not being held by one of the joint tenants. Therefore, the employee should tell the customer that an affidavit signed by all the joint tenants is needed as soon as possible. Depending on the customer's preference, the lost account affidavit may be mailed or picked up.

Requests for no mail delivery also require all joint tenants' signatures both to exercise and release. This is especially important when the joint tenants share the same address. The counselor should explain to the customers where their mail will be held and when and how to pick it up. This is especially important since some notices are required by law to be sent or given to customers. The counselor should also tell the customers that they must cancel the no mail request in writing in order to begin receiving mail again. In cases where the joint tenants do not live at the same address, the counselor can ask if any of the joint tenant addresses could receive mail rather than process a no mail request.

Right of Survivorship
A major distinguishing characteristic of the joint tenancy estate is the right of survivorship. The *right of survivorship* in joint tenancy means that when one joint tenant dies, the entire estate continues to be owned by the surviving joint tenant or tenants. The survivor or survivors of the decedent do not inherit the estate unless they are also the surviving joint tenants.

Assume that four joint tenants—John, Jane, Joe and Jill—own a deposit account. Jill dies, leaving John, Jane and Joe as the surviving tenants. Jill has heirs other than John, Jane and Joe, but this does not affect her ownership interest in the joint tenancy account. A pro rata interest in the account is not assigned to Jill and passed on to her heirs. John, Jane and Joe continue to own the account.

Common-Law Joint Tenancy versus Contractual Joint Tenancy

Joint tenancy is created either by common law or by contract, depending on the state in which the property

F I G U R E 6-3

Use of a Transfer Slip

SAVINGS ACCOUNT

964032
NUMBER

THIS CERTIFIES THAT

Joe LaMaster and Larry LaMaster as joint tenants with right

of survivorship and not as tenants in common

Holds a SAVINGS ACCOUNT in

STATE BANK

Transfer

Amount
Balance

Account __964032__   to Account __964223__   _____

Account _____   to Account _____   _____

Account _____   to Account _____   _____

_____   Total Checks _____

Authorized Signature

_____   Cash _____

Authorized Signature

_____   Total Amount __Balance__

Authorized Signature

Date 9-11-89   Approval

F I G U R E 6-3, Continued

SAVINGS ACCOUNT

964223
NUMBER

THIS CERTIFIES THAT

Joe LaMaster and Larry LaMaster and Curt LaMaster as joint tenants

with right of survivorship and not as tenants in common

Holds a SAVINGS ACCOUNT in

STATE BANK

---

is located. *Common law* is the body of law developed in England primarily from judicial decisions based on custom and previous decisions not documented in statute or code. It constitutes the basis of the U.S. legal system in all states except Louisiana.

In states where no specific laws exist for joint tenancy estates, the rules of common law prevail. Common-law states automatically presume the existence of a joint tenancy account when created for two or more persons, unless the account contains language that clearly spells out a tenancy in common. *Tenancy in common* means that two or more persons own the account, but each person owns a separate interest, usually divided on a pro rata basis; for example, each of two account holders could own

50% of the account. This type of ownership is explained in Chapter 7.

However, most states have statutes and laws pertaining specifically to joint tenancy estates.[2] These states reverse the common-law presumption of joint tenancy. Unless express language showing the intention to create a joint tenancy account is used, a tenancy in common is created. In these states, contracts are used to establish joint tenancy. To successfully create a joint tenancy account by contract, "words of survivorship" indicating the right of survivorship must appear in the contract.[3]

Obviously, the laws of the particular state in which a financial institution operates affect the manner in which joint tenancy accounts are established. Counselors should be aware of this, because it accounts for some of the differences among deposit account contracts discussed in this book.

DOCUMENTATION

The deposit contract spells out the intentions of the parties involved in a joint tenancy account. Employees who open such accounts must correctly document and identify joint tenancy ownership. Also, they must be prepared to explain the language contained in the deposit contract.

Intentions of the Parties

In both common-law and contractual joint tenancy, the intention of the parties to create joint tenancy is a necessary factor. Common law "presumes" that two or more persons involved in a conveyance—an instrument by which title to property is transferred—actually intend to create joint tenancy. As stated previously, in states where the presumption rule does not exist, a conveyance to two or more persons is presumed to create tenancy in common and not joint tenancy. This presumption points out the importance of joint tenancy language in the deposit account ownership.

When people contract to do something, they must intend to do that particular thing. For example, Pat and Dave may appear to have a contract, but Pat might think the contract means one thing, and Dave might believe it means something entirely different. When all parties to a contract do not agree on what was intended, a court may set aside, or nullify, the contract.

Counselors must be able to recognize situations where the joint tenancy form of ownership may be inappropriate for the customer's needs. From conversations with their customers, counselors must be able to identify any misunderstanding or intentional disregard of the required four unities. In addition, as depositors' intentions change, so may the appropriateness of the joint tenancy form of ownership for their situations. Keeping an effective line of communication open between employees and customers can help reveal any changes of intentions.

Two situations have frequently occurred that illustrate how customers' intentions in a joint tenancy can be misinterpreted. Both are usually characterized by a lack of unity of interest or of possession.

The first situation describes the interpretation of a joint tenancy as a "poor man's will," intended to provide for an easy transfer of fund ownership after the customer's death. Consider Mr. and Mrs. Eaton and their children, Barry and Barbara, all of whom are listed as joint tenants of a deposit account. Mr. and Mrs. Eaton knew about the rights of survivorship that joint tenancy confers and chose this form of ownership because they had no wills prepared. They thought it would be the most convenient way to pass their money on to their children in the event of their untimely deaths. Their only reason for naming their children as joint tenant owners was "just in case." Mr. and Mrs. Eaton did not actually intend to make Barry and Barbara equal owners with equal control over their life savings. In fact, their account is not a valid joint tenancy because the unities of interest and possession are missing.

The second situation concerns the "convenience joint tenancy account" in which the original owner names one or more joint tenants for convenience in making account transactions but does not intend to give up ownership of the funds. Consider Clara, an elderly widow in New York, who has two married sons, Peter and Paul, and one unmarried daughter, Mathilda. Both sons live on the West Coast and visit their mother only during the Christmas holiday. Mathilda lives in New York and usually calls her mother daily.

After talking with Mathilda one day, Clara transferred most of her life savings to a money market deposit account. She told the counselor to name herself and Mathilda as joint tenants so that her daughter could make account transactions for her. A few years later, Clara died. Peter and Paul flew to New York for the funeral. The day after the funeral, Mathilda closed the account she had shared with her mother, paid off the mortgage on her townhouse, bought a recreational vehicle and drove off to Canada.

Peter and Paul learned of the joint account later that morning upon seeing a monthly statement that Mathilda had inadvertently left on the kitchen table. When Mathilda had not returned by 3:30 p.m., they decided to go to the financial institution for more information. The counselor believed that Peter and Paul were Clara's sons, but she (correctly) explained that she could give them no information about the joint account without Mathilda's signature.

Peter and Paul finally located Mathilda. They tried to persuade her to share the funds, but she refused. Finally, Peter and Paul took their sister to court, and the judge ruled in the brothers' favor. The court determined that the joint account between Mathilda and Clara had been for convenience only, and therefore the joint tenancy was invalid. Mathilda had to sell the RV and take out another mortgage on her townhouse. The funds were then divided equally among Mathilda, Peter and Paul.

All of this might have been avoided if the counselor who opened the account had listened to Clara more closely. Clara's words "so that my daughter, Mathilda, can make transactions for me" should have prompted the counselor to question Clara's intentions. Here the unities of interest and possession were lacking, and a valid joint tenancy could not be created. An individual account with a power of attorney would have been more appropriate for Clara's purpose.

The Deposit Contract

The deposit contract should clearly indicate the parties' intentions. The language of the contract should avoid any ambiguity about whether the parties intend joint tenancy or tenancy in common.

Sample joint tenancy deposit contracts are illustrated in Figures 6-1 and 6-2. Notice that the deposit contract in Figure 6-2 is identical in every way to that in Figure 6-1 except in how it permits authorized withdrawals.

Figure 6-1 requires any one signature for withdrawals, and Figure 6-2 requires all signatures. Both contracts specify that the parties shall hold as "joint tenants with right of survivorship and not as tenants in common, and not as tenants by the entirety." These specific words establish beyond any doubt that a true joint tenancy exists.

Parties to the Contract

The documentation for a joint tenancy account is a three-party contract:

- The institution contracts with each joint tenant.

- The joint tenants contract with the institution.

- The joint tenants contract with each other.

No contract exists without the agreement of all concerned, evidenced by the signatures of all joint tenants.

Sometimes a customer who wishes to set up a joint tenancy account asks the counselor to overlook or waive the requirement for signatures of the other joint tenants on the deposit contract. The customer may wish to retain complete control over the account. Or perhaps he or she wishes to have the money paid to the other named individual(s) only upon his or her death. Both reasons are inappropriate for the joint tenancy form of ownership, because they violate the four unities required to establish a valid joint tenancy. A revocable trust account that names the depositor as trustee and the other individual(s) as beneficiary(ies), may be more appropriate in this case.

Adding a name to or deleting a name from an existing joint tenancy account invalidates the joint tenancy relationship because it violates the unities of time and title. The most effective procedure for changing ownership is to close the account and transfer the balance to a new account with a new contract. The counselor can use a transfer slip, similar to the one shown in Figure 6-3, to accomplish this. All the account owners must then provide their signatures for the institution's records. Even though any one joint tenant may be able to change ownership upon presentation of evidence of account, all account owners must sign the new contract.

Gift Language

Certain words in the joint tenancy deposit contract constitute gift language (see Figure 6-4). The *gift language* states that any funds placed in the account by one tenant are considered a gift to the other tenant(s). The gift language prevents a joint tenant from claiming an exclusive interest in the funds that he or she deposits. Also, it ensures that any balance in the account complies with the required unities of interest and possession. In short, gift language documents the fact and the intention that all the parties together own all the money in the account at all times. In today's litigious society, gift language can help a judge see that a joint tenancy was intended.[4]

And/Or Question

Throughout the country, there seems to be little uniformity among financial institutions in their use of the words *and* or *or* in joining the names of joint tenants. The word *and* can more accurately reflect the contractual relationship among the joint tenants and prevents any future question as to whether the account is held in joint tenancy or tenancy in common. However, on this issue, the most important language in the contract is that spelling out the incidents of joint tenancy. If a joint tenancy was clearly intended and specifically created, the use of *or* instead of *and* should not negate that intent. Legal

F I G U R E 6-4

Gift Language on the Joint Tenancy Deposit Contract

counsel for each institution may determine which wording the institution uses. However, in the past, the following points have been developed as support for using the word *and* to join the names of joint tenants.

First, *or* is a disjunctive word and implies a separateness that contradicts the very concept of a *joint* tenancy. *And*, on the other hand, is a conjunctive word that implies togetherness. One might point out that on jointly owned U.S. government savings bonds, the word *or* is printed on the face of the bond between the bond owners' names. However, ownership of a U.S. government bond is a federal matter, while ownership of a deposit account is a state issue—and what applies to federal law does not necessarily apply to state laws.

Second, consider the ways in which checks are made payable to multiple individuals. A check made payable to two or more payees that includes the word *and* between the names requires the endorsement of all payees for cashing, while a check that uses *or* requires only one payee's signature. However, the use of *or* on a check is simply the result of the payer exercising his or her power to specify to whom the check is *payable*. This is not the same situation as a joint tenancy account. A check differs in a significant way from a passbook, certificate or any other evidence of account: the check itself is negotiable, while the evidence of account by itself usually is not.

In conclusion, the important fact to remember is that ownership of a deposit account is determined by the records of the financial institution and not merely by what is typed on any evidence of account. For this reason, counselors may type *or* between the joint tenants' names on an evidence of account if their customers or institutions prefer to use *or*. However, counselors should be aware that the word *and* on any evidence of account can avoid uncertainty because that is the word used in the deposit contract.[5]

Preparing the Evidence of Account

Figure 6-3 illustrates the format for inserting two or more joint tenants' names on the evidence of account. Notice that the words "as joint tenants with right of survivorship and not as tenants in common" also appear on the evidence of account.

AUTOMATIC TERMINATION OF JOINT TENANCY

A joint tenancy may be terminated by any one of the following actions:

- a conveyance;

- a pledge;

- an appointment of a conservator or guardian.

However, specific language in the account contract can permit a joint tenant to pledge an account without terminating the joint tenancy.

Conveyance

A conveyance is the transfer of title to property (in this case, a deposit account) from one person to another. This can be done only on the records of the institution. When changing ownership, the funds are conveyed by closing one account and opening another. Regardless of whether or not the new account is a joint tenancy, this conveyance terminates the original joint tenancy.

Pledge

A pledge is the act of using money in an account as security or collateral to obtain additional money.

Pledged money may be used as security to back up a promise to repay a loan. The portion of the money equal to the outstanding loan balance must remain in the pledged account; the joint tenants regain full withdrawal rights when they pay back the loan. An example of a pledge that might terminate a joint tenancy is a deposit account loan to one joint tenant without the consent of the other joint tenant(s). Depending on the wording in the deposit contract, a pledge may or may not terminate the joint tenancy if all joint tenants' signatures are not present.

Some states have statutes that permit, in the absence of directions to the contrary, one joint tenant to pledge the entire deposit account without terminating the joint tenancy in whole or in part. In states without such a statute, the matter may be covered by specific words in the deposit account contract. These words explain exactly how the account can be pledged and its future status. A deposit contract can include language that permits any one joint tenant to pledge the account without severing the joint tenancy relationship (see Figure 6-5).

Appointment of a Conservator or Guardian

A joint tenancy may be terminated if a court declares a joint tenant incompetent or mentally incapable and appoints a conservator or guardian. In effect, the order appointing the conservator or guardian transfers the legal title of the incompetent person to the conservator or guardian and may terminate the joint tenancy. Thereafter, depending on state statute, the institution treats the account as a tenancy in common and pays half of it to the conservator or guardian and the other half to the other joint tenant (or pro rata if the account has more than two joint tenants).

F I G U R E 6-5

Language Permitting Pledges on the Joint Tenancy Account

| Taxpayer Identification Number | | | Account No._____ | 14610-0 JOINT (11/83) |

A,

and B,

and C,

Type All Names: (Last Name)   (First Name)   (Middle Name)
as joint tenants with right of survivorship and not as tenants in common, and not as tenants by the entirety, the undersigned hereby apply for a savings account in

and for the issuance of evidence thereof in their joint names described as aforesaid. You are directed to act pursuant to any one or more of the joint tenants' signatures, shown below, in any manner in connection with this account and, without limiting the generality of the foregoing, to pay, without any liability for such payment, to any one or the survivor or survivors at any time. This account may be pledged in whole or in part as security for any loan made by you to one or more of the undersigned. Any such pledge shall not operate to sever or terminate either in whole or in part the joint tenancy estate and relationship reflected in or established by this contract. It is agreed by the signatory parties with each other and by the parties with you that any funds placed in or added to the account by any one of the parties *are and shall be conclusively intended to be a gift and delivery* at that time of such funds to the other signatory party or parties to the extent of his or their pro rata interest in the account. You are authorized to accept checks and other instruments for credit to this account, whether payable to one or more of the parties, and to supply any needed endorsement. You are relieved of any liability in connection with collection of all items handled by you without negligence, and shall not be liable for acts of your agents, sub-agents or others or for any casualty. Withdrawals may not be made on account of such items until collected, and any amount not collected may be charged back to the account, including expense incurred, and any other outside expense incurred relative to this account may be charged to it.

By signing this signature card, I(we), under penalty of perjury, certify that (a) the number shown on this card is my(our) correct taxpayer identification number(s), and (b) I(we) are not subject to backup withholding. [If either of the signers have been notified by the IRS that they are subject to backup withholding, delete the language in (b) above.]

A
_____
Signature   (Type) Street   City & State   Phone
B
_____
Signature   (Type) Street   City & State   Phone
C
_____
Signature   (Type) Street   City & State   Phone

DATE_____

SAF Systems and Forms

ACCOUNTS-IN-TWO-NAMES STATUTES

To protect financial institutions from liability when a joint tenancy account is in dispute, the legislatures of all states plus the District of Columbia have passed *accounts-in-two-names* statutes. Such statutes protect the institution when it pays out to one or more of the parties after the death of one joint tenant. The statute makes it clear that the institution may pay out to the survivor—whether or not the survivor is ultimately determined to be the owner—without liability.

The scope of this protection varies widely among states, because there are basically two kinds of accounts-in-two-names statutes: (1) exculpatory, which relieve the institution from any liability for paying out to the survivor of a joint tenancy account, even where a court later finds that a valid joint tenancy never existed; and (2) ownership-fixing, which create a legal presumption that valid joint tenancy was established wherever right-of-survivorship language was used in creating the account.

These protective accounts-in-two-names statutes greatly reduce financial institutions' exposure to costly lawsuits when honoring withdrawal requests from joint tenancy accounts. Institutions are not required to know when each of their many account holders dies or loses his or her competence. Unless told of an account owner's death or in receipt of notice of a court declaration of incompetence, an institution may honor a withdrawal request upon presentation of any authorized signature according to the deposit contract without risk of liability to any other joint tenant(s) on the account.

Accounts-in-two-names statutes further protect institutions from certain risks associated with accounts opened by mail. Frequently, an institution may be unaware of the absence of one or more of the required four unities.

Consider an account opened through the mail involving one joint tenant who makes only deposits and another joint tenant who makes only withdrawals. The first tenant may decide to keep the passbook, thus restricting the other tenant's withdrawals. This action will invalidate the joint tenancy, since it will have violated the unity of title. If the second tenant obtains the passbook and closes out the account, the financial institution will not be liable to the first tenant.

Nevertheless, if an institution has received notice that the ownership of a joint tenancy account is in dispute and believes the dispute is valid, it should not pay out to the survivor or the heirs pending receipt of a signed release from all parties or a court order. In this situation, accounts-in-two-names statutes provide no protection from liability.[6]

SUMMARY

Joint tenancy is a popular form of ownership available in all states. Joint tenancy is created either by common law or by contract, depending on the state. The right of survivorship in joint tenancy permits the surviving joint tenant(s) to continue to own the funds when one joint tenant dies.

The four unities of time, title, interest and possession must be present to most effectively establish a valid joint tenancy. If any of these unities is missing, the account should be established in another form of ownership. The best opportunity for counselors to note whether any of the required unities is missing is the time at which the account is opened.

Properly documenting the intentions of the three parties to the deposit account contract is the responsibility of the counselor who opens the account. Counselors should verify that customers understand the terms they have agreed to. They also should be able to explain the meaning of gift and other language contained in the deposit contract.

Once the account is opened, both the institution and each of the joint tenants have rights and responsibilities. Employees who deal with deposit accounts should know these rights as well as the conditions necessary for canceling them. Joint tenants should be aware of their rights, know how to exercise them and understand the actions required to release any imposed restrictions.

Joint tenants should know how their actions may terminate the joint tenancy. They should also understand that a court appointment of a conservator or guardian may terminate a joint tenancy. Joint tenants should be made aware that ownership can be changed only by changing the records of the institution. Counselors can explain to joint tenants the language contained in the deposit contract that would permit the account to be pledged without severing the joint tenancy. Accounts-in-two-names statutes protect savings institutions from liability when honoring withdrawals from joint tenancy accounts.

FOOTNOTES

[1]For further information on the four unities of joint tenancy, see reference books on property law, such as Jon W. Bruce, James W. Ely, Jr., and C. Dent Bostwick, *Modern Property Law, Cases and Materials*, (St. Paul, Minn.: West Publishing, 1984), p. 323, and Roger A. Cunningham, William B. Stoebuck and Dale A. Whitman, *The Law of Property* (St. Paul, Minn.: West Publishing, 1984), pp. 202–207.

[2]Every state has joint tenancy statutes *except* KY, LA, OH and OR.

[3]See "Statutory Presumption of Joint Tenancy Held Conclusive," *Legal Bulletin*, XXIX (March 1963), pp. 85–90.

[4]See "Comprehensive Signature Card Held Key in Establishing Joint Ownership," *Legal Bulletin*, XXXII (March 1966), pp. 95–99; "Signature Card 'Gift Language' Establishes Joint Tenancy," *Legal Bulletin*, XLII (November 1976), pp. 323–25;

"Joint Tenancy Ownership Requires Signatures of All Parties," *Legal Bulletin*, XLVIII (May 1982), p. 103. See also *Austin* v. *Summers*, 118 S.E. 2d 684.

[5]See "The And/Or Controversy in Joint Accounts," *Legal Bulletin*, XX (March 1954), pp. 17–24.

[6]See "Accounts-in-Two-Names Statute, Establishing Joint Tenancy, Held Constitutional," *Legal Bulletin*, LI (September 1985), pp. 286–288.

CHAPTER 7

Other Multiple Owner Accounts

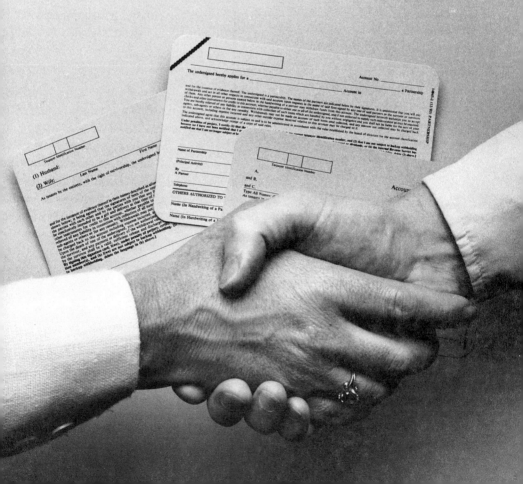

KEY CONCEPTS

- Differences between the corporate and partnership forms of account ownership;

- Purpose of a partnership agreement;

- Three situations that may change a joint tenancy into a tenancy in common;

- Differences between individually owned property and community property;

- Four ways a husband and wife can terminate a joint tenancy, a tenancy by the entirety or a community property account;

- Similarities and differences among joint tenancy, tenancy in common, tenancy by the entirety and community property with respect to ownership, withdrawal and survivorship rights.

The various forms of multiple ownership include joint tenancy, partnerships, tenancy in common, tenancy by the entirety and community property. Chapter 6 covered joint tenancy in detail. This chapter examines the other forms of multiple ownership. It compares each form with respect to ownership, withdrawal and survivorship rights. It also explains the opening and closing procedures for accounts that fall under these forms of ownership.

Counselors and other customer service employees need to be familiar with the documentation required by each form of ownership in order to protect the rights of both the account owners and the institution and to ensure that customers hold the appropriate form of ownership for their needs.

The wording in deposit contracts for each form of ownership also differs. Counselors need to be able to explain this wording to their customers in everyday terms. When customers understand the specific conditions that differentiate the various forms of ownership, fewer difficulties are likely to arise and customers can feel more confident in their choices.

PARTNERSHIPS

A *partnership* is a form of business organization in which two or more persons join together in a business enterprise and agree by contract to share profits and risks. It exists only for as long as all partners stay in the business. Also, a partnership issues no stock. Lawyers, doctors, accountants and other professionals frequently form partnership relationships, as do store owners and other tradespeople.

Ownership and Withdrawal Rights

Partnership laws vary among the states; however, they are essentially the same in principle.[1] In general, any one of the partners is authorized to act on behalf of the partnership. Also, each partner usually is responsible for and bound by the business contracts the other partners make. For example, John and Carolyn are lawyers who establish a partnership. Carolyn can sign a contract to rent an office for the business, and John will be bound by that contract.

This element of personal liability sets the partnership entity apart from the corporation, which ordinarily does not entail such liability. Persons who deal with a partnership have the right to assume, unless they are advised differently, that all partners have equal rights in the management and conduct of the business. Unless specifically spelled out to the contrary in the partnership documentation, each partner has the above-mentioned authority and liability. These general characteristics of personal liability and authority may not apply, however, in the case of a limited partnership (discussed below).

A partnership may consist of two kinds of partners: a general partner and a limited partner. A *general partner* shares equally, or as contractually agreed upon, with the other general partners in the partnership's profits and losses. A general partner can act alone in binding the partnership and, in turn, is bound by the business actions of the other general partners. Also, a general partner can lose more than his or her individual investment in the business. With regard to deposit accounts, general partners share equally, or as contractually agreed upon, in terms of ownership and withdrawal rights.

A *limited partner* is restricted in the amount of profits he or she can take from the partnership. Also, a limited partner cannot lose more than his or her individual investment in the business and therefore has limited power to act on behalf of the partnership. With regard to deposit accounts, limited partners do not have all the ownership and withdrawal rights that general partners have. However, if the depository institution is not "on notice" that a partner is limited in his or her authority, it may assume that in ordinary matters, such as opening a deposit account and making withdrawals from it, each partner has full partnership powers.

Partnerships differ from corporations in still another significant way. As stated in Chapter 5, the ownership of a corporate account does not change when a corporation changes the individuals authorized to transact business on the account. The corporation simply passes a resolution and completes the necessary account documents to notify the depository institution of the change. With a partnership, however, if the partners change, the partnership terminates. Whenever a partner leaves or joins the business, therefore, the partnership account is closed and a new account is opened.

Unlike in a joint tenancy, the owners of a partnership do not share the unities of interest or possession. This characteristic is reflected in the following elements of a partnership account:

- Partners may own a pro rata, or equal fractional interest, or some other specified percentage of the business.

- Partners have no automatic right of survivorship. In most states, a surviving partner has the absolute right to conclude the affairs of the partnership and the responsibility to account to the estate of the deceased partner.

- The owners of a partnership account do not have the authority to grant a power of attorney.

Documentation

The documentation of a partnership account shows that the account has been opened in the name of the partnership. Typically, the evidence of account includes only the name of the partnership and omits the names of the partners. Also, the partnership deposit contract does not contain a resolution authorizing changes in partners. Therefore, the deposit contract must be changed when partnership owners change. This requires closing the original deposit account and opening a new one, even if the partnership name remains the same.

Who should sign the deposit contract documents? Since a general partner has unlimited liability, all general partners should be present to sign the signature card when opening a partnership account (see Figure 7-1). Any limited partners who are authorized to make transactions on the account should also sign the signature card at this time. The scope of the partners' authority is spelled out in the *partnership agreement*, which is part of the deposit contract. A copy of the agreement goes to the partnership's files.

Unincorporated Joint Ventures

Sometimes an unincorporated joint venture of two or more persons appears to be a partnership, but this similarity may be misleading. An *unincorporated joint venture* has been defined as an association of persons formed

F I G U R E 7-1

Signature Card for Partnership Account

Account No. _____

_____ a Partnership

The undersigned hereby applies for a _____ Account in

and for the issuance of evidence thereof. The undersigned is a partnership. The names of the partners are indicated below by their signatures. It is understood that you will pay withdrawals and act in all other respects in connection with said account upon requests in the name of said firm signed by any one of said partners or the survivor or survivors of them. Any other person or persons named below in the handwriting of a partner may withdraw funds from this account. The undersigned herewith authorize you to accept checks and other instruments for credit to this account, whether payable to either one or all of the undersigned, and if not endorsed to supply such endorsement as may be required. You are hereby relieved of any liability in connection with collection of such items which are handled by you without negligence and you shall not be liable for the acts of your agents, sub-agents or others or for any casualty. Withdrawals may not be made on account of such items until collected, and any amount not collected may be charged back to this account, including expense incurred and any other outside expense incurred relative to this account may be charged to it.

The undersigned agree that this account is subject to and is to be administered in accordance with the rules established by the board of directors for the account classification indicated above, and acknowledge receipt of a copy of said rules.

Under penalties of perjury, I certify (1) that the number shown on this form is my correct taxpayer identification number, and (2) that I am not subject to backup withholding because (a) I have not been notified that I am subject to backup withholding as a result of a failure to report all interest or dividends, or (b) the Internal Revenue Service has notified me that I am no longer subject ot backup withholding. [If the Internal Revenue Service has notified the payee that she/he is subject to backup withholding, delete (2) above.]

Signatures of all partners:

Name of Partnership _____

(Principal Activity) _____

By _____
A Partner

Telephone _____ Date _____ Address _____

OTHERS AUTHORIZED TO WITHDRAW:

Name (In Handwriting of a Partner) _____   Signature of Authorized Person _____

Name (In Handwriting of a Partner) _____   Signature of Authorized Person _____

1845-2 (12/85) PARTNERSHIP

SAF Systems and Forms

for the purpose of carrying out a single business enterprise for profit. Once the specific purpose of the joint enterprise has been accomplished, the relationship established among the participants terminates. A partnership, on the other hand, generally is established for a continuing purpose. Although the rules of partnership are sometimes applied to the unincorporated joint venture, the features of a specific purpose and informality, or looseness, of or-

ganization that characterize the unincorporated joint
venture create major distinctions between the two types
of relationships. When two or more people wish to place
the funds of an unincorporated joint venture in a deposit
account, the voluntary association form of ownership may
be appropriate because many voluntary associations are
unincorporated (see Chapter 5).

TENANCY IN COMMON

Tenancy in common is a form of ownership in which two
or more parties own property but each party owns a separate interest—usually a pro rata or equal fractional interest, unless specified otherwise. For example, Cal and
Emily each own 50% of a tenancy in common account.

Tenancy in common, like joint tenancy, originated
from common law. Unlike in a joint tenancy, however,
the owners of a tenancy in common account have no right
of survivorship. When one owner dies, the decedent's
share of the account passes to his or her heirs rather than
to the remaining owner(s).

Creation of a Tenancy in Common

Individuals may establish tenancy in common accounts
for a variety of reasons. For example, Jan and Joe are
two cousins who both wish to invest $5,000 in certificate
accounts. Normally, each would open a separate account
but a particularly high-yielding account requires a minimum balance of $10,000. To qualify to open this account,
the two friends pool their funds and open a tenancy in
common account.

In addition, three situations may automatically create a tenancy in common: a defective attempt to create a joint tenancy; the severance of a joint tenancy by one of the tenants; or termination of a joint tenancy by mutual agreement. A tenancy in common can result from a defective attempt to establish a joint tenancy. For example, assume one of the joint tenants does not intend to share ownership rights with the other joint tenants. In this case, a court of law may determine whether the joint tenancy account lacks any of the required four unities. If it does, the account becomes a tenancy in common account.

Second, a tenancy in common can result when a joint tenancy account has been conveyed, pledged or otherwise terminated by one of the tenants without the consent of the others. An example could be a loan made on the account by one tenant without the authorization of the others. Chapter 5 covers specific language to include in the deposit contract that will allow a joint tenant to pledge the account without severing the joint tenancy and thus causing it to become a tenancy in common.

Third, a joint tenancy can become a tenancy in common due to termination of the account by mutual agreement of all the tenants. This may happen, for example, if the joint tenants eventually decide they no longer desire the right of survivorship. In such a case, the tenants may close the joint tenancy account and transfer the funds to a tenancy in common account using the appropriate deposit contract.

Ownership Rights

Ordinarily, each owner in a tenancy in common deposit account owns an undivided pro rata interest. This means that each is assumed to own an equal fraction of the balance on deposit. For example, if there are three tenants, each owns a third; if four tenants, each owns a fourth; and so on. Sometimes, however, each tenant owns an unequal pro rata interest in the account funds. For example, in a tenancy in common account with two owners, one tenant may own two-thirds and the other only one-third of the account.

In a tenancy in common account, any of the tenants may grant a power of attorney. Power of attorney enhances the convenience and accessibility to the funds on deposit without altering ownership of the account.

Withdrawal Rights

A tenancy in common account requires all of the owners' signatures for withdrawals from the account. The wording in the deposit contract includes language such as "the signatures of all tenants in common are required for withdrawals on or cancellation of the account." The tenancy in common account signature card shown in Figure 7-2 illustrates another example of appropriate wording.

Employees need to be extremely careful when handling accounts that require all owners' signatures. As in the case of withdrawals, employees should obtain all the signatures whenever they cash a check against such an account. Cashing a check without all the signatures could make the institution liable for an improper payout if the check is returned unpaid and the institution must deduct that amount from the account. In a practical sense, such a payment would be similar to a withdrawal made without all the owners' signatures.

Sometimes tenants in common give one another a power of attorney so that withdrawals and other

F I G U R E 7-2

Signature Card for Tenancy in Common— All Signatures

transactions on the account can be handled with one tenant's signature. For example, take a brother and sister who hold a tenancy in common account. Because both have spouses and children, they do not wish to have survivorship rights on the account. However, they trust each other enough to feel that only one signature is needed to transact business on the account. Thus, they give each other a power of attorney. In this case, each deposits a few dollars a week into the account so that once a year both families can vacation together.

Documentation

The deposit contract contains the critical elements that differentiate tenancy in common account ownership from other types of joint ownership. The counselor can point out these elements in the documents to help customers verify that this form of ownership meets their needs. Three points that need verification are:

- *Pro rata interest of each owner.* Deposit contract documents include language such as "unless noted on the face of this card, the Bank will assume that each person deposited an equal amount." Other typical wording concerning this element is "unless otherwise stated hereon, the ownership of this account is prorated."

  For an account whose owners actually own an equal fraction of the balance, the counselor need not add this information to the document. However, if each tenant owns an unequal pro rata interest in the account funds, this information must be entered into the deposit contract document. Otherwise, the institution will assume that all tenants have an equal fractional interest.

- *All signatures required.* The counselor should point out this requirement to the customer.

- *No right of survivorship.* The counselor can show where this language appears on joint tenancy account documents and then point out that it does not appear on tenancy in common documents. These actions can help the counselor make this important difference clear to the customer.

The evidence of account also includes language that indicates the account is held in the tenancy in common

F I G U R E 7-3

Passbook: Tenancy in Common

SAVINGS ACCOUNT

676890
NUMBER

THIS CERTIFIES THAT

Ralph Wentworth and Alice Jensen as tenants in common

Holds a SAVINGS ACCOUNT in

FIRST BANK

---

form of ownership. Figure 7-3 shows typical wording for tenancy in common account holders' names on a passbook. Note that the words "as tenants in common" appear after the tenants' names on the evidence of account.

TENANCY BY THE ENTIRETY

Tenancy by the entirety is a form of joint tenancy ownership in which a husband and wife hold the right of survivorship exclusively. Originally, under common law, a tenancy by the entirety was the only form of joint ownership possible between husband and wife because the spouses were considered to be one person, that is, a single entity. In the nineteenth century, the single entity concept was almost completely eliminated by the adoption of the Married Women's Property Acts, which allowed married women to own property in their own name, and by the change in public policy toward the rights of women in general. This form of ownership is slowly being abolished nationwide and today is recognized only in certain states.[2]

Ownership and Withdrawal Rights

A tenancy by the entirety includes the rights of survivorship, but it differs from a joint tenancy ownership in some significant ways. First, a tenancy by the entirety is possible only for a husband and wife, while a joint tenancy may rest in two or more persons who may or may not be related. Second, a tenancy by the entirety cannot be terminated by one party's signature. A tenancy by the entirety terminates if:

- the husband and wife, acting together, transfer or convey the account to someone else;

- either spouse dies;

- the husband and wife voluntarily separate; or

- the marriage is dissolved. A divorce will cause the tenancy by the entirety to become a tenancy in common unless the parties agree to another arrangement or the divorce decree states otherwise.

Third, neither the husband nor the wife can ordinarily grant a power of attorney to the other spouse. However, either spouse may grant a power of attorney to a third party.

Another characteristic of tenancy by the entirety concerns the disposition of the funds. When either spouse dies, the survivor receives the account balance free and clear of any debts the deceased spouse may have placed on the account independently.

Documentation

In states that recognize tenancy by the entirety, counselors should know how to document this form of ownership correctly. If a husband and wife wish to create a tenancy by the entirety, both should sign a deposit contract similar to the one shown in Figure 7-4.

Figure 7-5 illustrates how a sample evidence of account is prepared for a tenancy by the entirety. The words "Husband:" and "Wife:" should precede the spouses' names. Following their names, enter the words "as tenants by the entirety, with the right of survivorship."

The institution should take extra care in states that recognize tenancy by the entirety whenever a husband and wife open an account together. This especially applies when the couple actually request a joint tenancy. In that case, the words "and not as tenants by the entirety" should appear on the signature card and any evidences of account.

COMMUNITY PROPERTY OWNERSHIP

Community property is a form of ownership available only to a husband and wife and recognized only in certain

F I G U R E 7-4

Signature Card for Tenancy by the Entirety— All Signatures

Taxpayer Identification Number	Account No. _____

(1) Husband: _____

(2) Wife: _____

Last Name   First Name   Middle Name

As tenants by the entirety, with the right of survivorship, the undersigned hereby apply for a savings account in

and for the issuance of evidence thereof in their names described as aforesaid. You are directed to act pursuant to writings bearing the tenants' signatures shown below; it being agreed that the signatures of both of the tenants are required in all matters related to this account. It is agreed by both of the parties with each other and by the parties with you that any funds placed in or added to the account by any one of the parties *are and shall be conclusively intended to be a gift and delivery* at that time of such funds to the estate by the entirety. You are authorized to accept checks and other instruments for credit to this account, whether payable to one or the other of the parties, and to supply any needed endorsement. You are relieved of any liability in connection with collection of all items handled by you without negligence, and shall not be liable for acts of your agents, sub-agents or others or for any casualty. Withdrawals may not be made on account of such items until collected, and any amount not collected may be charged back to this account including expense incurred, and any other outside expense incurred relative to this account may be charged to it. Upon the death of one of the undersigned, you are authorized to act without further inquiry in accordance with writings bearing the signature of the survivor, and any payment or delivery of the withdrawal value of this account, or other rights relating thereto or a receipt or acquittance signed by the survivor shall be a valid, sufficient release and discharge of said institution.
By signing this signature card, I(we), under penalty of perjury, certify that (a) the number shown on this card is my(our) correct taxpayer identification number(s), and (b) I(we) are not subject to backup withholding. [If either of the signers have been notified by the IRS that they are subject to backup withholding, delete the language in (b) above.]

(1) Signature _____

(2) Signature _____

Street Address   City & State   Telephone

Dated_____

14615-9 JOINT/ENTIRETY (11/83)

SAF Systems and Forms

states.[3] *Community property* is all property belonging to married people provided that:

- it was not owned individually at the time of marriage; and

- it was not acquired during the course of the marriage by the husband or wife through an inheritance, will or gift.

F I G U R E 7-5

Passbook: Tenancy by the Entirety

SAVINGS ACCOUNT

<u>261794</u>
NUMBER

THIS CERTIFIES THAT

Husband: John Wentworth—Wife: Lisa Wentworth as tenants by

the entirety, with the right of survivorship

Holds a SAVINGS ACCOUNT in

STATE BANK

Community property, then, is all property that either spouse gains or earns during the course of the marriage.

Community property is a form of joint ownership that originated in the civil law of Spain and France. All of the community property states, except Wisconsin, inherited the concept from their colonial forebears. Wisconsin is the only state that has independently enacted community property legislation modeled after the Uniform Marital Property Act (UMPA).

A spouse can terminate community property ownership in the same ways he or she can terminate a tenancy by the entirety.

Community Property versus Individually Owned Property

When people open community property deposit accounts, their rights depend on state law. In states that recognize community property, two categories of property belong to married people: individually owned property and community property. Spouses may have individually owned property in a community property state in four situations:

- *Property that the husband or wife owned individually before the marriage continues to be owned individually by him or her.* For example, Susan Graham owned a late-model sports car before she married William Wait. When Susan and William got married, the car did not become community property; it remained individually owned property in Susan's name. Prior to the marriage, William held title to 500 shares of AT&T stock. Like the car, the stock did not automatically become community property; it remained individually owned property in William's name. However, William opened a regular savings account with his payroll check shortly after the marriage. Unlike the car and the stock, the savings account was considered community property, and therefore both Susan and William held an interest in it. This is because William earned the funds *during* the marriage.

- *Property either spouse acquired during the marriage by inheritance, will or gift is considered individually owned property.* For example, one year after Susan and William married, Susan's Aunt Harriet gave Susan a thoroughbred horse. The horse became individually owned property in Susan's name. Gifts given to only one spouse remain individually owned by that spouse; they do not become community property.

- *Property that a spouse purchases with individually owned funds remains individually owned property.* For example, Susan was afraid of horses and decided to sell the thoroughbred. With the proceeds of the sale, she purchased a video shop. The video shop also was considered individually owned property because she had purchased it with her individually owned funds.

- *Property that a spouse purchases from the proceeds, such as interest, profits, yield or appreciation, of individually owned property continues to be individually owned.* Continuing the example, Susan's video shop was so successful that from the profits she expanded the store and parking lot by purchasing the adjacent corner lot. The expanded business continued to be individually owned by Susan. Also, Susan used some of the profits from her store to buy valuable paintings and collector plates, which she displayed in the home she and William have. However, even though the home was community property, on which William continued to pay the mortgage, the artwork was not considered community property.

In states with community property laws, community property includes all property that is not individually owned. The reasoning is that a husband and wife should share equally in property acquired through their joint efforts during marriage. Each spouse, therefore, owns one-half of everything earned or gained, regardless of his or her individual contribution. This differs from the common law prevailing in most states under which each spouse owns whatever he or she earns.

Ownership and Withdrawal Rights

The following are important rights in a community property account:

- Depending on the deposit contract chosen upon opening the account, either or both signatures are required for all matters relating to the account.

- Like a tenancy in common, community property has no right of survivorship. The surviving spouse takes one-half of the account, and the remaining heirs of the deceased spouse take the other half.

- Neither husband nor wife may grant a power of attorney with a community property account.

Documentation

The spouses can own funds placed in a community property account in a variety of ways. Part of the funds may already be community property. However, some portions of the funds may be separately owned by the husband, others separately owned by the wife and still others owned in joint tenancy.

Under these circumstances, in order to make a standardized community property deposit contract possible, the laws of the state involved would have to permit the combining of the spouses' separately or jointly owned property into community owned property by agreement of the spouses. Institutions in community property states recognize these circumstances when developing standard documents.[4]

Certain information is designated on the account documentation. At the time the account is opened, the husband and wife should specify on the contract whether either or both signatures will be required for all matters relating to the account. Also, depending on institution policy, the counselor may prepare evidence of a community property account by indicating "Husband:" before the husband's name and "Wife:" before the wife's name, followed by the words "as owners in community" (see Figure 7-6).

Joint Tenancy Ownership in a Community Property State

Some married people living in a community property state may prefer a joint tenancy deposit account over a community property account because they want the features of a joint tenancy. The spouses' commitment to each other creates a willingness or intention to maintain the four required unities—time, title, interest and possession—of a valid joint tenancy. The spouses may also prefer the right of survivorship over the manner of disposition of a community property account. In these situations, counselors should proceed cautiously. The joint tenancy account documents (illustrated in Chapter 6,

---

F I G U R E 7-6

Passbook: Community Property

SAVINGS ACCOUNT   379516
                                    NUMBER

THIS CERTIFIES THAT

Husband: John Wentworth—Wife: Lisa Wentworth as owners in

community

Holds a SAVINGS ACCOUNT in

STATE BANK

Figures 6-1 and 6-2) should include the words "and not as owners in community" after the words "and not as tenants by the entirety."

SUMMARY

Partnership, tenancy in common, tenancy by the entirety and community property deposit accounts are all types of multiple owner accounts. Financial institution employees can refer to Figure 7-7 to review and compare the various forms of multiple ownership covered in this and the preceding chapter.

F I G U R E 7-7

Comparison of Multiple Ownership Accounts

	Interest	Signatures Required for Withdrawal	Rights of Survivorship Interest
Joint Tenancy	all owners are equal	anyone, unless specified otherwise	yes
Partnership	prorata	anyone, unless specified otherwise	none; deceased's interests passes to heirs; surviving partner may close account and account to deceased's heirs
Tenancy in Common	prorata	all signatures	none; deceased's interest passes to heirs
Tenancy by the Entirety	both owners are equal	one or both signatures as specified	yes
Community Property	some interest owned individually; some interest shared equally	one or both signatures as specified	none; deceased's interest passes to heirs

All states recognize both partnership and tenancy in common accounts. Partnerships are a form of business ownership. A partnership ceases every time a partner

F I G U R E 7-7, Continued

Who Is Eligible to Open Account	Authority to Grant Power of Attorney	Ability of Any One Account Holder to Pledge
any two or more competent individuals (four unities required)	yes	depends on contract; may sever the ownership
two or more legal partners	no	yes; contract may require more than one signature
any two or more competent individuals	yes	no; all signatures required
a husband and wife only in certain states	yes; but may not name the other spouse as an attorney in fact	yes; contract may require both signatures
a husband and wife only in certain states	no	yes; contract may require both signatures

leaves or a new partner joins the business. Financial institution employees must follow the relevant provisions of the partnership agreement, because the business actions of one partner bind all partners. Tenancy in common accounts differ from joint tenancy accounts in that they do not have a right of survivorship. They also require all signatures for withdrawals and provide for pro rata ownership of the funds.

Tenancy by the entirety is recognized only in certain states. It is similar in many ways to a joint tenancy but differs in three important respects:

- Tenancy by the entirety may be established only by a husband and wife, while joint tenancy may be created by two or more persons regardless of their relationship to each other.

- With a tenancy by the entirety, either spouse may grant a power of attorney, but not to each other, as they can with a joint tenancy.

- Tenancy by the entirety never loses the right of survivorship.

Also, the right of survivorship includes protection from creditors of the deceased spouse.

Only certain states recognize community property ownership. This form of ownership also is available only to a husband and wife. The laws in community property states determine whether property belonging to a married couple is considered individually owned or community property.

FOOTNOTES

[1]The Uniform Partnership Act (UPA) was created by the American Law Institute and the National Conference of Com-

missioners on Uniform State Laws and has been adopted by all the states except GA and LA.

[2]The only states that have tenancies by the entirety are AR, DE, FL, MD, MA, MS, MO, PA, RI, TN and VT.

[3]The states that have community property laws are AZ, CA, ID, LA, NV, NM, TX, WA and WI.

[4]"Signature Card Developed for Use in Six Community Property States," *Legal Bulletin*, XXVII (May 1961), pp. 162–163.

CHAPTER 8

Fiduciary Accounts

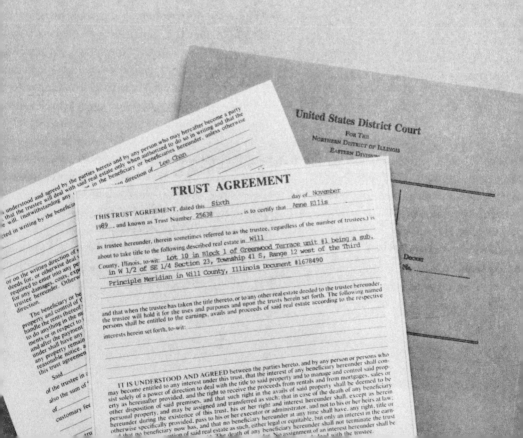

KEY CONCEPTS

- Definition and types of fiduciaries;

- Development and major provisions of Uniform Transfers to Minors Act;

- Forms of legal guardianship;

- Differences between a guardian and a conservator, a natural guardian and a legal guardian, and an administrator and an executor;

- Purpose of a representative payee account;

- Reasons for establishing trusts;

- The three parties to a trust and the relationship among them;

- Requirements for a valid trust;

- Purpose of accounts-in-trust statutes;

- Five items addressed by the provisions of a trust agreement;

- Methods for naming more than one trustee and/ or beneficiary to a valid trust account.

A nother type of ownership that may be appropriate or useful for certain customers' needs is some form of fiduciary account. A *fiduciary* is a person or corporation responsible for holding or controlling property for another; therefore, a fiduciary account is any deposit account one person holds for another. An example of a fiduciary account is the discretionary revocable trust account that many depository institutions offer.

This chapter explores the many types of fiduciaries and how and why they use deposit accounts. A major portion of the chapter is devoted to trusts, the most common type of fiduciary account. Topics include basic trust terminology, the reasons why people open trusts, the relationship among the parties to a trust, the requirements of a valid trust and the specific items that make a trust agreement complete.

The chapter differentiates among the various forms of trust account ownership so that counselors can match the proper documentation to a customer's request. It includes many examples illustrating how to document the various trust arrangements and clarifies the differences between revocable and irrevocable trusts.

TYPES OF FIDUCIARIES

The types of fiduciaries include:

- custodian;
- guardian;
- conservator;
- executor;

- administrator;

- representative payee;

- trustee.

Some fiduciary appointments are changeable and others are not. Figure 8-1 illustrates a fiduciary signature card.

Custodian

A *custodian* is a fiduciary who has control and possession (or "custody") of something that belongs to somebody else and is responsible for its care and preservation. A custodian does not hold legal title. A *custodial gift* is a gift given to a minor child by an adult who retains control over the gift, or grants control to another adult, until the child reaches the age of majority and can legally accept responsibility for the gift.

Uniform Transfers to Minors Act
The *Uniform Transfers to Minors Act* provides a simplified way to transfer any kind of property to minors under adult custodianship. It is a model law approved in 1983 by the National Conference of Commissioners on Uniform State Laws, an organization that promotes the passage of uniform legislation in local jurisdictions. Only in states whose legislatures have adopted this model law can depository institutions open deposit accounts under its provisions.

Relationship to Earlier Laws The Uniform Transfers to Minors Act as approved in 1983 is the latest version in a series of uniform laws on transferring property

F I G U R E 8-1

Fiduciary Signature Card, Side 1

Taxpayer Identification Number				Account No. _____

A,

B,_____
Type All Names: (Last Name)   (First Name)   (Middle Name)

The undersigned, as _____
(Full Title of Fiduciary as Authorized by Source of Authority)

as officially affirmed on _____ by the _____
           (Date)   (Name of Court or other Source of Authority)

hereby applies for a _____ Account in

and for the issuance of evidence thereof. In consideration of your acceptance of this application, I hereby certify that the funds which are offered to you concurrently herewith for placement in the account indicated above and any funds which later may be placed in the same account are funds properly within my custody which may be lawfully invested in or placed in an account in said institution in accordance with authority duly vested in me as fiduciary, all as described above. A specimen of my signature is shown below and you are hereby authorized to act without further inquiry in accordance with writings bearing such signature, it being agreed that if more than one signature is affixed hereto, all such signatures shall be required in all matters related to this account. You are authorized to supply any endorsement for me on any check or other instrument tendered for this account and you are hereby relieved of any liability in connection with collection of such items which are handled by you without negligence, and you shall not be liable for the acts of your agents, sub-agents or others or for any casualty. Withdrawals may not be made on account of such items until collected, and any amount not collected may be charged back to this account, including expense incurred, and any other outside expense incurred relative to this account may be charged to it. In this instrument except as otherwise indicated the singular includes the plural.

The undersigned agree that this account is subject to and is to be administered in accordance with the rules established by the board of directors for the account classification indicated above, and acknowledge receipt of a copy of said rules.

to minors. The earliest version, the Model Gifts of Securities to Minors Act, was developed by the New York Stock Exchange and the Association of Stock Exchange Firms and covered only gifts of securities. In 1956, the Conference developed the original version of the Uniform Gifts to Minors Act (UGMA) and broadened the previous model act to include gifts of money as well as securities. In 1965 and 1966, the Conference revised the Uniform

F I G U R E 8-1, Continued

Fiduciary Signature Card, Side 2

Under penalties of perjury, I certify (1) that the number shown on this form is my correct taxpayer identification number, and (2) that I am not subject to backup withholding because (a) I have not been notified that I am subject to backup withholding as a result of a failure to report all interest or dividends, or (b) the Internal Revenue Service has notified me that I am no longer subject to backup withholding. [If the Internal Revenue Service has notified the payee that she/he is subject to backup withholding, delete (2) above.]

* _____

A _____ as _____
    Signature of Fiduciary   Title

_____
    Address

B _____ as _____
    Signature of Fiduciary   Title

_____
    Address

_____ Date _____
    Counter-Signature, if required

* If, in addition to the signature of the fiduciary or co-fiduciaries, a court order or other authority requires a counter-signature (such as a bondsman, court officer, or other party), a provision to this effect entered on this line should suffice. For example; "Counter-signature of_____is required for any withdrawal, transfer, or hypothecation." A specimen of the counter-signature should be obtained at the time the account is opened on the line for this purpose.

Gifts to Minors Act to expand the number of types of financial institutions (including savings and loan associations) that could accept funds under the provisions of the act. Subsequently, many states (but not all) adopted the revised version.

Between the development of the revised version of the UGMA and the early 1980s, many states added or revised provisions in their laws. The result was substantial divergence among the states' laws. To address the problem of potential conflicts of law in gift-to-minor transactions, the Conference developed the Uniform Transfers to Minors Act.

The law has several significant provisions. Following the expanded approach introduced by some states, it allows transfer of *any* kind of property to a custodian for the benefit of a minor. It also permits *any* adult to act as custodian rather than only an adult member of the minor's family, as some earlier versions required. In addition, it has broadened the definition of financial institution to include banks, trust companies, savings institutions, and credit unions chartered and supervised under state or federal law.

General Provisions   The majority of the states have adopted the Uniform Transfers to Minors Act; the remaining states continue to follow earlier versions of the law.[1] Because the states have adopted different versions and some have altered the model law upon its enactment, depository institutions need to be aware of the details of their respective state laws.

The following items constitute the general provisions of the Uniform Transfers to Minors Act, as well as earlier versions of the legislation. These provisions especially apply to depository institutions:

- The custodian has direct control over the property and can sell and reinvest its proceeds for the minor. The minor's social security number is used on the account, and any gains or income earned on the account are taxable to the minor.

- The minor's income from the property cannot be combined with the custodian's property. For example, the custodian (e.g., a parent) may not use this income for personal items such as a car or vacation.

- The custodian must deliver the property, or the remainder thereof, to the minor when the latter attains the age of majority (18, 19 or 21 years, depending on state law) or, in the event of the minor's death prior to reaching that age, to his or her estate.

- The transfer of the property to the minor is irrevocable, i.e., it cannot be changed or taken back. The minor receives vested legal title to the transferred property subject only to the custodian's powers of control during the time of minority. For example, the custodian can make decisions on how to invest funds, but the principal and earnings remain the property of the minor.

Documentation

Figure 8-2 shows a signature card for a Uniform Transfers to Minors or UGMA account. The gift may involve only one minor and one custodian. As stated previously, any adult, or in some states any adult member of the minor's family, may act as custodian. The Uniform Transfers to Minors Act also allows for the appointment of a successor custodian; this is incorporated on the back of the signature card form shown in Figure 8-2. Note that the form in Figure 8-2 provides a space to indicate the original state statute under which the account was opened. The evidence of account in Figure 8-3 is prepared similarly to the form in Figure 8-2.

If the custodian moves from the state in which the account was originally opened, he or she may transfer the

F I G U R E 8-2

Signature Card for a Uniform Transfers/ Gifts to Minors Account, Side 1

```
┌─────────────────────────────────────────────────────────────────────────┐
│  ┌──────┬──────┬──────┐                                                   │
│  │      │      │      │                                                   │
│  └──────┴──────┴──────┘                                                   │
│    Taxpayer Identification Number              Account No. _____     │
│                                                                           │
│  _____   _____   _____         │
│  (Last Name of Custodian)         (First Name)     (Middle Name)          │
│                                                                           │
│  as Custodian for _____       │
│                    (Last Name of Minor)   (First Name)   (Middle Name)    │
│                                                                           │
│  under the _____        │
│              (Designate State Statute; for example, "Illinois Uniform Gifts to Minors Act.") │
│  hereby applies for a _____ Account in the    │
└─────────────────────────────────────────────────────────────────────────┘
```

and for the issuance of evidence thereof in my name described as aforesaid. A specimen of my signature is shown below and you are hereby authorized to act without further inquiry in accordance with writings bearing such signature. You are authorized to supply any endorsement for me on any check or other instrument tendered for this account and you are hereby relieved of any liability in connection with collection of such items which are handled by you without negligence, and you shall not be liable for acts of your agents, sub-agents or others, or for any casualty. Such funds are not withdrawable until collected. Any amount not collected may be charged back to this account, including expense incurred, and any other outside expense incurred relative to this account may be charged to it. The terms of this account contract hereby are deemed to include the provisions of said Statute of this State as it is now or hereafter may be amended.

The undersigned agree that this account is subject to and is to be administered in accordance with the rules established by the board of directors for the account classification indicated above, and acknowledge receipt of a copy of said rules.

Under penalties of perjury, I certify (1) that the number shown on this form is my correct taxpayer identification number, and (2) that I am not subject to backup withholding because (a) I have not been notified that I am subject to backup withholding as a result of a failure to report all interest or dividends, or (b) the Internal Revenue Service has notified me that I am no longer subject ot backup withholding. [If the Internal Revenue Service has notified the payee that she/he is subject to backup withholding, delete (2) above.]

```
_____            _____as Custodian for
         (Signature)

_____
        (Name of Minor)

_____            Date _____
      (Designate State Statute)
```

14846-0 (12/85) CUSTODIAN

© SAF Systems and Forms

funds to a depository institution in the new state. When the new institution accepts the funds from the out-of-state institution, the customer should not execute the gift transfer portion of the deposit contract for the custodian deposit account. Rather, the institution that accepts the transfer of the custodian account should designate on the deposit contract the original state statute under which

F I G U R E 8-2, Continued

Signature Card for a Uniform Transfers/ Gifts to Minors Account, Side 2

GIFT TRANSFER TO MINOR (1)

I hereby deliver $_____to

for credit to the account indicated on the reverse side in the said institution in the name of

_____
(Name of Custodian)

as Custodian for _____
(Name of Minor)

under the _____
(Designate State Statute)

This gift of money to the minor named, which gift shall be deemed to include all earnings thereon and any future additions thereto, is irrevocable and is made in accordance with and to include all the provisions of the said Statute of this State as it is now or hereafter may be amended.

_____   _____
(Date)   (Signature of Donor)

DESIGNATION OF SUCCESSOR CUSTODIAN (2)

_____
(Name of Eligible Successor Custodian)

is appointed successor custodian of the gift property described in the Gift Transfer above, such appointment to take effect when and in the event of my resignation, death or becoming legally incapacitated and when the institution named in the account contract on the reverse side of this instrument shall deliver said account, together with a true copy of this instrument of designation, into the custody of the successor custodian herein named, and the said financial institution, upon its receipt of actual or written notice of such event, is directed to make such delivery.

_____   _____
(Date)   (Signature of Custodian)

                                       _____
                                       (Signature of Witness to Signature of Custodian)

(1) The use of this form is optional but recommended.
(2) For use in states which have enacted the REVISED Uniform Gifts to Minors Act (Revised as of August 5, 1965), and where the donor has executed Gift Transfer above.

the account was opened as the applicable state statute controlling the account.

Deposit accounts, of course, may be accepted from any custodian holding funds for another, whether or not the custodianship is of the Uniform Transfers to Minors type. An example is a third party acting under court order who

---

F I G U R E 8-3

Passbook: Uniform Transfers to Minors

SAVINGS ACCOUNT 27-49017
NUMBER

THIS CERTIFIES THAT

Frank Crowell as custodian for Frank Crowell Jr. under the

(state name) uniform transfers/gifts to minors act

Holds a SAVINGS ACCOUNT in

FIRST BANK

---

takes charge of a debtor's assets for the benefit of the debtor's creditors as a whole. In cases of ordinary custodianship, the fiduciary account deposit contract shown in Figure 8-1 is appropriate.

Tax Considerations

The Tax Reform Act of 1986 contained provisions affecting taxation of the income from Uniform Transfers to Minors Act accounts. Prior to the Tax Reform Act of 1986, children with investment income possessed certain tax advantages. For example, they filed tax returns only if their income exceeded $1,000. Any amount over $1,000 was taxable at the child's rate, frequently the former minimum of 11%. Therefore, a child could receive a substantial amount of investment income, yet pay lower taxes than an adult who owned those funds would have had to pay. This income-shifting provision made Uniform Transfers to Minors Act accounts very attractive.

The Tax Reform Act of 1986 changed these rules. Now, the first $500 of a child's investment income is essentially tax-exempt, and the next $500 is taxed at the child's rate (usually the minimum rate). If the child's investment income exceeds $1,000 and the child is under 14 years of age, the additional amount is still taxable to the child but at the parent's rate, which usually is considerably higher. Once the child reaches age 14, the investment income is taxed at the child's tax rate.

These changes may reduce the attractiveness of income shifting through large gifts to minors. However, substantial gifts can still provide some tax benefits for parents while building funds for their children's future.

Counselors cannot give legal or tax advice to customers, but they can convey the previous factual information if customers request it. For advice or further information, counselors should direct customers to professionals such as tax accountants and lawyers.

Guardian and Conservator

A *guardian* is a type of fiduciary with the legal power and duty to manage the property and rights of another person who—because of age, disability, degree of understanding or self-control, or some other reason—is considered incapable of handling his or her own affairs. Guardians use the general fiduciary deposit contract or similar document shown in Figure 8-1.

Three forms of guardianship are common. A *conservator* is a legally appointed guardian for an incompetent person. A conservator may be an individual or a corporation. A child's guardian can be a natural and/or a legal guardian. A child's *natural guardian* is the parent who has custody of the child and has the duty to provide him or her with financial support, education and shelter. Custody of the child, however, does not extend to the child's property. Under common law, the parent has no rights in or control over the child's property, with the exception of the child's earnings. This common law rule applies even if the child received the property from the parent. To be able to exercise control over the child's property, the parent must first be appointed by a court as the child's *legal guardian.*

Other forms of legal guardianship include:

- guardian by will, whom the parent appoints in his or her will to exercise custody over both the child's person and property until the child reaches maturity;

- special guardian (usually an attorney), whom a court names to protect the minor's rights if he or she is involved in probate proceedings, has an interest in a decedent estate or is insane; and

- guardian ad litem, whom a court designates to prosecute or defend a lawsuit on behalf of the child.

Executor and Administrator

Two types of fiduciaries handle decedent estates. An *executor/executrix* is an individual appointed in a will and approved by a probate court to administer the disposition of an estate according the will's instructions. An *administrator* is a person to whom the court has granted the authority to administer the estate of a deceased person. The executor's and administrator's responsibilities are similar, except that the administrator is appointed by a court if the deceased has not left a will or has not named an executor in his or her will. Both an executor and an administrator may open a deposit account using a fiduciary contract similar to the one shown in Figure 8-1. Both executors and administrators are explained in Chapter 10.

Representative Payee

A *representative payee* is a type of fiduciary whom the federal government appoints to handle certain federal benefit payments on behalf of another person. A representative payee's responsibilities are similar to those of a custodian or agent; however, a representative payee retains only control of funds and not legal title.[2]

Persons under 18 years of age or disabled or incompetent adults are entitled to old age, survivors or disability insurance benefits payable by the government under federal Social Security legislation. For these people, federal officials may designate a representative payee to receive and disburse benefit payments for the "use and benefit" of the entitled individual.

Federal regulations permit a representative payee to invest funds not needed for the current maintenance of the beneficiary in an insured deposit account in the beneficiary's behalf. The representative payee account must clearly show that the representative payee has only a fiduciary and not a personal interest in the funds. The fiduciary deposit contract illustrated in Figure 8-1 is also appropriate for opening a representative payee account.

The potential benefits to institutions that offer representative payee accounts are tremendous. About 1 million such accounts exist, into which approximately $100 million of federal benefits flow every month.

To protect depository institutions in the handling of these accounts, the Social Security Administration has issued a statement saying, in effect, that a depository institution need not consider the reason for any withdrawal by a representative payee. This statement relieves the institution of liability for withdrawal of funds by a representative payee who misuses them, unless the institution was aware of such misuse.

Trustee

Another type of fiduciary responsible for handling another person's funds is a trustee. The remainder of this chapter and Chapter 9 explain various kinds of trustees.

TRUSTS

A *trust* is a completed transfer of ownership of property by the owner (grantor) to another individual (trustee) for the immediate or eventual benefit of a third person (beneficiary).

Trust accounts may be either revocable or irrevocable. A *revocable trust* allows the original owner of the funds to change the terms of the trust agreements to adapt to possible changes in intentions. An *irrevocable trust* permits no changes in the trust agreement and therefore is less flexible.

One may establish a trust for any lawful purpose, such as to:

- defer a gift;

- receive occasional periodic gifts;

- segregate special-purpose funds;

- protect oneself against possible later incompetency;

- secure deposit insurance coverage;

- avoid the delays and expenses of probate;

- minimize the possibility of a will contest;

- defer federal taxes; or

- provide for anticipated expenses.

The customer's attorney or tax advisor may be able to offer additional advantages. Under no circumstances should a depository institution attempt to analyze the tax consequences of opening a trust account for a customer.

Parties to a Trust Agreement

Trust accounts consist of the following six components:

- the funds;

- the grantor;

- the trustee;

- the beneficiary;

- the agreement between the grantor and the trustee;

- the deposit account contract with the financial institution.

When a trust is established, the two elements of complete ownership—the legal title and the right to use or benefit from the funds, called the beneficial interest—are separated. The grantor gives the legal title to the trustee and the beneficial interest to the beneficiary. A trust does not exist until this separation takes place.

Grantor

The *grantor*—sometimes called the *settlor, trustor* or *donor*—is the owner of the account and the party who establishes the trust. The grantor makes a settlement or creates a trust of property. Often grantors name themselves as trustees on trust accounts.

Trustee

The *trustee* is the legal title holder and controller of the funds in a trust account established for the benefit of another according to a trust agreement. Both individuals and corporations may be named trustees for a variety of purposes.

Beneficiary

The *beneficiary* is the person designated to receive the benefits accruing from the funds in the trust account.

Trusts generally are grouped according to how the trust funds are to be distributed to the beneficiaries. Categories of trusts include:

- trusts in which the income is periodically paid over to the grantor; to the grantor's spouse, child, parent, or other designated party; or to a specified charitable or other institution;

- trusts established in which the income is accumulated for a minor until the minor reaches the age of majority;

- trusts in which the principal is paid to one beneficiary when he or she reaches a certain age and the income is paid to the same or another beneficiary; and

- trusts in which the principal is paid to the beneficiary upon his or her marriage. Although it is permissible to establish a trust for someone to get married, since it is common to give gifts to our relatives and friends when they get married, one cannot create a trust for the purpose of preventing marriage.[3]

Requirements of a Valid Trust

To be valid, a trust must conform with certain legal requirements. Compliance with the following eight requirements and, frequently, with the relevant laws of the particular state ensures the establishment of a valid trust:

1. The grantor of the trust must be legally competent. Any person who is legally competent to make a will or enter into a contract may create a trust.

2. The property interest the grantor holds must be equal to or greater than the interest he or she wishes to convey in trust. This simply means that a person cannot establish a trust account for the benefit of another with funds that he or she has no title to or interest in.

3. The grantor's expression of intention to create a trust must be evident. A written trust agreement is the most direct and conclusive form of evidence of intention.

4. The trust agreement must specify disposition of the estate in terms that will enable a court to enforce its execution. Ownership of the trust property must have the title in the name of the trustee and the beneficial ownership in the name of the beneficiary or beneficiaries.

5. There must be at least one trustee and one beneficiary. If the trust agreement does not name a successor trustee, the court may appoint one if necessary.

6. The trust must be for a legal purpose. A trust would be invalid if:
   a. the trustee committed a criminal or tortious act, such as an unlawful business transaction. (A tortious act is one that can result in a civil suit.)
   b. enforcement of the trust terms would be against public policy even if the trustee's performance would not be a criminal or tortious act. For example, provisions that offered someone a financial reward for divorcing or separating from his or her spouse, for neglect-

ing parental duties, for refraining from marriage, for changing his or her religious faith, or for refraining from performing acts that would benefit the nation or the state would be against public policy but would not constitute a criminal or tortious act on the part of the trustee.

c. the purpose of the person creating the trust was fraudulent, such as transferring property into a trust to defraud creditors.

d. the considerations, if any, for the creation of the trust were illegal, for example, creating a trust for a person who agreed to perform an illegal act.

7. The trust must comply with the *rule against perpetuities*. This rule states that for a trust to be valid, the interest (title) must pass, take effect or *vest* no later than 21 years and 9 months after a life or lives in being at the time of the creation of the trust. (Some states stipulate a shorter time period than this.) The purpose of the rule against perpetuities is to prevent the locking up of trust funds beyond a reasonable length of time. Once vested, the beneficiary has complete ownership of the account, which cannot be forfeited and which is no longer contingent upon a certain time or event. The rule against perpetuities exists in about 14 states and the District of Columbia.

An example of a violation of the rule against perpetuities is a husband and wife who plan to have a child in two years and decide to open a trust account for the child now. If they do this, they will be opening a trust account for an indefinite period of time. To comply with the rule against perpetuities, they may open the trust after the baby's birth or even during the pregnancy, but not before.

8. The trustee must have active duties. Generally, if the trustee's duties are substantial, or if the trustee is free to act or judge in order to exercise his or her duties, the duties are considered active. The courts will consider the grantor's purpose or intent when determining whether a trust of personal property is active or passive.

The Trust Agreement

The *trust agreement* is a written agreement under which the grantor transfers legal ownership of property to another person or entity (the trustee) for the benefit of a third person (the beneficiary) subject to the various terms and provisions of the trust.

Objectives of the Agreement

A trust agreement should be complete and clear in its terms and provisions so that a court will correctly carry out the grantor's intentions. The following five specifications are part of the trust agreement:

- duties of the trustee pertaining to the manner and nature of withdrawals from or pledging of the account.

- specification of whether and how the grantor may alter the terms of the agreement. With an irrevocable trust, the grantor cannot subsequently change any of the provisions. If the trust is revocable, the agreement should explain how the grantor can change its terms.

- the automatic succession or appointment of a successor trustee or trustees in certain events. A *successor trustee* is a person whom the trust agreement or a court designates as trustee in the event the original trustee dies, resigns, is removed or becomes legally incompetent.

- the duration of the trust, how the trust may be terminated and who is to receive the funds upon termination.

- the division of beneficial interest if the trust has more than one beneficiary. The agreement should spell out whether each beneficiary is to receive an equal (pro rata) or specific percentage of the funds.

Terms and Provisions

Proper use of a trust fund is the responsibility of the trustee and not of the depository institution.

Exculpatory Language   A standard trust agreement is usually printed on the reverse side of a trust account signature document and contains exculpatory language permitting the trustee sole discretion in handling the funds (see Sentences 1 and 5 in Figure 8-4). This means that withdrawals may be paid to any trustee, as trustee, under the terms of the trust agreement. Employees need not ask the trustee to explain the purpose of the withdrawal; however, employees should never knowingly assist a trustee or other fiduciary in diverting funds for the trustee's personal use. For example, employees should not allow a trustee to deposit a check made payable to him or her for a named beneficiary into the trustee's personal account. There have been cases in

F I G U R E 8-4

Trust Agreement for Revocable Trust—
Single Trustee/Single Beneficiary

DISCRETIONARY REVOCABLE TRUST AGREEMENT

Trust Agreement No._____

The funds in the account indicated on the reverse side of this instrument, together with earnings thereon, and any future additions thereto are conveyed to the trustee as indicated for the benefit of the beneficiary as indicated. The conditions of said trust are: (1) The trustee is authorized to hold, manage, pledge, invest and reinvest said funds in his sole discretion; (2) The undersigned grantor reserves the right to revoke said trust in part or in full at any time and any partial or complete withdrawal by the original trustee if he is the grantor shall be a revocation by the grantor to the extent of such withdrawal, but no other revocation shall be valid unless written notice is given to the institution named on the reverse side of this card; (3) In the event of the death, resignation, removal, or incompetence of said trustee,

_____
is appointed successor trustee, and in the event of his death, resignation, removal, or incompetence,

_____
is appointed successor trustee, or in the event no successor trustee is named herein or the successor or successors die, resign, are removed, become incompetent, or fail to act, the institution named on the reverse side hereof is authorized to appoint a successor trustee, and such successor trustee shall have the powers of the original trustee; (4) This trust, subject to the right of revocation, shall continue for the life of the grantor and thereafter until the beneficiary is_____years of age, or until his death if he dies before such age, and then the proceeds may be delivered by the institution to the beneficiary, or to his heirs, or to the trustee on his or their behalf, and if the age of the beneficiary is not specified this trust is for twenty-one years; (5) The institution in which such funds are invested is authorized to pay the same or to act in any respect affecting said account before or after the termination of this trust upon the signature of the trustee and has no responsibility to follow the application of the funds. In this instrument the singular includes the plural and the masculine includes the feminine and the neuter.

This_____day of_____, 19_____

_____
Grantor

which the courts found the institution liable to the beneficiary of the trust for knowingly helping the trustee to divert the money.[4]

Revocation of the Trust   Sentence 2 in Figure 8-4 spells out how a grantor may revoke a trust agreement. It states that if the grantor and the trustee are the same person, a withdrawal by the grantor/trustee constitutes a revocation of the trust to the extent of that withdrawal. In these situations, the institution can, upon the trustee's request, make a check withdrawal payable to anyone, including the trustee personally. Recommended procedure dictates that check withdrawals be made payable to the trustee as trustee. If the trustee requests otherwise, the employee should consult a supervisor before taking action.

Successor Trustee Most trust agreements name a close relative of the trustee, such as a sibling or spouse, as a successor trustee. Sentence 3 in Figure 8-4 provides a space for the grantor to name a first and second successor trustee. The sentence also authorizes the depository institution to appoint a successor trustee if none is named or if those named are unable to serve for the stated reasons. In such situations, the institution can appoint anyone who is legally competent; usually institutions appoint one of their own officers. If the trust agreement does not provide for the appointment of a successor trustee, a court can and normally will appoint one. Figure 8-5 shows a form used for the appointment of a successor trustee.

Termination of the Trust If the beneficiary is a minor, the trust customarily terminates when the child reaches a specified age, such as 21 years. At the time of termination, the trustee delivers the entire proceeds of the trust to the beneficiary. To avoid conflict with the rule against perpetuities, the trust agreement also should provide for trust termination at the child's death if that occurs before the age of majority.

In many trust agreements, the timing of two events determines the timing of the termination of the trust: the death of the grantor and the achievement of a certain age by the beneficiary. For example, Sentence 4 in Figure 8-4 specifies:

F I G U R E 8-5

Letter of Appointment of Successor Trustee

**LETTER OF APPOINTMENT
OF A SUCCESSOR TRUSTEE**

To _____   _____
      (Successor Trustee)   (Date)

in accordance with condition (3) of the Trust Agreement executed by

_____ on _____
      (Name of Grantor)   (Date)

in favor of _____, the _____
              (Name of Beneficiary)   (Name of Financial Institution)

hereby appoints you Trustee on Savings Account No. _____ to succeed

_____, to act in all matters pertaining to this
      (Name of Trustee)

account in full accordance with the terms of the said Trust Agreement in

behalf of _____ until such time as the trust
                  (Name of Beneficiary)

terminates according to its terms or the operation of law at which time the
funds remaining in the account are to be transferred or paid to the beneficiary
or beneficiaries as specified in said Trust Agreement.

_____
(Authorized Signature of Officer)

_____
(Title)

Accepted this _____ day

of _____, 19 _____

_____
(Signature of Successor Trustee)

This trust, . . . shall continue for the life of the grantor and thereafter until the beneficiary is _____ years of age . . . and then the proceeds may be delivered to the beneficiary.

If these two factors are present in the trust agreement, lower courts may not be tempted to hold such a trust account to be an attempted testamentary disposition and thus a violation of the statute of wills.

The institution can still use the trust agreement shown in Figure 8-4 if the grantor wishes the trust to terminate immediately after his or her death and the beneficiary is an adult. When making this request, the grantor should fill in the beneficiary's age plus one additional year in the appropriate blank. In this situation, the beneficiary's attainment of the specified age usually occurs relatively quickly and, when the grantor eventually dies, the trust can be terminated. If the grantor dies before the beneficiary reaches the specified age, the beneficiary has only a short time to wait before the termination of trust.

However, counselors should be aware that if no age is filled in, the trust may terminate 21 years after its creation in compliance with the rule against perpetuities. This emphasizes the importance of filling in the age blank in all trust agreements, even if the beneficiary is an adult.

Trust agreements that provide for two or more beneficiaries may be similar to the one shown in Figure 8-4 with respect to the first three sentences. Figure 8-6 shows a trust agreement that provides for multiple beneficiaries. Sentences 4, 5 and 6 in Figure 8-6 indicate, respectively, when each beneficiary will receive his or her share, how the funds are to be divided among the beneficiaries, and the duration of the trust if no beneficiary age is specified.

F I G U R E 8-6

Trust Agreement for Revocable Trust—
Single Trustee/Multiple Beneficiaries

ONE TRUSTEE DISCRETIONARY REVOCABLE TRUST AGREEMENT FOR TWO OR MORE BENEFICIARIES

Trust Agreement No. _____

The funds in the account indicated on the reverse side of this instrument, together with the earnings thereon, and any future additions thereto are conveyed to the trustee as indicated for the benefit of the beneficiary or beneficiaries as indicated. The conditions of said trust are: (1) the trustee is authorized to hold, manage, pledge, invest and reinvest said funds in his sole discretion; (2) The undersigned grantor reserves the right to revoke said trust in part or in full at any time and any partial or complete withdrawal by the original trustee, if he is the grantor, shall be a revocation by the grantor to the extent of such withdrawal, but no other revocation shall be valid unless written notice is given to the institution named on the reverse side of this card; (3) In the event of the death, resignation, removal, or incompetence of said trustee,

_____

is appointed successor trustee, and in the event of his death, resignation, removal, or incompetence

_____

is appointed successor trustee or in the event no successor trustee is named herein or the successor or successors die, resign, are removed, become incompetent, or fail to act, the institution named on the reverse side hereof is authorized to appoint a successor trustee, and such successor trustee shall have the powers of the original trustee; (4) This trust, subject to the right of revocation, shall continue until the last surviving beneficiary either lives to the age specified below, or dies before reaching such age; (5) As each beneficiary reaches the age of _____years, the trust shall terminate at that time but only as to such beneficiary, and his pro rata share shall then belong and be distributed by the trustee to such beneficiary. The pro rata share of each beneficiary upon reaching the specified age shall be determined by dividing the amount of the trust funds then existing by the number of the beneficiaries then living as to whom such pro rata distribution has not previously been made. If any beneficiary should die prior to reaching the specified age, his pro rata beneficial interest in the trust funds shall terminate at that time and such funds shall continue to be trust funds subject to all of the other terms of the trust agreement. In the event that the last surviving beneficiary shall die before reaching the age specified, the trust shall then terminate and the funds shall revert to the sole ownership of the grantor or of his estate if he be deceased; (6) If the age at which each beneficiary is to receive distribution is not specified in the space provided therefor, this trust shall terminate twenty one years after its execution, and the proceeds shall belong and be delivered by the trustee to the beneficiaries then surviving, in equal shares, or if none suvives, to the grantor or to his estate if he be deceased; (7) The institution in which such funds are invested is authorized to pay the same or to act in any respect affecting said account before or after the termination of this trust upon the signature of the trustee, or successor trustee, duly appointed, and has no responsibility to follow the application of the funds.

In this instrument, except as otherwise indicated, the singular includes the plural and the masculine includes the feminine and the neuter.

This _____day of _____, 19_____

_____ Grantor

Totten Trusts

A written trust agreement is the most direct form of evidence of intention. However, one may establish a trust account without a written trust agreement. Such a trust account is called a *Totten trust*. The term originated from a lawsuit in New York concerning an account that had been opened without a written trust agreement by a "trustee" named Totten.[5] While lawyers and financial institutions have continued to use the term Totten trust to describe any trust without a written trust agreement, some courts prefer the term *tentative trust*.

An individual creates a Totten trust by depositing funds in his or her own name as trustee for another person without any written trust agreement. The grantor names himself or herself as trustee and holds title to the funds for the named beneficiary. The trustee may change or revoke the trust. Upon the trustee's death, since no written trust agreement exists, no one can change or revoke the trust and the tentative trust is presumed to become an existing one.

Because a Totten trust lacks a written trust agreement, the grantor's intentions are often vague and might be challenged in court after his or her death. The only indication that the account is intended as a trust may be wording such as "John Atkins, Trustee" or "John Atkins, Trustee for Jane Atkins" on the signature card. Use of the word *trustee* in this manner usually gives rise to a presumption that the account holder intended the account as a trust.

A financial institution can encounter difficulties in paying out the account upon the account holder's death. The heirs of the deceased account holder may wish to have the funds pass to them instead of to the named beneficiary and may dispute the existence of the trust. If the deceased account holder left a will, the courts may decide that the will revoked the trust.[6] This finding may be unknown to the financial institution.

To protect financial institutions from involvement in costly litigation, some states have enacted accounts-in-trust statutes.[7] *Accounts-in-trust statutes* protect the institution with respect to payouts to a beneficiary under a Totten trust. This protection is similar to the way accounts-in-two-names statutes protect institutions that pay out to a surviving joint tenant. However, accounts-in-trust statutes do not determine ownership of the money; they merely protect the institution in making such a payout where no one else has made a claim on the account. Totten trusts can be particularly troublesome for institutions in states without these protective accounts-in-trust statutes.

Financial institutions can best eliminate the legal confusion and risk of liability associated with Totten trusts by simply using deposit contract documents that clearly spell out the grantor's intent to create a trust and name a trustee and beneficiary.

Revocable Trusts

Because of their flexibility, revocable trusts are popular forms of deposit account ownership. They are adaptable to the changing needs of grantors, and grantors may add or change both trustees and beneficiaries at any time. This section shows counselors how to open various revocable trust accounts.

Co-Trustees and Multiple Beneficiaries

Legal title to funds may be given to two or more trustees, who then become *co-trustees*. The term *co-trustees* is more accurate than *joint trustees*, because the latter term may imply erroneously that the co-trustees are joint tenants. Generally, when one co-trustee dies, the surviving trustee(s) continues to control the account. Sometimes, however, the terms of the trust agreement may specify other provisions for control of the account.

A trust originally set up with co-trustees must retain its validity upon the death of one of the co-trustees. Recall that for a trust to be valid, the two elements of complete ownership—legal title and beneficial interest—must be separated. The legal title belongs to the trustee and the beneficial interest belongs to the beneficiary. However, the same person may be both a trustee and a beneficiary if other individuals share one of these positions; for example, A and B can be trustees for A, the beneficiary. However, when the same person is named as both a co-trustee and a beneficiary, that individual obtains full control of the two elements of ownership upon the death of the other co-trustee. At that point, the trust becomes invalid.

To understand this concept, compare a valid trust to a numerical fraction. The top half of a fraction is the numerator, and the bottom half is the denominator. When both the numerator and the denominator are the same in a numerical fraction, the result is equal to 1, which is no longer a fraction:

$$\frac{1}{1} = 1$$

This analogy may be applied to trusts. Assume the numerator of the fraction is the trustee and denominator is the beneficiary:

$$\frac{\text{Trustee}}{\text{Beneficiary}}$$

If the same person becomes both the only trustee and the only beneficiary on the account, the trust becomes invalid. For example, suppose A and B are trustees and A is the beneficiary:

$$\frac{\text{A and B}}{\text{A}}$$

If B dies, then:

$$\frac{\text{A}}{\text{A}} = \text{A}$$

The above is an invalid trust because A possesses both elements of ownership.

For this reason, financial institution employees should always recheck the validity of a trust account upon the death of a trustee or beneficiary to verify that the two elements of complete ownership have not recombined. To prevent this possibility from occurring, the account might be set up with three or more co-trustees, multiple beneficiaries and/or a named successor trustee. Trusts with multiple beneficiaries are common, and the number of beneficiaries a trust may have is unlimited. Parents who wish to name all their children as beneficiaries typically do so on their trust accounts.

Documentation

Counselors who open new trust accounts need to be familiar with a variety of revocable deposit contracts. The various contracts, trust agreements and evidences of account are prepared similarly.

Deposit Contracts   Figures 8-7 through 8-10 show types of deposit contracts typically used to establish revocable trust accounts. The trust agreements often appear on the reverse sides of the contracts.

Sometimes a customer who already has established a special trust agreement may wish to open a trust ac-

F I G U R E 8-7

Signature Card for Revocable Trust— Single Trustee/Single Beneficiary

count. A special trust deposit contract is used in these cases; it usually provides a space for indicating the date the special trust is established. A fiduciary contract such as that in Figure 8-1 is also appropriate. For such accounts, the institution may require a copy of the trust agreement for its files.

F I G U R E 8-8

Signature Card for Revocable Trust—Co-Trustees/Single Beneficiary, Side 1

Taxpayer Identification Number

Account No. _____

(1)

and (2)

For _____   Co-Trustees

(Last Name)   (First Name)   (Middle Name) _____ , Beneficiary

As Co-trustees with right of survivorship, the undersigned hereby apply for a savings account in

and for the issuance of evidence thereof in their names as trustees described as aforesaid. You are directed to act pursuant to any one or more of the trustees' signatures, shown below, in any manner in connection with this account and to pay, without any liability for such payment, to any one or the surviving of said trustees at any or on the signature of a duly appointed successor trustee. It is agreed by the signatory parties with each other and by the parties with you that any funds placed in or added to the account by any one of the parties whether in his trustee or individual capacity, **is and shall be conclusively intended to be a gift and delivery** at that time of such funds to the trust estate you are authorized to accept checks and other instruments for credit to this account, whether payable to one or more of the parties, and to supply any needed endorsement. You are relieved of any liability in connection with collection of all items handled by you without negligence, and shall not be liable for acts of your agents, subagents or others or for any casualty. Withdrawals may not be made on account of such items until collected, and any amount not collected may be charged back to this account including expense incurred, and any other outside expense incurred relative to this account may be charged to it.

Under penalties of perjury, I certify (1) that the number shown on this form is my correct taxpayer identification number, and (2) that I am not subject to backup withholding because (a) I have not been notified that I am subject to backup withholding as a result of a failure to report all interest or dividends, or (b) the Internal Revenue Service has notified me that I am no longer subject ot backup withholding. [If the Internal Revenue Service has notified the payee that she/he is subject to backup withholding, delete (2) above.]

Signature _____   as Co-Trustee

Signature _____   as Co-Trustee

Street Address _____ City and State _____

As Trustee for _____ , Beneficiary

as specified in trust agreement on reverse side hereof. Dated _____

Optional: Beneficiary is the _____ of Grantor No.1 of this trust and the _____
of grantor No.2 of this trust. (Insert Spouse, Child or Grandchild, whichever applies)

Preparing the Evidence of Account Figure 8-11 shows how a typical trust arrangement would appear in an evidence of account. The word "and" is used between each trustee and each beneficiary. The words "as trustee(s) for" appear after the trustee's or trustees' name and before the beneficiaries' names. For accounts

F I G U R E 8-8, Continued

Signature Card for Revocable Trust—
Co-Trustees/Single Beneficiary, Side 2

Trust Agreement No. _____

The funds in the account indicated on the reverse side of this instrument, together with earnings thereon, and any future additions thereto are conveyed to the trustees as indicated for the benefit of the beneficiary as indicated. The conditions of said trust are: (1) The trustees are authorized to hold, manage, pledge, invest and reinvest said funds in their sole discretion, or at the discretion of any one of them acting; (2) The undersigned grantor or grantors, reserve the right to revoke said trust in part or in full at any time and any partial or complete withdrawal by the original trustee if they are the grantors shall be a revocation by the grantor to the extent of such withdrawal, but no other revocation shall be valid unless written notice by both or either of such grantors is given to the institution named on the reverse side of this card; (3) In the event of the death, resignation,

removal, or incompetence of both of said trustees, _____ is

appointed successor trustee, and in the event of his death, resignation, removal, or incompetence, _____ is appointed successor trustee, or in the event no successor trustee is named herein or the successor or successors die, resign, are removed, become incompetent, or fail to act, the institution named on the reverse side hereof is authorized to appoint a successor trustee, and such successor trustee shall have the powers of the original trustee; (4) This trust, subject to the right of revocation, shall continue for the life of the grantors and thereafter

until the beneficiary is _____ years of age, or until his death if he dies before such age, and then the proceeds may be delivered by the institution to the beneficiary, or to his heirs, or to the trustee on his or their behalf, and if the age of the beneficiary is not specified this trust is for twenty- one years; (5) The institution in which such funds are invested is authorized to pay the same or to act in any respect affecting said account before or after the termination of this trust upon the signature of either of the trustees, or successor trustee, duly appointed and has no responsibility to follow the application of the funds. In this instrument except as otherwise indicated the singular includes the plural and the masculine includes the feminine and the neuter.

This _____ day of _____ , 19 _____

(1) _____   (2) _____
                        Grantor   Grantor

                                                                                    SAF Systems and Forms

14627-4 (12-85) CO-TRUSTEE/1 BENEF.

opened under separate special trusts, the words "under trust agreement dated month/date/year" also appear after the beneficiary's name.

Irrevocable Trusts

An irrevocable trust is a trust in which the grantor does not reserve the right to change or annul the trust agreement. An irrevocable trust must continue until the time

F I G U R E 8-9

Signature Card for Revocable Trust—
Single Trustee/Multiple Beneficiaries

ONE TRUSTEE DISCRETIONARY REVOCABLE TRUST ACCOUNT FOR TWO OR MORE BENEFICIARIES

Taxpayer Identification Number

Account No. _____

Trustee,

(1)   Beneficiary

(2)   Beneficiary

(3)   Beneficiary

(4) _____ Beneficiary,
           (Last Name)   (First Name)   (Middle Name)

I hereby apply for a _____ Account in

and for the issuance of evidence thereof. A specimen of my signature is shown below and you are hereby authorized to act without further inquiry in accordance with writings bearing such signature. It is agreed that any funds placed in or added to this account by the undersigned, whether in his trustee or individual capacity, *is and shall be conclusively intended to be a gift and delivery* at that time of such funds to the trust estate. You are authorized to supply any endorsement for me on any check or other instrument tendered for this account and you are hereby relieved of any liability in connection with collection of such items which are handled by you without negligence, and you shall not be liable for the acts of your agents, subagents or others or for any casualty. Withdrawals may not be made on account of such items until collected, and any amount not collected may be charged back to this account, including expense incurred, and any other outside expense incurred relative to this account may be charged to it. The undersigned agree that this account is subject to and is to be administered in accordance with the rules established by the board of directors for the account classification indicated above, and acknowledge receipt of a copy of said rules.

Under penalties of perjury, I certify (1) that the number shown on this form is my correct taxpayer identification number, and (2) that I am not subject to backup withholding because (a) I have not been notified that I am subject to backup withholding as a result of a failure to report all interest or dividends, or (b) the Internal Revenue Service has notified me that I am no longer subject of backup withholding. [If the Internal Revenue Service has notified the payee that she/he is subject to backup withholding, delete (2) above.]

Signature _____ as Trustee

Street Address _____

City and State _____ Telephone

As Trustee for _____ Beneficiary;

_____ Beneficiary;

_____ Beneficiary;

_____ Beneficiary;

as specified in trust agreement on reverse side hereof. Dated _____

OPTIONAL: List family relationships, i. e., spouse, child or grandchild, of each Beneficiary to Grantor

_____

_____

_____

_____

14869-4 (12/85) 1 TRUSTEE, MULTI. BENEF.

SAF Systems and Forms

F I G U R E 8-10

Signature Card for Revocable Trust— Co-Trustees/Multiple Beneficiaries

(Taxpayer Identification Number)	(Date)	(Account Number)

(1)

and (2)   Co-Trustees

(3)   Beneficiary

(4)   Beneficiary

(5)   Beneficiary

(6)   (Last Name)   (First Name)   (Middle Name)   Beneficiary

As co-trustees with right of survivorship, the undersigned hereby apply for a Savings Account in

and for the issuance of evidence thereof in their names as trustees described as aforesaid. You are directed to act pursuant to any one or more of the trustees' signatures shown below in any manner in connection with this account and to pay, without any penalty for such payment, to any one of the surviving of said trustees at any time or on the signature of a duly appointed successor trustee. It is agreed by the signatory parties with each other and by the parties with you that any funds placed in or added to the account by any one of the parties, whether in his trustee or individual capacity, *is and shall be conclusively intended to be a gift and delivery* at that time of such funds to the trust estate. You are authorized to accept checks and other instruments for credit to this account, whether payable to one or more parties, and to supply any needed endorsement. You are relieved of any liability in connection with collection of all items handled by you without negligence, and you shall not be liable for the acts of your agents, subagents or others or for any casualty. Withdrawals may not be made on account of such items until collected, and any amount not collected may be charged back to this account, including expense incurred, and any other outside expense incurred relative to this account may be charged to it.

By signing this signature card, I(we), under penalty of perjury, certify that (a) the number shown on this card is my(our) correct taxpayer identification number(s), and (b) I(we) are not subject to backup withholding. [If either of the signers have been notified by the IRS that they are subject to backup withholding, delete the language in (b) above.]

Signature _____as Co-Trustee

Signature _____as Co-Trustee

Address _____

As Trustee for _____ Beneficiary,

_____ Beneficiary,

_____ Beneficiary,

_____ Beneficiary,

as specified in trust agreement on reverse side hereof. Dated _____

OPTIONAL: List family relationships, i. e., spouse, child or grandchild, of each Beneficiary to Grantor

_____

_____

_____

_____

146324 (11/83) CO-TR/MULT. BEN. PD. UPON GRANTORS' DEATHS

SAF Systems and Forms

F I G U R E 8-11

Passbook: Co-Trustees/Multiple Beneficiaries

SAVINGS ACCOUNT
73-68915
NUMBER

THIS CERTIFIES THAT

John Pannkoke and Mary Pannkoke as Trustees for Joseph

Pannkoke and Linda Pannkoke

Holds a SAVINGS ACCOUNT in

FIRST BANK

of termination specified in the trust agreement. The grantor may terminate an irrevocable trust only with the written consent of the beneficiary.

Because of the irrevocability feature, depositors who wish to open such a trust should fully understand all the possible consequences. Also, because trusts require tax and estate planning advice that counselors are not qualified to give, counselors should advise customers to direct any questions pertaining to taxes and estate planning to their tax attorneys.

Trusteed Retirement Plans

Various retirement plans are established as irrevocable trusts with a depository institution or other corporation named as trustee. Retirement plans must be irrevocable in order to receive special tax treatment and to guarantee the interests of the beneficiaries. The details of retirement plans are covered in the next chapter.

Other Irrevocable Trusts

The revocable trust account discussed earlier in this chapter also may be opened as an irrevocable trust. Basically, Sentence 2 in the trust agreement in Figure 8-4 specifies whether the trust is revocable or irrevocable. Irrevocable trusts may be specially drawn up by an institution that has trust powers or by the grantor's attorney.

SUMMARY

A fiduciary is a person or corporation responsible for holding or controlling property for another. The various types of fiduciaries include administrators, executors, conservators, custodians, guardians, representative payees and trustees.

The establishment of a trust entails fulfilling eight legal requirements and creating a specific ownership relationship among the trust parties. The parties to a trust agreement are the grantor (who owns the funds), the trustee (who controls the funds) and the beneficiary (who possesses the beneficial interest in the funds). The trust agreement documents in writing how the trust is to be handled; it is often contained in the deposit contract. Trust accounts may be revocable or irrevocable. Irrevocable trusts require special planning and advice, which customers should obtain from professionals outside the institution. Trusteed retirement plans must be irrevocable in order to receive special tax treatment and ensure that beneficiaries' interests are protected.

FOOTNOTES

[1]The following states have adopted the Uniform Transfers to Minors Act: AL, AZ, AR, CA, CO, FL, HI, ID, IL, IA, KS, KY, LA, ME, MA, MN, MO, MT, NV, NH, NJ, NC, ND, OH, OK, OR, RI, SD, VA, WV, WI, WY and the District of Columbia. However, because the Act is fairly recent, states are likely to have adopted it since publication of this text.

[2]For further information on representative payee accounts, see Thomas C. Parrott, "Representative Payee Savings Accounts," *Legal Bulletin*, XXIX (November 1963), pp. 328–334.

[3]Glenn G. Munn and F.L. Garcia, *Encyclopedia of Banking and Finance*, 8th ed. (Boston: Bankers Publishing Co., 1983), p. 943.

[4]*Schofield* v. *Trust Co.*, 78 N.E. 2d 167.

[5]See *In re Totten*, 7 N.E. 748. For further information on Totten trusts, see William L. Papke, "Trustee Savings Accounts— Are Valid Trusts Created?", *Legal Bulletin*, XXIX (March 1963), pp. 59–62; *Illinois Bar Journal*, 50, 3 (November 1962), p. 238. See also Horace Russell, "Some Observations on Trust Accounts," *Legal Bulletin*, XXIX (March 1963), pp. 55–58; *Illinois Bar Journal*, 51, 5 (January 1963), p. 404.

[6]See *In re Stein's Will*, 249 N.Y.S. 2d 223.

[7]The following states have enacted accounts-in-trust statutes: AL, AR, CA, CT, FL, ID, IL, MI, MN, MT, NE, NJ, NY, OK, PA, TN, VA, WI, WY.

CHAPTER

Retirement Plans

KEY CONCEPTS

- The five types of IRA contributions and the eligibility and contribution limits for each;

- Eligible compensation for calculating allowable retirement plan contributions;

- IRAs, SEPs and Keogh plans and the leeway period for making contributions to each;

- How nondeductible IRA contributions affect IRA distributions;

- The documents required to establish IRAs;

- IRA participants' reporting requirements;

- Exceptions that permit participants to take allowable distributions before age 59½;

- Difference between defined contribution and defined benefit plans and between money-purchase and profit-sharing Keogh plans in terms of contribution limits;

- Difference between a salary reduction plan and a thrift/savings plan.

A retirement plan is any method of saving or accumulating funds that an individual intends to use upon retiring. To encourage people to plan for their retirement, the government has provided tax incentives to establish qualified retirement plans since 1926. Through the years, many changes in tax law have occurred. These changes have enhanced the incentives for businesses to provide qualified retirement plans for their employees, helped ensure that all employees receive equitable treatment and allowed individual workers to establish their own tax-deferred plans. Today hundreds of millions of dollars are deposited in retirement plans at financial institutions. These plans can provide an important source of stable, long-term funds for an institution.

This chapter gives an overview of the various retirement plans depository institutions offer. Initially, the chapter approaches retirement plans from a broad perspective by describing their advantages and disadvantages and defining the fiduciary responsibilities of the financial institution. The remainder of the chapter gives basic information on Individual Retirement Accounts, qualified plans and other retirement plan options. This chapter is not intended to give detailed coverage of each retirement plan and their many technicalities, since that is beyond the scope of this book.[1]

ADVANTAGES AND DISADVANTAGES OF RETIREMENT PLANS

Tax-deferred retirement plans provide four main advantages for customers. First, they offer immediate income tax benefits. Generally, contributions made to tax-deferred retirement plans can be either fully or partially deducted from income. Second, earnings on all contributions remain tax deferred until withdrawn. Third, retirement plans provide a means of generating funds to supplement other retirement income. Fourth, these benefits will seem enhanced because during retirement, the customer usually is in a lower tax bracket, and distributions from the retirement plan may be taxed at a lower income tax rate than during the individual's working years.

Disadvantages of tax-deferred qualified retirement plans include complex restrictions and requirements on eligibility, contributions and distributions. If the participant or employer does not follow the rules as specified in the Internal Revenue Code (hereinafter referred to as "the Code"), the IRS may impose tax penalties or disqualify the plan from favorable tax treatment. Retirement plan participants at depository institutions therefore need to be more careful with these investments than they need to be with other deposit accounts.

RETIREMENT PLAN RESPONSIBILITIES OF FINANCIAL INSTITUTIONS

Typically, a financial institution enters into a fiduciary relationship under the retirement plan agreement wherein the institution agrees to serve as trustee of the funds deposited on behalf of plan participants. In addition to exercising care and prudence in handling retirement funds, the institution's fiduciary responsibilities may include:

- preparing required IRS reports completely and accurately and filing them in a timely manner;

- providing annual reports of account balances for individual participants; and

- paying the proper amount of benefits to designated beneficiaries.

INDIVIDUAL RETIREMENT ACCOUNTS (IRAs)

An *Individual Retirement Account (IRA)* is a tax-deferred, trusteed deposit account into which certain eligible individuals contribute funds for retirement up to annual contribution limits. Approved investment vehicles for IRAs include deposit accounts and certificates of deposit at financial institutions, individual retirement annuities, mutual fund offerings and securities.

In general individuals can make five types of contributions into IRAs:

- *Contributory.* This type of IRA is opened by individuals who deposit up to $2,000 of their yearly compensation; also called a *regular IRA.*

- *Spousal.* This type of contribution enables a working spouse to establish an IRA for his or her "nonworking" spouse who earns little or no compensation during the year. Also, the married couple must file a joint tax return in order to make spousal contributions. Spousal IRA contributions were created by the Tax Reform Act of 1976.

- *Third-party Sponsored.* This type of contribution (also called *employer IRAs*) is made by employers for the exclusive benefit of their employees or employees' beneficiaries, or by an association of employees for the exclusive benefit of its members or their beneficiaries. It is also called a Section 408(c) IRA, in reference to a section of the Code.

- *Simplified Employee Pension Plan (SEP).* This is an arrangement in which employers make SEP contributions to the IRAs of eligible employees. Under SEP arrangements, employers are subject to certain nondiscrimination and employee eligibility requirements. SEP contributions differ from employer IRAs in that under a SEP, the employer is *required* to provide equitable coverage for all employees.

- *Rollover.* This type of IRA contribution is made by employees who receive a distribution from one of the following: a qualified pension plan, such as a Keogh plan, Section 403(b) tax-sheltered annuity or custodial account; a qualified retirement bond purchase plan; or another qualified retirement savings plan. Individuals choose this type of contribution because they wish to defer taxes by depositing all or part of the funds into an IRA. Usually employees receive such distributions upon employment termination or upon termination of the employer's qualified plan.

  Because of recent tax law changes to Code requirements on qualified plans for businesses, financial institutions can expect that more individuals will elect rollover treatment for their qualified plan distributions. For example, as of 1989, employers who provide qualified plans must provide more rapid vesting schedules to employees than were previously required. More rapid vesting schedules increase the likelihood that employees who change jobs or leave employment for some other reason will be entitled to qualified plan benefits.

Since IRAs were first allowed in 1974, six major tax acts and three technical correction acts have affected IRA rules. The most recent changes described in this text were enacted under the Tax Reform Act of 1986 and subsequently corrected and clarified by the Technical and Miscellaneous Revenue Act of 1988.

Eligibility

Most retirement plans must meet certain eligibility requirements in order to qualify for tax-favored treatment. Some of these are described in the following sections and summarized in Figure 9-1.

Age

A participant's age can affect his or her eligibility to make IRA contributions. Any individual under the age of 70½ who works and earns income can open an IRA and make regular contributions, even if he or she is covered by a company pension plan, profit-sharing plan or government retirement plan. However, the deductibility of IRA contributions may be restricted for some individuals who also participate in employer retirement plans. (Deductibility of contributions is covered later in this chapter.)

Under a SEP, the employer makes contributions for a given calendar year on behalf of every employee who has attained age 21 and performed service for the employer during at least three of the immediately preceding five calendar years. The employer may establish a lower age or fewer years of service as conditions of eligibility, as long as such conditions apply equally to all employees.

F I G U R E 9-1

IRA Eligibility Requirements

Age	Compensation
A participant cannot contribute for or after the taxable year in which age 70½ is reached (except for spousal, rollover and SEP contributions).	A participant must have earned income such as: • salaries • wages • professional fees • commissions • tips • bonuses

Special rules allow some participants over age 70½ to make or receive contributions made on their behalf:

- *Spousal contributions.* IRA rules allow a working individual who is over age 70½ to contribute to an IRA for a nonworking spouse who is under 70½.

- *SEP contributions.* Employers may make SEP contributions for employees over 70½ years of age until such employees retire. However, these employees must take required minimum distributions.

- *Rollovers.* If the recipient of a distribution that is eligible for rollover treatment is over age 70½, the rollover contribution is still permitted. However, the recipient must take required minimum distributions.

Compensation

The second IRA eligibility requirement is that the participant have received compensation. *Compensation* means salaries, wages, professional fees and other amounts received for personal services actually rendered. Examples of compensation include commissions, tips, bonuses and income earned from self-employment in which personal services were rendered.

Income from investments (e.g., interest, dividends, capital gains and rental fees) is not considered compensation. This important point eludes some IRA participants who do not readily distinguish between income and compensation. The Code, however, does make this distinction. Compensation is defined as payment for services actually rendered, while income from investments does not involve services performed by the individual. Therefore, an IRA participant who earns $1,000 in salary and $5,000 from various investments over the taxable year has only $1,000 in compensation; the $5,000 in investment income cannot be considered compensation.

The participant's compensation requirement has some exceptions. The first is that both spouses need not receive compensation in order for one to be eligible to make spousal IRA contributions for the other. The second permits a nonworking spouse who is a surviving beneficiary to treat the deceased spouse's IRA as his or her own. The third exception permits a person who receives a distribution from another plan to redeposit it as a rollover contribution. The fourth allows a divorced spouse to include taxable alimony received as compensation.

Rules on eligible compensation for contributions have varied over the years. At one time, in order to be eligible to make spousal contributions, one spouse could not have received *any* compensation in the taxable year for which the spousal contributions were being made. However, the Tax Reform Act of 1986 eliminated this requirement. Under the changed law, a spouse who earned compensation in a given taxable year may elect to be considered noncompensated for spousal IRA contribution purposes.

General Rules Concerning Allowable Contributions

The Code regulates contributions to tax-deferred retirement plans in three ways:

- the allowable maximum amount of contributions;

- when the contributions may be made for a tax year;

- the nature of those contributions.

The amount of contribution is subject to limitations. For all types of contributions into IRAs except rollovers, the Code defines the limitations on allowable contributions as the lesser of either a stated dollar amount or a percentage of a participant's compensation. The Code does not require that eligible individuals use a minimum amount to establish or contribute to an IRA. Therefore, a participant may establish and contribute to any number of IRAs at different trustee institutions as long as the *total* amount contributed does not exceed the annual IRA limit. Institutions, however, are free to set their own customer policies regarding minimums required to establish or add to an IRA account. Figure 9-2 shows the contribution limits for each type of IRA.

F I G U R E 9-2

Allowable Contribution Limits

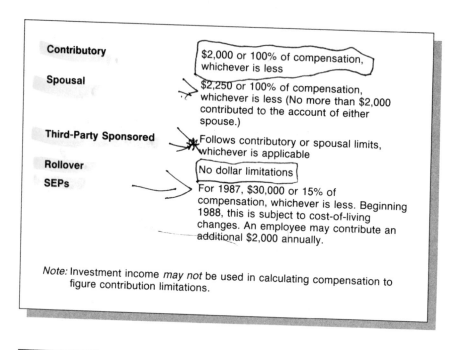

Contributory
$2,000 or 100% of compensation, whichever is less

Spousal
$2,250 or 100% of compensation, whichever is less (No more than $2,000 contributed to the account of either spouse.)

Third-Party Sponsored
Follows contributory or spousal limits, whichever is applicable

Rollover
No dollar limitations

SEPs
For 1987, $30,000 or 15% of compensation, whichever is less. Beginning 1988, this is subject to cost-of-living changes. An employee may contribute an additional $2,000 annually.

Note: Investment income *may not* be used in calculating compensation to figure contribution limitations.

Contributions also must be made within specified time periods, usually the taxable year plus the leeway period. The *leeway period* is the period of time in which individuals may establish IRAs or make IRA contributions applying to the preceding taxable year. For regular, spousal, third-party-sponsored and SEP contributions, the leeway period includes the time after the end of the taxable year (usually January 1) to the day income tax returns are due (normally April 15). No extensions of the due date are granted for either IRA or SEP contributions. For IRA contributions made during the first 3½ months of a year, institutions typically require customers to designate the year for which they are making the contributions.

All IRA contributions, with the exception of rollover IRA contributions, must be made in *cash*. Thus, an individual cannot make a contributory, spousal, third-party-sponsored or SEP contribution in the form of stocks or bonds. Of course, cash contributions can then be used to invest in a variety of approved investment vehicles. With rollover IRAs, financial institutions may have the implied power to receive noncash property as a rollover contribution and convert it to cash for deposit to accounts in their own institutions. Under the Code, a rollover of noncash property does not result in a taxable event for the person making the rollover. Figure 9-3 lists both allowable and barred investments for retirement savings plans. In general, IRAs are barred or prohibited from investing in collectibles.

Allowable Contributions by Type

As previously mentioned, specific contribution limits apply to each of the five types of IRA contributions. In addition, specific rules apply to each type of contribution.

Contributory or Regular

In some cases, an individual's amount of annual compensation may determine the limitation on regular contributions. Individuals who earn less than $2,000 per year may contribute any amount up to a maximum of 100% of their compensation. Individuals who earn more than

F I G U R E 9-3

Allowed and Barred Investments for IRAs

Allowed IRA Investments	Barred IRA Investments
Bonds	Collectibles:
Stocks	artworks
Money market instruments	rugs
Mutual funds	antiques
Insurance annuities	metals
Government securities	gems
Government agency notes	stamps
Treasury bills	alcoholic beverages
Certificates of deposit	
	Tangible personal property
Stocks:	
growth	Most coins and any fashioned
high-yield	into jewelry
blue-chip	
Bonds:	
corporate	
convertible	
discount	
high-yield	
Certain coins, e.g., "American	
Eagle" gold and silver coins	
(U.S. Treasury-minted) and	
state-issued coins	

$2,000 per year may contribute any amount up to a maximum of $2,000. Whether this contribution is tax-deductible by the individual will depend on the individual's adjusted gross income if the individual is covered by a retirement plan at work.

The eligibility and contribution limits are the same for a married individual. However, deductibility limitations will apply if either spouse is covered by an employer-provided qualified retirement plan. Also, a divorced spouse may consider taxable alimony received to be compensation.

Spousal Contributions

Spousal contributions may be made up to $2,250 or 100% of the working spouse's compensation, whichever is less. Spouses may choose to deposit any portion of the allowable spousal contribution *up to $2,000* in either spouse's IRA.

Third-Party-Sponsored Contributions

The same contribution rules that apply to regular and spousal IRA contributions pertain to third-party-sponsored contributions. In addition, with this form of contribution, an employee may contribute the difference between the employer's contribution and the regular IRA limits to his or her own regular IRA. For example, if Bud Selkirk receives contributions of $1,000 from his union to a Section 408(c) IRA, he may contribute another $1,000 to his IRA. If Bud's union contributes $2,000 for him in any year, Bud cannot contribute any amount for that year.

SEP Contributions

The yearly SEP contribution limit to an IRA is $30,000 from the employer or 15% of compensation, whichever is less. Employees may make their $2,000 IRA contributions to the same IRA that is holding employer SEP contributions.

The Tax Reform Act of 1986 made a significant tax change relating to SEP agreements affecting small firms (25 employees or fewer). The act allows employees of such firms to elect to defer some of their income from taxation by making voluntary pretax contributions under the employer's SEP.

Technically, these arrangements are called salary reduction arrangements or *SARSEPS*. When SARSEPS were first introduced, employees could defer up to $7,000 of their annual salaries in addition to their employers' contributions. Beginning in 1988, however, the amount became subject to annual cost-of-living adjustments (COLA). For example, the dollar limit for elective-deferral arrangements for 1989 was $7,627. Employee salary deferrals are counted with employer contributions in order to limit total SEP contributions to the lesser of the employee's 15% of compensation or the $30,000 allowable SEP contribution limit.

The Code permits employers to maintain SARSEPS if at least half of the employees who are eligible to participate in the plan elect deferrals.

Rollover Contributions

Unlike all other types of contributions to IRAs, the Code sets no maximum dollar limitations on the amount of rollover IRAs. However, several significant points affect the composition of rollover contributions:

- An employee may rollover funds from a qualified pension plan (such as a Keogh plan), a retirement annuity or an IRA to an IRA.

- Rollovers from a qualified plan may not include after-tax contributions made by the employee to the plan, because these amounts already have been declared as income and taxed. Only amounts yet to be declared as income qualify for rollover treatment.

- Rollovers may include employer contributions and earnings on both employer and employee contributions.

- Individuals are required to deposit (rollover) the distributed funds into an IRA within 60 days after receiving a distribution.

- The distribution may be either a lump-sum or a partial distribution. A lump-sum distribution is the total amount of the employee's vested benefits accrued in a qualified plan. A partial distribution will qualify for rollover treatment if:
  1. the distribution equals at least 50% of the participant's balance in the qualified plan;
  2. the distribution is not one of a series of periodic payments; and
  3. the distribution is made for one of the following three reasons:
     —death of the participant;
     —disability of the participant;
     —separation from service.

- An employee may choose to rollover all or any portion of the eligible funds. Any eligible distribution that is not rolled over may be subject to income tax. In addition, if the recipient is under age 59½ or does not meet other requirements, such amounts may be subject to penalty taxes.

Additional information on distribution rules is covered in a later section of this chapter.

- Rollovers from one IRA to another are restricted to a maximum of one every 12 months per plan. The 12-month period begins on the date the funds are distributed from the first IRA to the participant for rollover purposes. Thus, if a participant receives a partial or full distribution from his or her IRA on October 24 of one year, he or she may not receive another distribution from that IRA for rollover purposes until October 24 of the next year; and so on. This 12-month rule applies only to rollovers from one IRA to another; rollovers from a qualified pension plan to an IRA or vice versa are not restricted.

Participants who make rollover contributions properly will have no immediate tax liabilities as a result of the rollover transaction. The funds moved from one tax-deferred plan to another continue to be tax deferred.

Besides receiving the funds from one IRA and complying with the time and frequency restrictions of rollovers, a participant may direct his or her trustee to transfer the funds to another trustee. Such a *direct transfer* is done between IRA trustees only, with no check made payable to the participant. The IRS imposes no time or frequency restrictions on direct transfers.

Deductibility of Contributions

The Tax Reform Act of 1986 retained the *eligibility* requirements for IRA participation. However, the tax *deductibility* of contributions may be limited depending on how three factors pertain to the participant:

- status as an active participant in a qualified pension plan;

- tax filing status (single, married filing jointly, married but living apart); and

- amount of adjusted gross income.

The first factor to consider is whether an individual or his or her spouse is an active participant in a qualified plan. The employer must inform the employee of his or her active participant status on the annual W-2 form. The employer uses this form to report to the IRS on the employee wages earned and taxes withheld for the previous year. The employees must receive the W-2 forms from the employer by January 31 of each year.

The active participant status of employees or their spouses determines whether the employees will be affected by deduction limitations. After ascertaining whether the individuals are active participants, the following rules for deductibility of contributions will apply:

- Nonactive participants may continue to make fully deductible IRA contributions without regard to their income or tax filing status.

- Active participants must consider their tax filing status and amount of adjusted gross income to determine whether their contributions will be fully deductible, partially deductible or nondeductible (see Figure 9-4 for specific information). Also, the federal income tax return includes instructions for participants to follow to help them determine the deductibility of their IRA contributions.

A common misconception among customers is that they must contribute their full eligible amount in order

What constitutes earned income

earnings are still deductible for partially deductible for non deductible

F I G U R E 9-4

IRA Contributions for Active Participants

If your filing status is:	and you are in an employer-sponsored qualified plan with an adjusted gross income of:		
Single	$25,000 or less	$25,001 to $34,999	$35,000 or more
Married, filing jointly	$40,000 or less	$40,001 to $49,999	$50,000 or more
Married, filing singly	Not applicable	Under $10,000	$10,000 or more
Married, filing singly and living apart	$25,000 or less	$25,001 to $34,999	$35,000 or more
Your IRA contribution is:	Fully Deductible	Partially Deductible	Not Deductible

to qualify for a partial deduction. This is not true. However, deductions are limited to the actual amount contributed if the participant contributes less than his or her maximum deductible amount.

The IRS requires that once a participant makes a nondeductible contribution into an IRA, he or she must file Form 8606 as required until all IRA funds are ultimately distributed. This form is used to account for the participant's total deductible and nondeductible contributions in all IRAs. This information is important for the participant because only deductible contributions will be subject to income taxes upon withdrawal. The IRS can assess a participant a $50 penalty for failing to file Form 8606 if required. Also, the IRS may impose a $100 penalty if a participant overstates the amount of a nondeductible IRA contribution on his or her tax return.

Rollover transactions and direct transfers merely maintain the tax-deferred status of funds being moved from one plan to another. Therefore, rollover contributions and direct transfers are *not* subject to deduction limitations.

Excess Contributions

An *excess contribution* is an amount greater than the IRA participant's allowable contribution. The IRS imposes a 6% penalty on the participant for any excess contribution. The penalty applies for each year that an excess occurs. The IRS has specific procedures for correcting, or curing, an excess. However, additional distribution penalties may apply when an excess is cured.

Participants usually make excess contributions unintentionally. One situation in which excess contributions result occurs when a participant contributes early in the calendar year for that tax year and then fails to earn the anticipated compensation. Another situation is one in which a participant contributes to several IRAs at different institutions and the total amount contributed to all IRAs exceeds the annual contribution limits.

IRA trustees must have procedures for limiting certain excess contributions. However, financial institutions are responsible only for monitoring the amounts contributed into their institutions for a particular tax year. Generally, institutions cannot accept IRA contributions in excess of $2,000. Since IRA contributions by a calendar-year taxpayer can be made between January 1 and April 15 of the following year, institutions can require customers to designate the tax year for which they are making contributions. However, *institutions are not required to monitor the percentage limitations pertaining to a participant's income*; this is the participant's responsibility.

Since 1987, the Code has permitted participants to withdraw any IRA contributions (regardless of whether they were excess, deductible or nondeductible) without tax penalties if:

- no deduction was taken for the contribution; and

- the withdrawal is made before the due date (including extensions) for filing the participant's income tax return for the applicable tax year.

In this case, the earnings on such IRA contributions must also be withdrawn and reported as income to the participant. Also, if the IRA participant is under age 59½, the IRS will impose a 10% early distribution penalty tax on the earnings attributable to the IRA contribution. Any earnings withdrawn after the close of the taxable year will be considered as earned in the taxable year in which the contributions were made. For example, Bob makes a regular IRA contribution of $2,000 on January 2, 19X1. Before filing his income tax return for 19X1 on April 14, 19X2, Bob changes his mind and decides he does not want to make a contribution for 19X1. Assuming the $2,000 contribution earned $180 in 19X1 and $45 in 19X2, Bob can withdraw $2,225. He reports the $2,225 as taxable income for 19X1. Also, if Bob is under age 59½, the $225 will be subject to a 10%, or $23, penalty tax.

Documentation

In addition to the institution's "new account" forms for opening any deposit account, certain other documents are completed when opening an IRA account:

- trust agreement, also called the plan agreement;
- disclosure statement; *hth. how much IRA can earn→*
- designation of beneficiary form;
- signature card (if necessary);
- deposit information.

Trust Agreement

A trust agreement is used to establish an IRA. Generally, it designates the financial institution as trustee and the participant as grantor. It also details the fiduciary relationship between the institution and the participant. Some basic provisions that a trust agreement may include are:

- the participant's nonforfeitable, or fully vested, interest in the account balance;

- the participant's agreement to provide information the trustee needs to prepare required reports; and

- the trustee's agreement to submit reports to the IRS and to the participant.

The IRS has issued two model IRA agreements: Form 5305 for trusteed plans and Form 5305-A for custodial plans. A financial institution may use the model IRS forms, prepare its own trust account agreement (which the Internal Revenue Service may examine and approve), adopt a model plan prepared by a plan sponsor or adopt any other agreement (such as a prototype plan) that the IRS has already approved.

Figure 9-5 shows a trust agreement for a trusteed IRA plan. Figure 9-6 illustrates a plan agreement used for a SEP. When a SEP is opened, the agreements shown in both Figures 9-5 and 9-6 are used. The employer completes the SEP agreement while participants complete IRA agreements. With a SEP, the trustee must check the appropriate box on the IRA application that indicates a SEP agreement applies to the IRA.

Disclosure Statement

The *disclosure statement* is a nontechnical explanation of the terms and conditions of the IRA trust agreement. The law requires a financial institution, as IRA trustee, to furnish a disclosure statement and a copy of the trust agreement to the IRA participant. For every disclosure not made, the institution may be subject to a fine. Figure 9-7 shows a sample of a disclosure statement.

Typically, a disclosure statement has two main sections. The first section includes explanations of statutory and regulatory requirements about the operation and tax treatment of IRAs. The second section contains a financial disclosure. If an institution guarantees, or can reasonably project, the growth of an IRA, it is required to project the growth during the account's first five years and in the years in which the participant will attain the ages of 60, 65 and 70. This calculation assumes annual contributions of $1,000 made on the first day of each calendar year. The interest rate used in the projection must be no greater than the actual rate paid on the IRA investment at the time the IRA is opened. In other words, the financial institution uses the IRA rates detailed in its statement of terms and conditions for deposit accounts as the basis for this calculation. Additionally, projected amounts must take into consideration the terms of the investment currently in effect. Thus, projections must reflect potential investment penalties on early withdrawals.

Designation of Beneficiary

An IRA participant may designate a beneficiary as recipient of any assets remaining in the IRA at the participant's death. The beneficiary may be a person or an entity. Single or joint beneficiaries may be designated as primary beneficiaries or as contingent beneficiaries. A *primary beneficiary* would become the owner of the IRA participant's funds in the event the IRA owner dies. A *contingent beneficiary* would receive the IRA funds if the primary beneficiary predeceases the IRA grantor. The IRA participant may change the beneficiaries at any time by completing a new form and filing it with the IRA trustee.

Figure 9-8 shows a typical IRA application and designation of beneficiary form. After completion, the institution gives a copy to the participant and keeps the original in its files.

Deposit Information

Whenever an IRA is established or a subsequent contribution made, the institution should obtain and document the following information for required reporting:

- the deposit amount;

- the type of IRA contribution being made (e.g., regular, spousal, SEP, direct transfer or rollover);

F I G U R E 9-5

Form 5305, Side 1

Form 5305
(Rev. December 1987)
Department of the Treasury
Internal Revenue Service

INDIVIDUAL RETIREMENT TRUST ACCOUNT
(Under Section 408(a) of the Internal Revenue Code)

Do NOT file
with Internal
Revenue Service

The Grantor who completes and signs the Application is establishing an individual retirement account (under section 408(a) of the Internal Revenue Code) to provide for his or her retirement and for the support of his or her beneficiaries after death.

The Trustee named in the application has given the Grantor the disclosure statement required under the Income Tax Regulations under section 408(i) of the Code.

The Grantor and the Trustee make the following agreement:

Article I

The Trustee may accept additional cash contributions on behalf of the Grantor for a tax year of the Grantor. The total cash contributions are limited to $2,000 for the tax year unless the contribution is a rollover contribution described in section 402(a)(5), 402(a)(7), 403(a)(4), 403(b)(8), 408(d)(3) of the Code or an employer contribution to a simplified employee pension plan as described in section 408(k).

Article II

The Grantor's interest in the balance in the trust account is nonforfeitable.

Article III

1. No part of the trust funds may be invested in life insurance contracts, nor may the assets of the trust account be commingled with other property except in a common trust fund or common investment fund (within the meaning of section 408(a)(5) of the Code.)

2. No part of the trust funds may be invested in collectibles (within the meaning of section 408(m) of the Code.)

Article IV

1. The Grantor's entire interest in the trust account must be or begin to be distributed by the Grantor's required beginning date, the April 1 following the calendar year end in which the Grantor reaches age 70½. By that date, the Grantor may elect, in a manner acceptable to the trustee, to have the balance in the trust account distributed in:

(a) A single sum payment.

(b) An annuity contract that provides equal or substantially equal monthly, quarterly, or annual payments over the life of the Grantor. The payments must begin by April 1 following the calendar year in which the Grantor reaches age 70½.

(c) An annuity contract that provides equal or substantially equal monthly, quarterly, or annual payments over the life and last survivor lives of the Grantor and his or her designated beneficiary. The payments must begin by the April 1 following the calendar year in which the Grantor reaches age 70½.

(d) Equal or substantially equal annual payments over a specified period that may not be longer than the Grantor's life expectancy.

(e) Equal or substantially equal annual payments over a specified period that may not be longer than the joint life and last survivor expectancy of the Grantor and his or her designated beneficiary.

Even if distributions have begun to be made under option (d) or (e), the Grantor may receive a distribution of the balance in the trust account at any time by giving written notice to the trustee. If the Grantor does not choose any of the methods of distribution described above by the April 1 following the calendar year in which he or she reaches age 70½, distribution to the Grantor will be made not later than that date by a single sum payment. If the Grantor elects as a means of distribution (b) or (c) above, the annuity contract must satisfy the requirement of section 408(b)(1), (3) and (4) of the Code. If the Grantor elects as a means of distribution (d) or (e) above, the annual payment required to be made by the Grantor's required beginning date is for the calendar year the Grantor reached age 70½. Annual payments for subsequent years, including the year the Grantor's required beginning date occurs, must be made by December 31 of that year.

2. If the Grantor dies before his or her entire interest is distributed to him or her, the entire remaining interest will be distributed as follows:

(a) If the Grantor dies on or after the Grantor's required beginning date, distribution must continue to be made in accordance with paragraph 1.

(b) If the Grantor dies before the Grantor's required beginning date, the entire remaining interest will, at the election of the beneficiary or beneficiaries, either

(i) Be distributed by the December 31 of the year containing the fifth anniversary of the Grantor's death, or

(ii) Be distributed in equal or substantially equal payments over the life or life expectancy of the designated beneficiary or beneficiaries.

The election of either (i) or (ii) must be made by December 31 of the year following the year of the Grantor's death. If the beneficiary or beneficiaries do not elect either of the distribution options described in (i) or (ii), distribution will be made in accordance with (ii) if the beneficiary is the Grantor's surviving spouse and in accordance with (i) if the beneficiary or beneficiaries are or include anyone other than the surviving spouse. In the case of distributions under (ii), distributions must commence by December 31 of the year following the year of the Grantor's death. If Grantor's spouse is the beneficiary, distributions need not commence until December 31 of the year the Grantor would have attained age 70½, if later.

(c) If the Grantor dies before his or her entire interest has been distributed and if the beneficiary is other than the surviving spouse, no additional cash contributions or rollover contributions may be accepted in the account.

3. In the case of distribution over life expectancy in equal or substantially equal annual payments, to determine the minimum annual payment for each year, divide the Grantor's entire interest in the trust as of the close of business on December 31 of the preceding year by the life expectancy of the Grantor (or the joint life and last survivor expectancy of the Grantor and the Grantor's designated beneficiary, or the life expectancy of the designated beneficiary, whichever applies). In the case of distributions under paragraph (1), determine the initial life expectancy for joint life and last survivor expectancy) using the attained ages of the Grantor and designated beneficiary as of their birthdays in the year the Grantor reaches age 70½. In the case of distribution in accordance with paragraph 2(b)(ii), determine life expectancy using the attained age of the designated beneficiary as of the beneficiary's birthday in the year distributions are required to commence. Unless the Grantor (or spouse) elects not to have life expectancy recalculated, the Grantor's life expectancy (and the life expectancy of the Grantor's spouse, if applicable) will be recalculated annually using their attained ages as of their birthdays in the year for which the minimum annual payment is being determined. The life expectancy of the designated beneficiary (other than the spouse) will not be recalculated. The minimum annual payment may be made in a series of installments (e.g., monthly, quarterly, etc.) as long as the total payments for the year made by the date required are not less than the minimum amounts required. [See Article IX for additional rules concerning distributions.]

Article V

Unless the Grantor dies, is disabled (as defined in section 72(m) of the Code, or reaches age 59½ before any amount is distributed from the trust account, the Trustee must receive from the Grantor a statement explaining how he or she intends to dispose of the amount distributed.

Article VI

1. The Grantor agrees to provide the Trustee with information necessary for the Trustee to prepare any reports required under section 408(i) and the Code and related regulations.

2. The Trustee agrees to submit reports to the Internal Revenue Service and the Grantor as prescribed by the Internal Revenue Service.

Article VII

Notwithstanding any other articles may be added or incorporated, the provisions of Articles I through III and this sentence will be controlling. Any additional articles that are not consistent with section 408(a) of the Code and related regulations will be invalid.

Article VIII

This agreement will be amended from time to time to comply with the provisions of the Code and related regulations. Other amendments may be made with the consent of the persons whose signatures appear on the Application.

Article IX

1. **Definitions.**

(a) **Application:** The Individual Retirement Account Application and Beneficiary Designation incorporating this Agreement by reference.

(b) **Grantor:** The individual who establishes an individual retirement account by executing the Application, also referred to as the "Participant" in the Application and related administrative rules.

(c) **Beneficiary:** A person or entity (including but not limited to the Grantor's estate, dependent or dependents) other) designated by the Grantor (or, if Section 13 applies, the Grantor's surviving spouse) in writing furnished to the Trustee during the Grantor's (or surviving spouse's) lifetime or (2) specified under this agreement, to receive benefits payable under this agreement subsequent to the death of the Grantor (or surviving spouse).

(d) **Trustee:** Financial Institution named in the Application as trustee.

2. **Investment Authority. (Investment Direction by Grantor.)**

(a) At the direction of the Grantor, the Trustee may invest in such certificates of deposit or other savings instruments as are chosen by the Grantor from among those designated from time to time by the institution to be within the class or classes of deposits offered for the investment of IRA funds. If such deposits

19416 (8/88)

Copyright © 1988 United States League of Savings Institutions

SAF Systems and Forms, Inc.
1-800-323-3000

F I G U R E 9-5, Continued

Form 5305, Side 2

are not automatically renewable, or if the Grantor fails to give timely directions for investment, the funds shall be invested by the Trustee in deposits paying the then current annual rate of interest being paid by the Institution on regular deposit accounts. A class may be established in the form of a common trust fund or common investment fund as described in Article III. If the Grantor elects self-direction in section 6 of the Application with the consent of the Trustee, the Trustee also may invest and reinvest any part of the IRA trust assets in such other investments as the Trustee legally is authorized to hold and as the Grantor may direct. Investment directions under this paragraph 2(a) shall be given by the Grantor in a reasonable and timely manner acceptable to the Trustee. If the Grantor fails specifically to elect self-direction in section 6 of the Application, the IRA trust assets shall be invested in deposits of the Institution.

(b) The Trustee may hold a reasonable portion of the trust account in cash, with no obligation for payment of interest, for payment of current expenses or benefits under the Agreement.

3. Judicial Settlement of Accounts.

The Trustee shall have the right to apply at any time to a court of competent jurisdiction for the judicial settlement of its accounts. In any such judicial action or proceeding it shall be necessary to join as parties the Trustee and the Grantor, (or Beneficiary if Grantor is deceased). Any judgment or decree entered therein shall be conclusive upon all persons claiming any interest in the IRA.

4. Expenses and Compensation.

The Trustee may charge against and deduct from the IRA, or receive directly from the Grantor, reimbursement for all reasonable expenses incurred by the Trustee in the administration of the IRA, including, among others, costs of fiduciary insurance and counsel fees. The Trustee also may charge reasonable compensation for its services as Trustee or for providing administrative services for the IRA. The Trustee shall give the Grantor at least 30 days' prior written notice before first imposing a fee if the fee schedule is not set out in the disclosure statement, or before increasing the fee.

5. Fiduciary Responsibilities.

(a) The Trustee shall be responsible for the administration of the IRA, shall receive all contributions, shall invest the IRA assets pursuant to the direction of the Grantor and shall make distributions and pay benefits from the IRA, shall file such statements or reports as may be required of Trustees by law, and shall do such other things as may be required in the administration of the IRA. Unless otherwise directed in writing by the Grantor, the Trustee in its sole discretion from time to time shall cast any votes on any and all matters, or appoint any proxy to cast such votes as may be attributable to the Grantor's interest under this agreement. The Trustee shall use reasonable care, skill, prudence and diligence in the administration of the IRA and in executing the Grantor's written instructions as to the investment of the IRA assets and shall be entitled to rely on information submitted by the Grantor to the Trustee.

(b) The institution shall have no duties under this agreement and no responsibility for the administration of the IRA except for such duties imposed by law or this agreement on savings institutions which sponsor IRA programs. The Trustee shall have no liability regarding investments made at the direction of the Grantor other than to carry out the duties imposed under this Article.

(c) The United States League of Savings Institutions shall have no duties with respect to, or responsibility or discretionary control over the administration of the IRA established pursuant to this agreement, except that it may, from time to time, make amendments to the trust agreement consistent with Section 408 of the Code or other applicable law, regulations or administrative rulings, and with paragraph 7 hereof.

6. Resignation, Removal and Appointment of Trustee.

The Trustee acting hereunder may resign at any time by written notice of such resignation to the institution and the Grantor. The institution may remove any Trustee acting hereunder at any time by written notice thereof to such Trustee and the Grantor. The Institution shall fill any vacancy in the office of Trustee by written instrument appointing a successor Trustee, furnished to the successor Trustee and the Grantor, provided, however, that any successor Trustee so appointed shall be a savings and loan association, bank or trust company authorized to act as Trustee of trusts established under individual retirement accounts, organized under the laws of the United States or any State of the United States, and subject to supervision and examination by government authority.

7. Amendments

This IRA agreement is intended to be and to remain a qualified individual retirement account within the meaning of Section 408 of the Code. For the sole purposes of insuring the continued compliance of this agreement with the requirements of applicable law, or of conforming it to statutory or regulatory changes in allowable contribution limits, this agreement may be amended unilaterally from time to time, pursuant to the first sentence of Article VII, by the United States League of Savings Institutions by written instrument delivered to the Trustee. The United States League, pursuant to the second sentence of Article VIII, also may make such other amendments to this agreement from time to time as may be consistent with the provisions of applicable law, which amendments shall not be effective until the Trustee and the Grantor have consented thereto. No amendment to this agreement shall vest any right or interest in the IRA in any party other than the Grantor, (or beneficiary if Grantor is deceased). Any amendments to this agreement pursuant to this paragraph may be effective retroactively, provided that no amendment made pursuant to the second sentence of Article VIII shall deprive the Grantor, (or beneficiary if Grantor is deceased) of any benefit to which each may have been entitled as a result of contributions made prior to the amendment.

8. Records and Reports.

The Trustee shall maintain appropriate records for the IRA showing all contributions, disbursements and investments of IRA funds which shall be open for inspection by the Grantor during business hours of the Trustee. In addition to the reports by Trustee required under Article VI, the Trustee shall arrange for such reports and information to be provided to the Grantor regarding the investment of the IRA funds as may reasonably be necessary to enable the Grantor to direct the investment and reinvestment of his IRA funds.

9. Calculation of Life Expectancy.

Notwithstanding any provision in Article IV, section 3, the following shall apply:

(a) Unless the Grantor elects to recalculate life expectancies in writing furnished to the Trustee no later than the required beginning date, the Grantor's life expectancy (and the life expectancy of the Grantor's spouse, if any) will not be recalculated.

(b) If the beneficiary is the Grantor's surviving spouse and the Grantor dies before the Grantor's required beginning date, the Grantor's surviving spouse may elect to recalculate such spouse's life expectancy, but unless the Grantor's surviving spouse elects to recalculate his or her life expectancy in writing furnished to the Trustee no later than the date distributions are required to begin to such spouse under the applicable payment election, such spouse's life expectancy will not be recalculated.

(c) In addition to any other fees which the Trustee may impose under Article IX, section 4, the Trustee, in its discretion and immediately upon commencement of distribution, may impose a fee for its services under this section.

10. Failure of Grantor to Make Timely Election of Benefits.

If the Grantor fails to elect any of the methods of distribution described in Article IV, section 1 by April 1 following the calendar year in which the Grantor reaches age 70½, the single sum payment of the IRA balance required to be made on that date in the event of such failure will apply only if the balance in the account on such date is $3,500 or less. If such balance exceeds $3,500, payments will be made to the Grantor on an annual basis beginning on that date and extending over a period equal to the Grantor's single life expectancy for the year the Grantor reaches age 70½, such life expectancy to be nonrecalculated. During that period the Grantor, as permitted by Article IV, section 1, may elect to have distribution made on an accelerated basis at any time by giving written notice to the Trustee.

11. Other Provisions Governing Distributions.

(a) During the Grantor's lifetime, all payments from the account shall be made to the Grantor or on the Grantor's written direction. After the Grantor's death, all payments from the account shall be made to the beneficiary or beneficiaries designated by the Grantor or, if none, to the Grantor's estate.

(b) Except as otherwise provided by the Grantor or in Section 13, if a beneficiary dies before the complete distribution of his or her interest in the account, any benefits which would have been payable to such beneficiary shall be paid to such beneficiary's estate.

(c) Any beneficiary from time to time may elect to accelerate the distribution of his or her interest in the account, in whole or in part.

12. Administration after the Grantor's Death.

After the Grantor's death, the Grantor's beneficiaries shall have all of the rights and powers of the Grantor under this agreement with respect to the investment and administration of the account. Nothing in this section shall be construed, however, as permitting any beneficiary to change any beneficiary designation or distribution election made by the Grantor, to deprive any beneficiary of any benefit to which he or she otherwise would be entitled under this agreement, to designate a beneficiary to receive any payments or distributions from the account or to make additional contributions to the account (except to the extent permitted under Section 13).

13. Special Provisions Applicable to Grantor's Surviving Spouse.

Unless otherwise expressly provided by the Grantor, if the beneficiary is the Grantor's surviving spouse, the following provisions shall apply after the Grantor's death:

(a) The Grantor's surviving spouse may elect to treat such spouse's interest in the Grantor's IRA as the spouse's IRA, in which case all of the terms, conditions and restrictions of this agreement shall be applied as if the spouse were the Grantor. An election under this paragraph must be made by the Grantor's surviving spouse on or before December 31 of the year following the year of the Grantor's death and will be deemed to have been made if the spouse makes any additional contribution to the account.

(b) The Grantor's surviving spouse may designate in writing one or more beneficiaries to receive any benefits otherwise payable to such spouse under this agreement which are not completely distributed to such spouse prior to his or her death.

14. Notwithstanding any other provisions of this agreement, the Grantor's written instructions with respect to the distribution of the account shall control. The Grantor may limit or eliminate any right or power granted under this agreement to any beneficiary (including the Grantor's surviving spouse) by specifying in writing furnished to the Trustee the rights or powers so limited, the beneficiary or beneficiaries affected by the limitation, and the provisions which are to govern the distribution of the account in that event; provided, however, that no such writing shall be effective to the extent inconsistent with Section 408(a) of the Code and related regulations.

F I G U R E 9-6

Form 5305–SEP, Side 1

Form **5305-SEP** (Rev. June 1988) Department of the Treasury Internal Revenue Service	**Simplified Employee Pension-Individual** **Retirement Accounts Contribution Agreement** (Under Section 408(k) of the Internal Revenue Code)	OMB No. 1545-0499 Expires 7-31-91 **Do NOT File with Internal Revenue Service**

_____ makes the following agreement under the terms of section 408(k) of
(Business name—employer)

the Internal Revenue Code and the instructions to this form.

The employer agrees to provide for discretionary contributions in each calendar year to the Individual Retirement Accounts or Individual Retirement Annuities (IRA's) of all eligible employees who are at least _____ years old (not over 21 years old) (see instruction "Who May Participate") and worked in at least _____ years (enter 1, 2, or 3 years) of the immediately preceding 5 years (see instruction "Who May Participate"). This ☐ includes ☐ does not include employees covered under a collective bargaining agreement and ☐ includes ☐ does not include employees whose total compensation during the year is less than $300.

The employer agrees that contributions made on behalf of each eligible employee will:
- Be made only on the first $200,000 of compensation (as adjusted per Code section 408(k)(8)).
- Be made in an amount that is the same percentage of total compensation for every employee.
- Be limited to the smaller of $30,000 (or if greater, ¼ of the dollar limitation in effect under section 415(b)(1)(A)) or 15% of compensation.
- Be paid to the employee's IRA trustee, custodian, or insurance company (for an annuity contract).

_____   _____
Signature of employer   Date

By _____

Instructions for the Employer
(Section references are to the Internal Revenue Code, unless otherwise noted.)

Paperwork Reduction Act Notice.—The Paperwork Reduction Act of 1980 says we must tell you why we are collecting this information, how it is to be used, and whether you have to give it to us. The information is used to determine if you are entitled to a deduction for contributions made to a SEP. Your completing this form is only required if you want to establish a Model SEP.

Purpose of Form.—Form 5305-SEP (Model SEP) is used by an employer to make an agreement to provide benefits to all employees under a Simplified Employee Pension (SEP) plan described in section 408(k). This form is NOT to be filed with IRS.

What Is a SEP Plan?—A SEP provides an employer with a simplified way to make contributions toward an employee's retirement income. Under a SEP, the employer is permitted to contribute a certain amount (see below) to an employee's Individual Retirement Account or Individual Retirement Annuity (IRA's). The employer makes contributions directly to an IRA set up by an employee with a bank, insurance company, or other qualified financial institution. When using this form to establish a SEP, the IRA must be a model IRA established on an IRS form or a master or prototype IRA for which IRS has issued a favorable opinion letter. Making the agreement on Form 5305-SEP does not establish an employer IRA as described under section 408(c).

This form may not be used by an employer who:
- Currently maintains any other qualified retirement plan.
- Has maintained in the past a defined benefit plan, even if now terminated.
- Has any eligible employees for whom IRA's have not been established.

- Uses the services of leased employees (as described in section 414(n)).
- Is a member of an affiliated service group (as described in section 414(m)), a controlled group of corporations (as described in section 414(b)), or trades or businesses under common control (as described in section 414(c)), UNLESS all eligible employees of all the members of such groups, trades, or businesses, participate under the SEP.
- This form should only be used if the employer will pay the cost of the SEP contributions. This form is not suitable for a SEP that provides for contributions at the election of the employee whether or not made pursuant to a salary reduction agreement.

Who May Participate.—Any employee who is at least 21 years old and has performed "service" for you in at least 3 years of the immediately preceding 5 years must be permitted to participate in the SEP. However, you may establish less restrictive eligibility requirements if you choose. "Service" is any work performed for you for any period of time, however short. Further, if you are a member of an affiliated service group, a controlled group of corporations, or trades or businesses under common control, "service" includes any work performed for any period of time for any other member of such group, trades, or businesses. Generally, to make the agreement, all eligible employees (including all eligible employees, if any, of other members of an affiliated service group, a controlled group of corporations, or trades or businesses under common control) must participate in the plan. However, employees covered under a collective bargaining agreement and certain nonresident aliens may be excluded if section 410(b)(3)(A) or 410(b)(3)(C) applies to them. Employees whose total compensation for the year is less than $300 may be excluded.

Amount of Contributions.—You are not required to make any contributions to an employee's SEP-IRA in a given year. However, if you do make contributions, you must make them to the IRA's of all eligible employees, whether or not they are still employed at the time contributions are made. The contributions made must be the same percentage of each employee's total compensation (up to a maximum compensation base of $200,000 as adjusted per section 408(k)(8) for cost of living changes). The contributions you make in a year for any one employee may not be more than the smaller of $30,000 or 15% of that employee's total compensation (figured without considering the SEP-IRA contributions).

For this purpose, compensation includes:
- Amounts received for personal services actually performed (see section 1.219-1(c) of the Income Tax Regulations); and
- Earned income defined under section 401(c)(2).

In making contributions, you may not discriminate in favor of any employee who is highly compensated.

Under this form you may not integrate your SEP contributions with, or offset them by, contributions made under the Federal Insurance Contributions Act (FICA).

Currently, employers who have established a SEP using this agreement and have provided each participant with a copy of this form, including the questions and answers, are not required to file the annual information returns, Forms 5500, 5500-C, 5500-R, or 5500EZ for the SEP.

Deducting Contributions.—You may deduct all contributions to a SEP subject to the limitations of section 404(h). This SEP is maintained on a calendar year basis and contributions to the SEP are deductible for your taxable year with or within which the calendar year ends. Contributions made for a particular taxable year and contributed by the due date of your income tax return (including extensions) shall be deemed made in that taxable year.

Form **5305-SEP** (Rev. 6-88)

F I G U R E 9-6, Continued

Form 5305–SEP, Side 2

Form 5305-SEP (Rev 6-88)   Page 2

Making the Agreement.— This agreement is considered made when (1) IRA's have been established for all of your eligible employees, (2) you have completed all blanks on the agreement form without modification, and (3) you have given all your eligible employees copies of the agreement form, instructions, and questions and answers.

Keep the agreement form with your records; do not file it with IRS.

Information for the Employee

The information provided explains what a Simplified Employee Pension plan is, how contributions are made, and how to treat your employer's contributions for tax purposes.

Please read the questions and answers carefully. For more specific information, also see the agreement form and instructions to your employer on this form.

Questions and Answers

1. Q What is a Simplified Employee Pension, or SEP?

A A SEP is a retirement income arrangement under which your employer may contribute any amount each year up to the smaller of $30,000 or 15% of your compensation into your own Individual Retirement Account/Annuity (IRA)

Your employer will provide you with a copy of the agreement containing participation requirements and a description of the basis upon which employer contributions may be made to your IRA

All amounts contributed to your IRA by your employer belong to you, even after you separate from service with that employer

The $30,000 limitation referred to above may be increased by ¼ of the dollar limitation in effect under section 415(b)(1)(A).

2. Q Must my employer contribute to my IRA under the SEP?

A Whether or not your employer makes a contribution to the SEP is entirely within the employer's discretion. If a contribution is made under the SEP, it must be allocated to all the eligible employees according to the SEP agreement. The Model SEP specifies that the contribution on behalf of each eligible employee will be the same percentage of compensation (excluding compensation higher than $200,000) for all employees

3. Q How much may my employer contribute to my SEP-IRA in any year?

A Under the Model SEP (**Form 5305-SEP**) that your employer has adopted, your employer will determine the amount of contribution to be made to your IRA each year. However, the contribution for any year is limited to the smaller of $30,000 or 15% of your compensation for that year. The compensation used to determine this limit does not include any amount which is contributed by your employer to your IRA under the SEP. The agreement does not require an employer to maintain a particular level of contributions. It is possible that for a given year no employer contribution will be made on an employee's behalf

Also see Question 5.

4. Q How do I treat my employer's SEP contributions for my taxes?

A The amount your employer contributes for years beginning after 1986 is excludable from your gross income subject to certain limitations including the lesser of $30,000 or 15% of compensation mentioned in 1 A above and is not includible as taxable wages on your Form W-2

5. Q May I also contribute to my IRA if I am a participant in a SEP?

A Yes. You may still contribute the lesser of $2,000 or 100% of your compensation to an IRA However, the amount which is deductible may be subject to various limitations

Also see Question 11.

6. Q Are there any restrictions on the IRA I select to deposit my SEP contributions in?

A Under the Model SEP that is approved by IRS, contributions must be made to either a Model IRA which is executed on an IRS form or a master or prototype IRA for which IRS has issued a favorable opinion letter

7. Q What if I don't want a SEP-IRA?

A Your employer may require that you become a participant in such an arrangement as a condition of employment. However, if the employer does not require all eligible employees to become participants and an eligible employee elects not to participate, all other employees of the same employer may be prohibited from entering into a SEP-IRA arrangement with that employer. If one or more eligible employees do not participate and the employer attempts to establish a SEP-IRA agreement with the remaining employees, the resulting arrangement may result in adverse tax consequences to the participating employees.

8. Q Can I move funds from my SEP-IRA to another tax-sheltered IRA?

A Yes, it is permissible for you to withdraw, or receive, funds from your SEP-IRA, and no more than 60 days later, place such funds in another IRA, or SEP-IRA. This is called a "rollover" and may not be done without penalty more frequently than at one-year intervals. However, there are no restrictions on the number of times you may make "transfers" if you arrange to have such funds transferred between the trustees, so that you never have possession

9. Q What happens if I withdraw my employer's contribution from my IRA?

A If you don't want to leave the employer's contribution in your IRA, you may withdraw it at any time, but any amount withdrawn is includible in your income. Also, if withdrawals occur before attainment of age 59 ½, and not on account of death or disability, you may be subject to a penalty tax

10. Q May I participate in a SEP even though I'm covered by another plan?

A An employer may not adopt this IRS Model SEP (**Form 5305-SEP**) if the employer maintains another qualified retirement plan or has ever maintained a qualified defined benefit plan. However, if you work for several employers you may be covered by a SEP of one employer and a different SEP or pension or profit-sharing plan of another employer.

Also see Questions 11 and 12.

11. Q What happens if too much is contributed to my SEP-IRA in one year?

A Any contribution that is more than the yearly limitations may be withdrawn without penalty by the due date (plus extensions) for filing your tax return (normally April 15th), but is includible in your gross income. Excess contributions left in your SEP-IRA account after that time may have adverse tax consequences. Withdrawals of those contributions may be taxed as premature withdrawals

Also see Question 10.

12. Q Do I need to file any additional forms with IRS because I participate in a SEP?

A No

13. Q Is my employer required to provide me with information about SEP-IRA's and the SEP agreement?

A Yes, your employer must provide you with a copy of the executed SEP agreement (**Form 5305-SEP**), these Questions and Answers, and provide a statement each year showing any contribution to your IRA

Also see Question 4.

14. Q Is the financial institution where I establish my IRA also required to provide me with information?

A Yes, it must provide you with a disclosure statement which contains the following items of information in plain, nontechnical language

(1) the statutory requirements which relate to your IRA;

(2) the tax consequences which follow the exercise of various options and what those options are;

(3) participation eligibility rules, and rules on the deductibility and nondeductibility of retirement savings;

(4) the circumstances and procedures under which you may revoke your IRA, including the name, address, and telephone number of the person designated to receive notice of revocation (**this explanation must be prominently displayed at the beginning of the disclosure statement**);

(5) explanations of when penalties may be assessed against you because of specified prohibited or penalized activities concerning your IRA; and

(6) financial disclosure information which

(a) either projects value growth rates of your IRA under various contribution and retirement schedules, or describes the method of computing and allocating annual earnings and charges which may be assessed;

(b) describes whether, and for what period, the growth projections for the plan are guaranteed, or a statement of the earnings rate and terms on which the projection is based;

(c) states the sales commission to be charged in each year expressed as a percentage of $1,000; and

(d) states the proportional amount of any nondeductible life insurance which may be a feature of your IRA.

See **Publication 590**, Individual Retirement Arrangements (IRA's), available at most IRS offices, for a more complete explanation of the disclosure requirements.

In addition to this disclosure statement, the financial institution is required to provide you with a financial statement each year. It may be necessary to retain and refer to statements for more than one year in order to evaluate the investment performance of the IRA and in order that you will know how to report IRA distributions for tax purposes.

☆ U.S. Government Printing Office: 1988–201-993/60256

F I G U R E 9-7

Sample Disclosure Statement, Side 1

INDIVIDUAL RETIREMENT ACCOUNT DISCLOSURE STATEMENT

I. **LEGAL REQUIREMENTS FOR INDIVIDUAL RETIREMENT ACCOUNTS: 7-DAY REVOCATION PROCEDURE**

   A. **INTRODUCTION.** This disclosure statement provides a general explanation of the rules governing the operation and tax treatment of your individual retirement account ("IRA"). A copy of the application and the Agreement establishing the IRA accompanies this disclosure statement. Specific questions you may have regarding applicability of this information to your own tax situation should be referred to your personal tax advisor.

   B. **7-DAY REVOCATION PROCEDURE.** IRS regulations provide that, if you wish, you may revoke your IRA within 7 days after you are given the IRA disclosure statement. Since this disclosure statement is being provided to you at the time that you establish your IRA, you are entitled to revoke the IRA within 7 days after the date of establishment. You may revoke only by written notice mailed or delivered to the authorized officer at the institution's address. The name of the authorized officer and the institution's address appear on the IRA application. If mailed, the revocation notice shall be deemed mailed on the date of the postmark (or if by registered or certified mail, the date of registration or certification) if deposited in the United States mail in an envelope or other appropriate wrapper, first class postage prepaid, properly addressed to the authorized officer. Upon revocation within the 7-day period, you will be entitled to the return of the entire amount paid by you into the IRA, without adjustment for penalties or other charges. If you have questions about the written revocation procedure, you may call the authorized officer at the institution phone number that appears on the IRA application.

   C. **QUALIFICATION OF AN IRA.** The agreement under which your IRA is established is approved as to form by the IRS, such approval being a determination only as to form and not as to the merits of the IRA. When you fully execute an application adopting the Agreement, and the IRA is administered in accordance with applicable rules, you will have an IRA meeting the requirements of Internal Revenue Code Section 408(a). The following rules apply:

      1. **Limitation on Contributions.**

         a. **Regular.** Contributions to an IRA (other than certain rollovers) must be made in cash, and except for rollovers or simplified employee pension (SEP) contributions, cannot exceed the lesser of $2,000 or the amount of your compensation for the taxable year. (Compensation includes salaries, wages, professional fees, self-employment income other than amounts contributed to a Keogh plan, and other income for personal services that is includible in your gross income, as well as certain taxable alimony payments. Income from property, such as dividends, interest, capital gains or rent, and pension or annuity payments or other deferred compensation do not qualify as compensation for IRA purposes.) If both you and your spouse receive compensation during the year, each of you may contribute to your respective IRAs. You may or may not be able to deduct your IRA contributions depending on: (1) whether or not you are (or your spouse, if any, is) an active participant in an employer's retirement plan; (2) whether or not you have reached age 70½; and (3) how much adjusted gross income you (and your spouse, if any) have for the year. See Subsection D.1. below. Contributions for a given year may be made up to the due date for filing your tax return, not including extensions, but you must designate the year for which the contribution is made.

         b. **Spousal.** You may make a contribution to your spouse's IRA based on your own compensation if you file a joint return, your spouse does not receive, or elects to be treated as not receiving, compensation for the year, your spouse does not reach age 70½ during the year and the aggregate amount contributed to your IRA and your spouse's IRA does not exceed $2,250, with no more than $2,000 going into either spouse's IRA.

         c. **SEP.** Your employer may adopt a SEP plan under which he makes contributions to your IRA in amounts up to the lesser of 15% of compensation or $30,000. Amounts so contributed are not taxable until distributed to you from the IRA. If your employer has established a SEP, he will provide you with further information about it. If SEP contributions are made for you (or salary reduction contributions are made by you under a SEP permitting such contributions), the deductibility of any IRA contributions you make to yourself may be cut back or eliminated depending on the amount of your adjusted gross income for the year and your filing status. See Subsection D.1. below.

         d. **Employer or employee association.** Under Code Section 408(c), an employer may make a contribution to your IRA which is in lieu of your own contribution and is subject to the regular or spousal contribution limits discussed above. Any such contribution would be includible in your taxable income and would be subject to the same deductibility rules as if you made it yourself.

         e. **Rollovers.** If you receive a lump sum distribution, a distribution of your accumulated deductible employee contributions, a plan termination distribution, or a qualifying "partial" distribution from a qualified employee retirement plan, you may roll over into an IRA all or any part of the distribution if you do it within 60 days after the date you receive it. A plan termination distribution includes a distribution from a profit-sharing or stock option plan that occurs on or after the date the plan administrator informs the IRS that it intends to permanently discontinue contributions to the plan. The amount rolled over cannot exceed the amount that would be includible in taxable income. If you receive a plan distribution of property other than cash, under certain circumstances you may either roll over the property, or sell the property and roll over the cash proceeds. Consult your personal tax advisor for guidance.

         You don't get a deduction for a rollover, but the tax deferral you had under the employee plan continues for the IRA rollover until subsequently distributed to you. Your spouse may make a rollover of part or all of an eligible distribution from your employer's plan after your death to the spouse's own IRA.

         A partial distribution from a qualified plan may be rolled over into an IRA by you (or your surviving spouse) if: (1) a distribution is made in one taxable year of 50 percent or more of your plan balance (determined without regard to accumulated deductible employee contributions); (2) with respect to distributions made after March 31, 1988, the distribution is not one of a series of periodic payments; (3) the distribution is on account of your disability, death or separation from service; (4) the rollover is elected in a manner prescribed by Treasury regulations; and (5) other rollover requirements are met as described above.

         Amounts rolled over to an IRA from a qualified plan must consist solely of employer and, if any, deductible employee contributions, plus earnings on either of these or on other employee contributions. Nondeductible contributions may not be rolled over, but they also are not included in taxable income. Any part of the distribution retained except nondeductible employee contributions are taxable to you in the year of distribution. The written election you make to roll over a partial or total plan distribution (by executing the application form on which you have checked "rollover") is, as required by the IRS, irrevocable; that is, it cannot be revoked (after the 7-day revocation period) by later declaring the amount rolled over as income on the tax return filed for the year of the plan distribution.

         You may withdraw all or part of the funds in your IRA and roll the amount withdrawn into another IRA without adverse tax consequences provided you have not taken another distribution from that IRA within the immediately preceding 12-month period and rolled it over. This limitation does not apply to rollovers between a qualified plan and an IRA, or to direct transfers between IRA trustees or custodians.

      2. **Exclusive Use.** The IRA must be created in the United States for the exclusive use of you or your beneficiaries.

      3. **Limitation on Investment of IRA Funds.** No part of the IRA funds may be invested in life insurance contracts or in collectibles as defined in Code Section 408(m) (e.g., art works, rugs, antiques, gems, stamps, alcoholic beverages, certain other tangible personal property and coins other than coins issued under the laws of any state which are acquired by the IRA after November 10, 1988, and certain gold and silver coins minted by the U.S. Treasury beginning October 1, 1986).

      4. **Investment and Holding of Contributions.** Contributions under the IRA plan are held for you or any beneficiary you name. Your beneficiary may be your spouse, your estate, a dependent or any other person you designate in writing delivered to the Institution. Your interest in your IRA is nonforfeitable.

19417 (Rev. 7/89)   Copyright © 1989 United States League of Savings Institutions

F I G U R E 9-7, Continued

Sample Disclosure Statement, Side 2

Your IRA funds may be invested in deposits chosen by you from the class or classes of deposits offered by the Institution for the investment of IRA funds. The Institution has discretion to determine what types of deposits will be offered. If permitted by law and by the terms of your IRA agreement, the Institution may invest part or all of the funds in such other investments as you may direct. You are solely responsible for directing investment of your IRA funds, and the Institution will carry out its administrative responsibilities only in response to your specific investment instructions, given in a manner acceptable to the Institution. As required by law, your IRA funds will not be commingled with other property except in a common trust or custodial fund or common investment fund.

5. **Distribution Rules.**

   a. **Retirement distributions.** Once you attain age 59½ or become disabled, you may receive distributions from your IRA without a premature distribution tax penalty. You MUST take or begin to take distribution by your required beginning date, April 1 of the year following the year you reach age 70½. If you elect to take periodic life expectancy payments, the first distribution must be made by your required beginning date; the second distribution must be made by December 31 of the year in which your required beginning date occurs; and the distribution for each subsequent year must be made by December 31 of that year. The minimum required distribution for each year including the year you reach age 70½ generally is determined by dividing the balance at the beginning of such year by your life expectancy (or the joint life expectancy of you and your designated beneficiary), determined as described in Paragraph (c) below.

   If you fail to elect a method of distribution by your required beginning date, distribution of the full balance in your IRA must be made to you in a single sum as of that date if the balance in your IRA is $3,500 or less; if the IRA balance is more than $3,500, distribution will be made over a period equal to your nonrecalculated single life expectancy. You may accelerate such distribution by written notice to the Institution.

   b. **Distributions after your death.** If you are living on your required beginning date and begin to receive distributions under the foregoing rules, but die with funds still remaining in your IRA, your beneficiary must take distribution of the remaining funds at least as rapidly as under the distribution method in use on the date of your death.

   If you die before required distributions to you begin under the required minimum distribution rules, distribution of your IRA funds must be completed within 5 years after the end of the year in which your death occurs. However, if certain conditions are met, a longer payout schedule may be followed and if you have designated a beneficiary and distributions begin within one year after the end of the year in which your death occurs, distributions may be made over a period not exceeding the beneficiary's life or life expectancy.

   If you have designated your spouse as your beneficiary, the date on which distribution to your spouse must begin may be as late as December 31 of the year in which you would have reached age 70½. If your spouse dies before distributions are required to begin to the spouse, then similar conditions to those described in the preceding paragraph apply to a beneficiary designated by your surviving spouse to take the spouse's interest in your IRA upon the spouse's death.

   c. **Special rules regarding distributions.**

      (1) **Calculation of life expectancies.** Generally your life expectancy, the joint life expectancy of you and your designated beneficiary, or the life expectancy of your designated beneficiary in the case of distributions to be made after your death, is determined as of the year for which the first distribution is required to be made, reduced by the number of years elapsing since that time. However, your life expectancy and, if your spouse is your designated beneficiary, the joint life expectancy of you and the single life expectancy of your surviving spouse) may be recalculated no more than once each distribution year if you (or your surviving spouse) so elect in writing no later than your (or your spouse's) required beginning date. If life expectancy is not recalculated, payments may continue on the same schedule after your death. However, if life expectancies are being recalculated, then upon the death of either you or your beneficiary the payment schedule will be based solely on the life expectancy of the survivor. The Institution may impose a fee for its services with respect to life expectancy calculation. The life expectancy of a nonspouse designated beneficiary cannot be recalculated under any circumstances.

      (2) **Beneficiary identity.** Generally, for purposes of calculating distribution periods, all of your beneficiaries must be individuals if you want to use any life expectancy other than your own. Under certain circumstances, the individual beneficiaries of an irrevocable trust that is the named beneficiary can be treated as individual beneficiaries of your IRA. Consult your legal counsel for further guidance.

      (3) **Minimum distribution incidental benefit.** Any minimum distributions you are required to take for calendar years after 1988 also may be subject to a minimum distribution incidental benefit ("MDIB") requirement which reflects a Congressional intention that IRAs be used primarily to provide retirement benefits rather than death benefits or estate enhancement. Under the MDIB rule, if you use a joint life expectancy calculation involving a nonspouse designated beneficiary who is more than 10 years younger than you are, then during your lifetime, you must take a distribution of at least an amount determined by using a recalculated joint life expectancy factor based on an age differential of 10 years.

      (4) **Divorce.** If any part of your IRA is awarded to your spouse in a divorce action, the amount awarded will be treated as the spouse's IRA rather than as a distribution to you for tax purposes.

      (5) **Penalty.** A penalty tax as described in Part II, Section D, may be imposed if the minimum distribution requirements in this Subsection 5 are not met.

   d. **Additional information regarding the minimum distribution rules is available in IRS regulations and publications.**

   e. **IRA funds acquired by surviving spouse.** If you die and your IRA is inherited by your surviving spouse, it may be maintained as the spouse's own IRA.

D. **INCOME TAX CONSEQUENCES OF ESTABLISHING AN IRA.**

   1. **Deductibility of Contributions.** Your IRA contribution made within prescribed contribution limits is completely deductible in a given tax year if you are not yet age 70½ by the end of the year and neither you nor your spouse is an active participant in an employer retirement plan such as a qualified pension, profit-sharing or annuity plan (including a so-called "Keogh" or "HR-10" plan for the self-employed), a government plan or a SEP plan. If you are an active participant, your employer should indicate this by marking the box labeled "Pensions" on your Form W-2. For taxable years beginning after 1987, the active participant status of one spouse will affect the IRA deduction limit for contributions attributable to the other spouse unless the married couple lives apart. Married individuals who live apart for an entire year are treated as single taxpayers for the purpose of determining the deductibility of IRA contributions if: (1) separate returns are filed for such year and (2) they do not live together at any time during such taxable year. If you are (or your spouse, if any, is) an active participant in an employer's retirement plan, you may have a full, partial or no IRA deduction depending on your aggregated adjusted gross income ("AGI") level and filing status as shown in the following chart:

(1) If your filing status is:	(2) Your IRA contribution is:		
	(a) Fully deductible if AGI is:	(b) Partly deductible if AGI is:	(c) Not deductible if AGI is:
Single	$25,000 or less	$25,001-$34,999	$35,000 or more
Married, filing jointly	$40,000 or less	$40,001-$49,999	$50,000 or more
Married, filing separately	Not Applicable	Under $10,000	$10,000 or more
Married, filing separately and living apart	$25,000 or less	$25,001-$34,999	$35,000 or more

   Where only a partial deduction is permitted (Chart, column 2(b)), the formula for determining the nondeductible portion calls for a loss of $10 of deduction for each $50 of AGI exceeding the threshold limit of $40,000 for married persons filing jointly, $25,000 for single persons and $0 for married persons filing separately. The formula is:

   Excess AGI/$10,000 x $2,000 ($2,250 if spousal contribution) = Nondeductible portion of maximum allowable contribution.

F I G U R E 9-7, Continued

Sample Disclosure Statement, Side 3

A special rule permits at least a $200 deduction in the final stage of the deduction phaseout, even though the formula literally calls for less. The deduction falls to zero at AGI levels of $35,000, $50,000 and $10,000 respectively. For dollar amounts not ending in a multiple of ten, the nondeductible amount is rounded down to the next lower multiple of ten.

2. **Income tax treatment of withdrawals and distributions.** Generally, amounts distributed to you from your IRA are includible in taxable income when received. Not includible are amounts properly rolled over, any contribution removed on a timely basis (except the allocable income that must accompany such a distribution is subject to income taxation for the year during which the contribution was made) and amounts you contributed as nondeductible contributions. Premature distribution penalty tax also may apply as described in Part II, Section C.

II. PENALTIES, PROHIBITIONS AND OTHER TAX INFORMATION

A. **PROHIBITED TRANSACTIONS.** If you or your beneficiary engages in a prohibited transaction as described in Code Section 4975(c) with respect to your IRA, the IRA will lose its tax exemption and you will have to include the fair market value of the IRA in your taxable income for the year in which the prohibited transaction occurred. Examples of prohibited transactions are borrowing from, or selling property to, your IRA.

B. **USE OF IRA TO SECURE LOAN.** If you use all or any portion of your IRA as security for a loan, the portion so used is treated as distributed to you and must be included in taxable income in the year the IRA is so used.

C. **PREMATURE DISTRIBUTION PENALTY TAX.** Generally, taxable distributions made (or deemed made on account of a prohibited transaction or loan involving your IRA) before you reach 59½ will be subject to a premature distribution penalty tax of 10 percent unless you have become disabled or have died, or you roll the amount distributed into an IRA within 60 days. The penalty will not apply if distribution begins before age 59½ and is made in a series of substantially equal payments (not less frequently than annually) over your life expectancy or your and your designated beneficiary's joint life expectancy, and you do not attempt to alter the payment arrangement before the later of five years after payments begin or when you reach 59½, unless you die or become disabled before this time.

D. **INADEQUATE DISTRIBUTION PENALTY TAX.** Under Code Section 4974, your failure to take the minimum distributions required after you reach age 70½ or your beneficiary's failure to take distributions required after your death, as described in Part I, Section C.5, will result in a penalty tax of 50 percent of the difference between the amount required to be distributed and the amount actually distributed. The penalty could be waived if the inadequate distribution is due to reasonable error and reasonable corrective steps are being taken.

E. **EXCESS CONTRIBUTION PENALTY TAX.** A penalty of 6 percent will be imposed under Code Section 4973 for any amounts you contribute to your IRA that, as of the close of the tax year, exceed the sum of the amounts you are permitted to deduct and the amounts that are nondeductible because of your (or your spouse's) active participation in an employer's retirement plan, up to the limits described in Part I, Subsections C.1. and D.1. The penalty also will apply to amounts rolled over that exceed amounts permitted to be rolled over to your IRA. You can avoid the penalty if you do not claim a deduction and you withdraw the excess contribution and earnings attributable thereto by the due date for filing your tax return, including extensions.

Withdrawal of an excess contribution after your return due date will not avoid one-time imposition of the penalty, but will avoid the penalty in future years following the withdrawal. If the amount of the aggregate contributions for the year the excess contribution was made exceeded $2,250 or a deduction was taken for the amount withdrawn, such amount will be included in taxable income, and if you have not reached age 59½ or become disabled when you make such a withdrawal, you also will be liable for the 10 percent premature distribution penalty described in Section C above. If an excess contribution results from a rollover made because of erroneous tax information supplied by your employer on which you reasonably relied, the excess may be removed without incurring the 10 percent penalty even though the $2,250 limit is exceeded.

If not withdrawn, and if no deduction has been claimed, an excess contribution may be corrected by applying it against the contribution limit in a following year, or in other words, by undercontributing in a subsequent year. If an excess contribution is not corrected either by removal or by undercontributing, the 6 percent penalty tax continues to apply each year that the excess remains in the IRA.

F. **EXCESS DISTRIBUTION PENALTY TAX.** Effective for excess distributions made after December 31, 1986, you will be subject to a 15 percent penalty tax on such amounts. The term "excess distribution" means the aggregate amount of your retirement distribution from any plan, contract or account that at any time has been treated as a qualified employer plan or IRA and the total you receive during any calendar year, less certain exclusions, exceeds the greater of $150,000 or $112,500 as indexed for cost-of-living adjustments. The excess distribution tax does not apply to: (1) distributions after the participant's death; (2) rollover distributions; (3) distributions that represent nondeductible contributions; and (4) distributions of contributions and allocable income pursuant to Code Section 408(d)(4). If you had an accrued balance in your retirement plans of more than $562,500 on August 1, 1986, a special grandfather rule permits you to elect, on a Form 5329 filed with a tax return filed for tax year 1987 or 1988, to exempt from the tax distributions attributable to your accrued balance as of August 1, 1986. (The election or nonelection becomes irrevocable after the filing deadline for the taxable year beginning in 1988 has passed.) Although exempt from the tax, such distributions are included in determining whether an excess distribution has been made, and the alternative threshold of $150,000 is not available.

The excess distributions tax does not apply to payments made after your death, but your estate may be subject to a 15 percent "excess retirement accumulations" tax on the amount by which the present value of undistributed amounts in IRAs, plus your interests in qualified plans or annuities, exceeds the present value of an annuity providing annual payments equal to the annual limitations described above for a fixed period equal to your life expectancy immediately prior to your death. The tax may not be offset by any credits against the estate tax, such as the unified credit. If you elect the grandfather provision described above, special rules apply.

The $112,500 threshold for both types of taxes is subject to cost of living indexing. Consult the IRS or your tax advisor if you need guidance as to the applicability of these penalty taxes to your IRA.

G. **TAXPAYER REPORTING REQUIREMENT.** If you choose to make a nondeductible IRA contribution, you must report the amount on Form 8606 and attach the form to your tax return (Form 1040, 1040A or 1040NR) for the year the contribution is made. If you are married and your spouse also chooses to make a nondeductible IRA contribution, your spouse must report the amount on a separate Form 8606. A $100 penalty will be imposed if you overstate the amount of your nondeductible contributions. If you are required to file a Form 8606 and you fail to do so, a $50 penalty will be assessed for each failure to file unless you can show that such failure was due to reasonable cause. If a transaction has occurred for which a penalty tax is imposed under Section C, D, E, or F, you are required by the IRS to attach to your annual income tax return an information return Form 5329 on which you report the transaction and calculate the penalty tax due. If your estate becomes subject to the excess retirement accumulations penalty tax, your executor must file Schedule S (Form 706) with the estate tax return.

H. **WITHHOLDING.** Federal income tax will be withheld from your IRA distributions, generally at the rate of 10 percent, unless you elect not to have tax withheld.

I. **ADDITIONAL INFORMATION.** Additional information about the rules governing your IRA is provided in IRS Publication 590, which is available at any IRS district office.

F I G U R E 9-7, Continued

Sample Disclosure Statement, Side 4

III. FINANCIAL DISCLOSURE

A. **VALUE OF YOUR IRA.** The balance in your IRA can be expected to increase as a direct result of your contributions and the return on the investment of IRA funds. Information about the projected financial future of your IRA is provided in:

☐ Optional statement 1 below   ☐ Optional statement 2 below   ☐ Attached supplemental statement

Optional Statement 1. Projection of IRA Value when amount is guaranteed over period of time or projection of growth in value can reasonably be made.

You have chosen to invest your contribution to this IRA in a _____ at an interest rate of _____ percent, compounded
                                        (type of deposit)

_____, for a term of _____
(interval)   (number of years, months or days)

The nature of the investments you have chosen to fund your IRA is such that it is possible to make a reasonable projection as to the amount that would be available to you if you withdraw your IRA balance at specified times in the future. To provide standard information that you can readily apply to your own situation, it is assumed that an annual contribution of $1,000 will be made on the first day of each taxable year* and that you withdraw your IRA balance at the end of the first five years and at the end of each of the years in which you reach age 60, 65 and 70.

*Note: If your initial and only contribution to the IRA is a rollover or transfer, the following projections are based on the assumption that the rollover or transfer is made in the amount of $1,000 on the first day of the year and that no other contributions are to be made.

The amounts shown below are projections only. The rates and terms of your investment are established by the terms of the contracts for the deposits or investments you have chosen. If the funds are invested in fixed-term certificates of deposit, the projected amounts may be reduced by imposition of a penalty for withdrawal prior to maturity, if so provided in the deposit contract. The amounts shown below are based on: an interest rate of _____ percent, a premature withdrawal penalty of _____ months, and an annual trustee/custodial fee of $_____. **

		Amount available to you after premature withdrawal, and
At end of:	Total accumulation	trustee/custodial fees, if any
First year	$ _____	$ _____
Second year	$ _____	$ _____
Third year	$ _____	$ _____
Fourth year	$ _____	$ _____
Fifth year	$ _____	$ _____
Year you reach age 60	$ _____	$ _____
Year you reach age 65	$ _____	$ _____
Year you reach age 70	$ _____	$ _____

**Note that the interest rate may be no greater than that of the investment you purchased to establish this IRA. The premature withdrawal penalty or trustee/custodial fees (indicated in B. below) must be as great as that, if any, associated with this investment. The interest compounding interval must be at least that associated with this investment, i.e., if the investment provides for quarterly compounding, the projections may be based on quarterly, semiannual or annual compounding.

These projections at the ages specified reflect the institution's policy that the penalty for early withdrawal from a fixed-term deposit _____ be waived when funds are withdrawn for retirement purposes.
(will or will not)

Optional Statement 2. Information provided to you in lieu of financial projections when amount is not guaranteed and projection of growth cannot reasonably be made.

The nature of the investments you have chosen to fund your IRA is such that a projection cannot reasonably be made. In its place, the following information describes, in nontechnical terms, the various factors that may affect the net amount available to you from your IRA:

(a) Type and amount of charge that may be made against a contribution: _____

(b) Method used for computing and allocating annual earnings: _____

(c) Charge or charges that may be applied to earnings in determining the net amount of money available to you: _____

(d) Growth in the value of your IRA is neither guaranteed nor projected.

(e) The portion of each $1,000 that is attributable to the cost of life insurance for each year during which contributions are to be made is $_____ (if none, state "0"). Any amount shown here is not deductible.

B. **INSTITUTION'S FEES AND OTHER CHARGES.** The institution may impose reasonable fees for its fiduciary services as trustee or custodian, including reasonable charges for preparing reports, keeping records, providing forms, and such other services as may be required to administer the IRA. The institution also may charge to the IRA account the reasonable costs of fiduciary insurance and counsel fees. Fees and costs imposed under this section B will not be charged directly to and deducted from the IRA if you pay them out-of-pocket.

Current fees or fee schedule: _____

F I G U R E 9-7, Continued

Sample Disclosure Statement, Side 5

The charts below and on the reverse side may be used to calculate the projected IRA balances to be provided in Optional Statement 1 of the Financial Disclosure Statement. The projections assume annual compounding and are illustrated assuming varying interest rates and premature withdrawal penalties. For purposes of the total accumulation column, use the results shown for no penalty. For the column that reflects premature withdrawal penalties, use the results shown for the closest penalty (i.e., equal to or greater than) to that of the investment the customer has chosen. If the institution waives penalties on distributions that occur after the customer reaches age 59½, use the no penalty results for projections of IRA balances at the end of the years in which the customer reaches age 60, 65 and 70. The charts below are to be used for regular contributions and the charts on the reverse side for other contributions, i.e., rollover and transfer contributions. The blank areas of the charts are for those ages that the customer has already reached prior to establishing this IRA and are not applicable. THESE CHARTS MAY NOT BE USED IF THE INSTITUTION CHARGES TRUSTEE/CUSTODIAL FEES.

REGULAR CONTRIBUTIONS

F I G U R E 9-7, Continued

Sample Disclosure Statement, Side 6

OTHER CONTRIBUTIONS

5% INTEREST

Year	No Penalty	3 Month Penalty	6 Month Penalty
1	1050	1037	1025
2	1102	1089	1076
3	1157	1143	1129
4	1214	1199	1185
5	1274	1259	1244

Age	No Penalty			3 Month Penalty			6 Month Penalty		
	$60	$65	$70	$60	$65	$70	$60	$65	$70
18	8082	10313	13159	7986	10190	13003	7890	10067	12846
19	7698	9822	12533	7604	9705	12384	7515	9588	12235
20	7332	9355	11937	7244	9243	11785	7157	9132	11653
21	6983	8910	11369	6900	8804	11233	6817	8698	11098
22	6651	8486	10828	6572	8385	10699	6493	8284	10570
23	6335	8082	10313	6259	7986	10190	6184	7890	10067
24	6034	7698	9822	5962	7604	9705	5890	7515	9588
25	5747	7332	9355	5678	7244	9243	5610	7157	9132
26	5474	6983	8910	5409	6900	8804	5344	6817	8698
27	5214	6651	8486	5152	6572	8385	5090	6493	8284
28	4966	6335	8082	4907	6259	7986	4848	6184	7890
29	4730	6034	7698	4673	5962	7604	4617	5890	7515
30	4505	5747	7332	4451	5678	7244	4398	5610	7157
31	4291	5474	6983	4240	5409	6900	4189	5344	6817
32	4087	5214	6651	4038	5152	6572	3990	5090	6493
33	3893	4966	6335	3846	4907	6259	3800	4848	6184
34	3708	4730	6034	3664	4673	5962	3620	4617	5890
35	3532	4505	5747	3490	4451	5678	3448	4398	5610
36	3364	4291	5474	3324	4240	5409	3284	4189	5344
37	3204	4087	5214	3166	4038	5152	3128	3990	5090
38	3052	3893	4966	3015	3846	4907	2979	3800	4848
39	2907	3708	4730	2872	3664	4673	2836	3620	4617
40	2769	3532	4505	2736	3490	4451	2703	3448	4398
41	2638	3364	4291	2606	3324	4240	2575	3284	4189
42	2513	3204	4087	2483	3166	4038	2453	3128	3990
43	2394	3052	3893	2365	3015	3846	2337	2979	3800
44	2280	2907	3708	2253	2872	3664	2226	2836	3620
45	2172	2769	3532	2146	2736	3490	2120	2703	3448
46	2069	2638	3364	2044	2606	3324	2020	2575	3284
47	1971	2513	3204	1947	2483	3166	1924	2453	3128
48	1878	2394	3052	1855	2365	3015	1833	2337	2979
49	1789	2280	2907	1767	2253	2872	1746	2226	2836
50	1704	2172	2769	1683	2146	2736	1663	2120	2703
51	1623	2069	2638	1603	2044	2606	1584	2020	2575
52	1546	1971	2513	1527	1947	2483	1509	1924	2453
53	1473	1878	2394	1455	1855	2365	1438	1833	2337
54	1403	1789	2280	1386	1767	2253	1370	1746	2226
55	1337	1704	2172	1321	1683	2146	1305	1663	2120
56	1274	1623	2069	1259	1603	2044	1244	1584	2020
57	1214	1546	1971	1199	1527	1947	1185	1509	1924
58	1157	1473	1878	1143	1455	1855	1129	1438	1833
59	1102	1403	1789	1089	1386	1767	1076	1370	1746
60	1050	1337	1704	1037	1321	1683	1025	1305	1663
61		1274	1623		1259	1603		1244	1584
62		1214	1546		1199	1527		1185	1509
63		1157	1473		1143	1455		1129	1438
64		1102	1403		1089	1386		1076	1370
65		1050	1337		1037	1321		1025	1305
66			1274			1259			1244
67			1214			1199			1185
68			1157			1143			1129
69			1102			1089			1076
70			1050			1037			1025

7% INTEREST

Year	No Penalty	3 Month Penalty	6 Month Penalty
1	1070	1052	1035
2	1144	1125	1107
3	1224	1204	1184
4	1309	1287	1266
5	1400	1377	1354

Age	No Penalty			3 Month Penalty			6 Month Penalty		
	$60	$65	$70	$60	$65	$70	$60	$65	$70
18	18237	25575	35868	17938	25156	35281	17640	24738	34695
19	17044	23902	33522	16765	23511	32973	16486	23120	32425
20	15929	22339	31329	15668	21973	30816	15408	21608	30304
21	14887	20878	29280	14643	20536	28801	14400	20195	28322
22	13914	19513	27365	13686	19194	26917	13458	18875	26470
23	13004	18237	25575	12791	17938	25156	12579	17640	24738
24	12154	17044	23902	11955	16765	23511	11756	16486	23120
25	11359	15929	22339	11173	15668	21973	10987	15408	21608
26	10616	14887	20878	10442	14643	20536	10269	14400	20195
27	9922	13914	19513	9759	13686	19194	9597	13458	18875
28	9273	13004	18237	9121	12791	17938	8970	12579	17640
29	8667	12154	17044	8525	11955	16765	8383	11756	16486
30	8100	11359	15929	7967	11173	15668	7835	10987	15408
31	7571	10616	14887	7447	10442	14643	7323	10269	14400
32	7074	9922	13914	6960	9759	13686	6845	9597	13458
33	6614	9273	13004	6506	9121	12791	6398	8970	12579
34	6182	8667	12154	6081	8525	11955	5980	8383	11756
35	5778	8100	11359	5683	7967	11173	5589	7835	10987
36	5400	7571	10616	5311	7447	10442	5223	7323	10269
37	5047	7076	9922	4964	6960	9759	4882	6845	9597
38	4717	6614	9273	4640	6506	9121	4563	6398	8970
39	4408	6182	8667	4337	6081	8525	4265	5980	8383
40	4121	5778	8100	4053	5683	7967	3986	5589	7835
41	3852	5400	7571	3789	5311	7447	3726	5223	7323
42	3600	5047	7076	3541	4964	6960	3482	4882	6845
43	3365	4717	6614	3310	4640	6506	3255	4563	6398
44	3145	4409	6182	3093	4337	6081	3042	4265	5980
45	2940	4121	5778	2892	4053	5683	2844	3986	5589
46	2748	3852	5400	2703	3789	5311	2658	3726	5223
47	2569	3600	5047	2527	3541	4964	2485	3482	4882
48	2401	3365	4717	2361	3310	4640	2322	3255	4563
49	2244	3145	4409	2207	3093	4337	2171	3042	4265
50	2098	2940	4121	2063	2892	4053	2029	2844	3986
51	1961	2748	3852	1929	2703	3789	1897	2658	3726
52	1833	2569	3600	1803	2527	3541	1773	2485	3482
53	1714	2401	3365	1686	2361	3310	1658	2322	3255
54	1602	2244	3145	1576	2207	3093	1550	2171	3042
55	1498	2098	2940	1473	2063	2892	1449	2029	2844
56	1400	1961	2748	1377	1929	2703	1354	1897	2658
57	1309	1833	2569	1287	1803	2527	1266	1773	2485
58	1224	1714	2401	1204	1686	2361	1184	1658	2322
59	1144	1602	2244	1125	1576	2207	1107	1550	2171
60	1070	1498	2098	1052	1473	2063	1035	1449	2029
61		1400	1961		1377	1929		1354	1897
62		1309	1833		1287	1803		1266	1773
63		1224	1714		1204	1686		1184	1658
64		1144	1602		1125	1576		1107	1550
65		1070	1498		1052	1473		1035	1449
66			1400			1377			1354
67			1309			1287			1266
68			1224			1204			1184
69			1144			1125			1107
70			1070			1052			1035

F I G U R E 9-8

Designation of Beneficiary

INDIVIDUAL RETIREMENT ACCOUNT
APPLICATION AND BENEFICIARY DESIGNATION

File or Account Number

State of_____
County of_____ } SS

INSTITUTION NAME
Street Address
City, State, Zip
Phone Number

NAME AND ADDRESS

1. Name of Participant _____ Date of Birth _____
2. Social Security Number _____ Home Phone (____)____—____
3. Street _____ City _____ State ___ Zip ___

ACCOUNT INFORMATION

4. Amount of Initial Deposit $_____ Allocated: $_____ for tax year _____
   $_____ for tax year _____
5. If not regular IRA contribution indicate type:
   ☐ Rollover ☐ Spousal ☐ Transfer ☐ Divorced Spouse ☐ Other
6. Investment direction by Participant (Choose one): ☐ Deposit Accounts only ☐ Alternative Investments (requires consent of Institution)

FUNDS INVESTED PURSUANT TO THIS AGREEMENT ARE NOT INSURED BY THE FEDERAL SAVINGS AND LOAN INSURANCE CORPORATION ("FSLIC") MERELY BECAUSE THE TRUSTEE OR CUSTODIAN IS AN INSTITUTION THE ACCOUNTS OF WHICH ARE COVERED BY SUCH INSURANCE. ONLY INVESTMENTS IN THE ACCOUNTS OF SUCH AN INSTITUTION ARE INSURED BY THE FSLIC, SUBJECT TO ITS RULES AND REGULATIONS.

BENEFICIARY DESIGNATION*

Primary Beneficiary	Contingent Beneficiary
In the event of my death, I name as Primary Beneficiary(ies):	If all of the Primary Beneficiaries die before me, I name as Contingent Beneficiary(ies):
1.	1.
Name _____ Relationship _____	Name _____ Relationship _____
Social Security Number _____ Date of Birth _____	Social Security Number _____ Date of Birth _____
Address	Address
2.	2.
Name _____ Relationship _____	Name _____ Relationship _____
Social Security Number _____ Date of Birth _____	Social Security Number _____ Date of Birth _____
Address	Address

(The foregoing beneficiary designation is subject to the conditions listed on the reverse side of this document.)

*If Applicant has attained age 70½ and is receiving required minimum distributions, a designation of beneficiary may affect the amount of the required payouts.

SIGNATURE AND ACCEPTANCE

By my signature below, I apply, and Institution by its signature accepts my application, to participate in the Individual Retirement Account Plan of the Institution subject to the terms of the U.S. League of Savings Institutions' IRA Agreement which is incorporated in this Application by reference and the rules applicable to the savings deposit or class of deposits or other investments, if any, available to participants in such plan for the investment of contributions thereunder.

I acknowledge that I have received a copy of the rules of deposit classification and an IRA disclosure statement. The Institution is authorized to act without further inquiry in accordance with writings bearing my signature. I understand that I may revoke the Agreement by written notice to the Institution within seven (7) days after the date of the Agreement as specified below.

Witness (Required for Beneficiary Designation): Date _____

Signature of Witness (Witness should not be a beneficiary) _____ Signature of Participant _____

Address of Witness _____ Name of Financial Institution _____

City _____ State _____ Zip _____ as Trustee or Custodian under the Agreement hereby acknowledges receipt of the above Designation of Beneficiary and Application to participate in the Individual Retirement Account Plan, consenting to all elections made herein.

By Authorized Officer _____

USL 19414 (3/88)   Copyright 1988 United States League of Savings Institutions   Customer Copy

F I G U R E 9-9

IRA Deposit Slip

IRA DEPOSIT AUTHORIZATION

DATE _____ SOCIAL SECURITY NUMBER_____ ACCOUNT NO. _____

NAME _____

ADDRESS_____

Type of Deposit:	Deposit Allocated		CASH	
☐ Regular or Spousal	$_____ for tax year _____	C H		
☐ Transfer	$_____ for tax year _____	E C		
☐ Rollover		K S		
☐ Other _____		TOTAL		
Under penalties of perjury, I certify that my contribution relates to the tax year I have indicated.		LESS CASH RECEIVED		
Depositor Signature _____		NET DEPOSIT		

- the tax year for which the contribution is being made (if applicable);

- any necessary investment information that pertains to the specific transaction;

- the participant's signature.

Generally, IRA applications for new plans request the applicant to indicate the type of IRA contribution being made. Also, some institutions have developed special deposit forms for participants to use when making additional IRA deposits. Figure 9-9 shows a sample IRA deposit form.

Optional Documentation

In addition to completing the above documents when establishing an IRA—the plan agreement, disclosure statement, application and designation of beneficiary and deposit information—individual institutions may require further documentation. IRA counselors may prepare certificates of deposit or other evidences of IRA investments such as statements or receipts. Some institutions also require employees to use special wording on evidences of account to indicate ownership of the accounts as IRAs.

Many institutions use signature cards (see Figure 9-10) to document ownership of their IRAs. Institutions commonly use signature cards to show that an account relationship exists. However, many institutions use other methods such as the IRA trust agreement as means of identification.

Distributions

Distributions are withdrawals from retirement plans. All tax-deferred retirement plan participants, or their beneficiaries, begin receiving distributions from their retirement plan funds at some point in time. To ensure that a participant uses such funds for retirement, the Code has established certain restrictions on the availability of retirement plan funds. The Code permits participants to take distributions as early as age 59½ without IRS penalty (or sooner for specific reasons such as disability). Participants also must take minimum distributions in a prescribed manner once they reach age 70½.

The IRS penalizes participants with excise taxes if they do not follow the retirement plan rules. Because the rules are complex, many participants depend on financial in-

F I G U R E 9-10

IRA Signature Card

Individual Retirement Account   Acct. No._____

_____, Fiduciary
(Name of Savings Institution)

The undersigned, as Fiduciary, officially affirmed on_____
(Date)
by an agreement known as the United States League of Savings Institutions Form 5305 (5305-A) Individual Retirement Account
as executed by

_____   _____
(Participant)   (Social Security No.)

hereby applies for a savings account in the savings institution specified as trustee or custodian ("Fiduciary") above and for
the issuance of evidence thereof. In consideration of your acceptance of this application, the undersigned hereby certifies that
the funds which are offered to you concurrently herewith for placement in a savings account and any funds which later may
be placed in the same savings account are funds properly within its custody which may be lawfully invested in or placed in the
same savings account in said institution in accordance with authority duly vested in the undersigned as fiduciary, all as described
above. A specimen signature of the Fiduciary is shown below and you are hereby authorized to act without further inquiry in
accordance with writings bearing such signature, or the signature of any duly authorized agent of the Fiduciary. You are authorized
to supply any endorsement for the undersigned on any check or other instrument tendered for this account and you are hereby
relieved of any liability in connection with collection of such items which are handled by you without negligence, and you shall
not be liable for the acts of your agents, sub-agents or others or for any casualty. Withdrawals may not be made on account
of such items until collected, and any amount not collected may be charged back to this account, including expense incurred,
and any other outside expense incurred relative to this account may be charged to it. In this instrument except as otherwise
indicated the singular includes the plural.

For identification:

Account of:_____   _____
(Participant)   (Name of Fiduciary Savings Institution)

By_____
_____   (Agent)
(Signature of Participant)

USL 19463 (3/88) IRA (Fiduciary)   ©1988 United States League of Savings Institutions

stitution employees to help them avoid penalty taxes. To
aid customers, employees can give general information
and refer customers to other sources for specific advice.
Employees should be able to explain general rules for permitted and required distributions. Employees also should
be able to make participants aware of those actions for
which the IRS will impose penalty taxes. In addition to
avoiding penalty taxes, many participants are interested

in minimizing the tax liabilities on their distributions. To help participants reduce their taxes, employees should advise them to consult an attorney or reliable tax advisor. Also, because the rules regarding distributions are complex, employees should be careful that participants do not mistake general information for specific advice applicable to individual circumstances.

Allowable Distributions

An IRA participant between the ages of 59½ and 70½ may take distributions for any amount, but the recipient's tax liabilities will depend on whether he or she made any nondeductible contributions. If the participant made deductible contributions only, any amount withdrawn that is not redeposited as a rollover contribution will be fully taxable to him or her. If the participant also made nondeductible (after-tax) contributions, a portion of the distribution will not be taxable. The participant is responsible for keeping track of deductible and nondeductible amounts held in his or her IRA by filing Form 8606. The IRS has developed a formula for calculating the nontaxable portion of a distribution when participants have made nondeductible contributions. The formula is as follows:

$$\text{Nontaxable Amount} = \text{Total Distributions for the Year} \times \frac{\text{Total Nondeductible Contributions}}{\text{Year-end Balance of All IRAs plus Distributions for the Year}}$$

The following seven exceptions to the general rules permit participants to take distributions before age 59½ without incurring a 10% tax penalty:

- To cure an excess contribution if a deduction has not been taken for such amount. Before the individual's filing date, however, earnings attributable to the excess contribution must also be withdrawn and are subject to the 10% penalty; after the individual's filing date, earnings attributable to the excess contribution are not withdrawn.

- To remove any nondeductible contribution (and earnings) made for a taxable year before the individual's filing date for that year. However, the earnings attributable to the contribution are subject to the 10% tax penalty.

- To make a rollover contribution within 60 days.

- To distribute funds to a beneficiary if the participant has died.

- To allow a disabled participant to withdraw funds.

- To transfer funds to a spouse's ownership due to a divorce.

- To establish annuitized payments over the individual's life expectancy.

Required Distributions

By April 1 of the calendar year following the year in which the participant attains age 70½, the participant must begin taking distributions of a prescribed amount, known as required minimum distributions.

The taxable year in which a participant reaches age 70½ is calculated from his or her birth date. Participants whose 70th birthdays are on or before June 30 must begin taking distributions by April 1 of the calendar year following the year in which they become 70 years old. Participants whose 70th birthdays are on or after July 1 must begin taking distributions by April 1 of the calendar year following the year in which they become age 71.

The participant may delay the first required distribution attributable to the 70½ year. If the participant delays receipt for the first year, two distributions will be required in the second year, because distributions must be taken *for* the year in which the participant reaches age 70½ and *every year thereafter.* In this case, the distribution attributable to the 70½ year (first required minimum distribution) must be made by April 1 following the 70½ year. The second distribution must be made by December 31 of the same year.

Participants should be aware that distributions are taxable income *in* the year of receipt. Receiving two years of required distributions in the same taxable year may not be advantageous to participants. Therefore, participants may need to seek professional tax advice before deciding to delay receipt of the first required distribution.

Some IRA plan agreements provide that if a participant has not made a decision regarding the terms and form of the minimum distribution payment by April 1 of the applicable year, the financial institution will distribute the funds to the participant as a lump sum. Then the funds will be included in the participant's gross income for the year and taxed as ordinary income. To avoid this harsh result, some IRA plans provide for lifetime installment payments in lieu of the lump sum distribution. As a matter of public relations, many institutions contact participants before they reach age 70 to set up a procedure for distribution.

Under the Code, a retirement plan participant has three methods of distribution from which to choose. The participant may:

- withdraw the entire IRA balance in a lump-sum distribution by April of the year following the year in which he or she reaches age 70½;

- direct the trustee to purchase a single life annuity or a joint life and last survivor annuity for the participant, covering the participant and his or her designated beneficiary; or

- begin to receive distributions from the IRA over a predetermined time period (called period certain) not longer than the life expectancy of the participant or the joint life and last survivor expectancy of the participant and his or her designated beneficiary.

These participant decisions are important because they affect the amount of taxable income to the participant. Also, irrevocable elections can affect the options available to surviving beneficiaries. Therefore, the participant should be strongly urged to seek the advice of a professional tax attorney *before* electing the choices available for receiving required distributions.

Because distributions are taxable, the Code provides procedures for withholding taxes from IRA, SEP and other plan distributions. Institutions must withhold income taxes from the IRA payments in an amount equal to 10% of the distribution unless the recipient elects no withholding. The trustee institution must notify payment recipients of their right to elect out of withholding. The

Code specifies how often the institution must notify participants of this election. Also, the IRS has procedures for institutions to follow in remitting amounts withheld from distributions to the U.S. Treasury.

Penalized Distributions

To discourage tax-deferred retirement plan participants from using their funds for other than retirement purposes, the Code permits the IRS to impose tax penalties for certain early or premature distributions, underdistributions or excess accumulations, and excess distributions. Examples of actions that may result in penalized distributions are the use of IRA funds as collateral for a loan or an attempt to accumulate IRA funds as an estate-building device rather than for their stated purpose of retirement funding. Since such tax penalties can be substantial, trustee institution employees should refer to the other publications listed in footnote 1 for detailed information.

Early (Premature) Distribution Penalties   Participants will incur tax penalties for withdrawals made before age 59½ if they do not qualify as one of the permitted exceptions previously explained.

Underdistribution (Excess Accumulation) Penalty
If required minimum distributions are not taken, the IRS may impose a 50% penalty on the excess accumulation—the difference between the amount that should have been distributed from the IRA and the amount actually distributed. The IRS can impose this penalty if the participant does not receive the required minimum distributions on a timely basis or a lesser amount than he or she

was required to receive. Also, beneficiaries can incur tax penalties if they fail to take their required minimum distributions.

The following example illustrates the tax consequences of an underdistribution or excess accumulation. Rudi Schmidt's required distribution for the taxable year was $10,000, but he received only $6,000. Therefore, Rudi is subject to a penalty tax of 50% of the excess accumulation of $4,000 (the difference between $10,000 and $6,000), which equals $2,000. The $2,000 penalty was in addition to Rudi's ordinary income tax on the $6,000 distribution and any other income he received that year.

Excess Distribution Penalties The IRS may impose excess distribution tax penalties in two situations. One involves the participant taking excess distributions. The other may occur after the participant's death if the decedent's total IRA and qualified plan funds exceed a certain amount. In both situations, the 15% tax on the excess is in addition to any regular income or estate tax that applies.

Reporting Requirements

As required by the Code and as part of their fiduciary responsibilities, trustee institutions must report certain information to the participant and to the appropriate government agencies. Basically this includes reporting all activity that has occurred on the account and identifying the tax year in which the activity applies.

In addition, IRA participants must supply certain information to the IRS. They must complete the appropriate lines on IRS Form 1040 if they have made deductible contributions or rollover contributions. They must also file Form 8606 if their account balances contain nondeductible contributions, even if they need not file a federal income tax return. Another reason a participant has to file additional tax forms is to report IRA transactions subject to IRS penalties. The form for reporting tax penalties applicable to penalized activities is Form 5329.

QUALIFIED PLANS

A *qualified retirement plan* is an employee benefit plan that contains provisions satisfying specific IRS guidelines. Plans that satisfy these guidelines "qualify" for special tax treatment under Internal Revenue Code Section 401(a). By meeting these requirements, the employer that establishes a qualified retirement plan and the employees who will benefit from it are entitled to favorable tax treatment. An easy way to distinguish between an IRA and a qualified plan is to keep in mind that an individual opens an IRA, while a business opens a qualified plan. Incorporated businesses must have approval of their board of directors before they can establish a qualified plan.

A Keogh plan is a special name for the type of qualified plan that is established for unincorporated businesses, such as self-employed individuals or partnerships. A *Keogh plan* is defined as a tax-deferred, trusteed savings plan that allows self-employed individuals (those who own their own unincorporated businesses) to accumulate funds for retirement. Employers who establish Keogh plans for themselves must make the benefits available to eligible employees. In general, the rules for Keogh plans are now basically the same as those applicable to corporate plans.

Qualified plans such as Keoghs and corporate plans may be either a defined contribution plan or a defined benefit plan. Under a *defined contribution plan*, the employer makes contributions to the accounts of plan participants according to an allocation formula. The participants' account balances at retirement age determine the retirement benefits.

The three basic types of qualified defined contribution plans are the money purchase pension, the profit-sharing plan and the thrift/savings plan. (The last type is covered in the next section of this chapter.) With a *money purchase pension plan*, the employer contributes a specified percentage of the employee's annual salary up to certain limits. A *profit-sharing plan* is similar to a money purchase plan except that employers can change the percentage contributed each year.

Under a *defined benefit plan*, each participant's benefit is determined from a formula that reflects the employee's retirement income needs. Generally, service, earnings and Social Security benefits are incorporated into the benefit formula. The amount of the annual plan contribution is calculated with an actuarial valuation and is the amount needed from year to year to accumulate plan assets sufficient to pay each participant's projected retirement benefit. Plan assets accumulate as they would in a defined contribution plan; however, contribution requirements rather than retirement benefit levels change. The Code specifies the maximum annual contributions or benefit for both types of plans.

Eligibility, Contributions and Distributions

Keoghs and other qualified retirement plans for businesses are subject to many rules affecting eligibility and contributions. This section briefly describes the general rules that apply to qualified plans pertaining to age, compensation, allowable contribution limits and distributions.

Age

Qualified plans have several age requirements. No minimum age is required for establishing a qualified plan, but if employers set a qualifying age for their employees, it may be no more than 21 years. Contributions for employees must continue regardless of their age until they retire. However, all employees must begin to receive required minimum distributions for the year in which they attain age 70½ and each year thereafter.

Compensation

Qualified plans have the following compensation-related requirements:

- In general, a qualified plan is one method for an employer to compensate employees. Self-employed individuals may also establish qualified plans, or Keoghs, if they have earned income.

- To be considered self-employed, the participant must render a personal service to the business. If an individual merely provides financial backing for a business and receives a share of the profits, he or she is not eligible to open a Keogh.

- Individuals who are self-employed part time and work full time at a different job are still eligible to open Keogh plans based on their income from self-employment.

- Self-employed individuals or owner-employees who have established Keogh plans for themselves must cover their employees also. Keogh plans must provide coverage for those employees who are age 21 or older and have one year of service. The cost of covering employees is a deductible business expense for the owner-employee.

Allowable Contributions

Different deadlines apply to establishing plans and making contributions. Qualified plans must be established no later than the last day of the employer's taxable year. Employers have until their filing date plus any extensions for making the balance of their allowable contributions applicable for the previous tax year.

In defined contribution plans, the contribution limits refer to the "annual additions" to a participant's account. Annual additions are funds contributed to a participant's account from three sources:

- employer contributions;

- all employee contributions except rollover contributions;

- forfeitures (nonvested employer contributions that other employees forfeit when they leave the company before becoming fully vested).

The deduction limits differ for the two basic types of defined contribution plans (money purchase and profit-sharing plans). Although the dollar limitation is the same for both types, the contribution percentage of compensation that may be deducted from income limitation differs.

Under defined contribution plans that are money purchase plans, the annual additions to a participant's account, which cannot exceed the lesser of:

- $30,000 (or, if greater, 25% of the indexed defined benefit plan dollar limit); or

- 25% of the participant's compensation (earned income for self-employed individuals) for the year.

Under defined contribution plans that are profit-sharing plans, the annual additions to a participant's account cannot exceed the lesser of:

- $30,000 (or, if greater, 25% of the indexed defined benefit plan dollar limit); or

- 15% of the participant's compensation (earned income in the case of self-employed individuals) for the year.

The highest annual benefit a participant in a defined benefit plan can receive is the lesser of:

- $90,000 subject to annual cost-of-living adjustments (COLA) ($98,064 for 1989); or

- 100% of the participant's (including self-employed individuals) average compensation for the three consecutive years with the highest compensation during which he or she was an active participant.

Because business owners can deduct the contributions made for employees as a retirement plan expense, self-employed individuals must adjust the percentage of compensation they are permitted to contribute into their own plans. Self-employed individuals must reduce their earned income by the amounts of their deductible Keogh contributions. This effectively lowers the self-employed person's contribution limit of 25% or 15% of compensation for money purchase and profit-sharing plans to 20% and 13.04%, respectively. Self-employed individuals can determine their appropriate percentages by formula or from tables.

Participants may be able to increase their allowable contributions. If their plans provide, participants may make nondeductible voluntary contributions. Although these additional contributions cannot be deducted, the income earned on them is tax deferred. Nondeductible voluntary contributions are counted toward the overall limit on annual additions. Also, in addition to making allowable contributions into a qualified plan, participants may have IRAs. However, the deductibility of their IRA contributions may be affected by their active participant status under a qualified plan. Employer contributions to a Keogh plan or other qualified plan that exceed the deductible limits are subject to 10% cumulative excise tax until the excess is eliminated. Therefore, a plan administrator must carefully monitor the amount of employer and employee contributions to avoid penalties.

Distributions
Generally, the same distribution rules that apply to IRAs apply to distributions from qualified plans. In addition, the Code requires married participants in certain qualified plans to follow special procedures to receive distributions in a form other than a survivor annuity. The request to receive distributions in a form other than a survivor annuity has certain age and spousal restrictions, as well as notice requirements, and is usually attached to or included on any designation of beneficiary and distribution forms.

Documentation and Reporting Requirements

The self-employed individual or employer must execute certain documents to establish a qualified plan. Regulations require employers to provide plan participants with a summary explanation of the plan as well as annual statements similar to those provided to IRA participants by the trustee institution.

The documents generally required for opening any qualified plan are:

- adoption agreement;

- plan and trust agreement; and

- designation of beneficiary.

As tax laws change, existing plans must be amended to comply with new regulations.

Some of the trustee institution's reporting requirements for IRAs also apply to qualified plans. The employer is responsible for the majority of the required reports to plan participants and federal government agencies.

OTHER RETIREMENT SAVINGS PLANS

In addition to IRAs and Keogh plans, there are many other types of retirement savings plans. This section gives a general overview of two employer-provided plans—401(k) or salary reduction plans, and thrift/savings plans. It also covers annuities offered through insurance companies. All three plans are used to defer income taxes.

Tax laws covering these plans are complex and often undergoing change. Like IRAs, which conform to exact specifications, many variations and combinations of plans are permitted by the Code. Companies that provide benefits through these plans may set their own eligibility, contribution and distribution limits within those requirements specified by the Code.

401(k) Plans

A *401(k) plan* is often referred to as a *salary reduction plan* but is actually a special feature of a profit-sharing plan. Such a plan allows employees to elect to have their employer contribute up to a specified percentage of their salaries (on a pretax basis). Employee elective deferrals, like other contributions, may be invested by the plan in one or more of several employer-selected investments such as money market instruments, deposit accounts, stocks or bonds. In some cases, the plan may permit employees to direct their plan investments.

Typically, employee contributions are made with payroll deductions of pretax dollars. Thus, the amounts contributed are not reported as income for federal income tax purposes. This contrasts with the procedures used by IRA participants who report all their income and then deduct their contributions. Also, most states do not consider 401(k) plan contributions as taxable income. Finally, an employer may totally or partially match an employee's elective deferral in some specified way.

Thrift/Savings Plans

A *thrift/savings plan* is a type of qualified defined contribution plan. It is a profit-sharing plan that encourages employee participation, using after-tax compensation, by providing for employer matching contributions. Like other profit-sharing plans, both employees and the employer contribute to it according to a specified formula. Employees make after-tax or nondeductible voluntary contributions to qualify for specified matched employer contributions. In order for the IRS to consider the plan as qualified (allowing the employer to deduct matching contributions), all benefits and employee contributions must be nonforfeitable, or fully vested. In addition to the specified mandatory contribution to participate, the plan may permit employees to make unmatched, nondeductible voluntary contributions.

All employee contributions are made with after-tax dollars, which are nondeductible. Therefore, when employees receive distributions, those portions representing their contributions are not subject to income taxes again. Also, these employee contributions cannot be rolled over into an IRA. However, all interest earned and all employer's contributions are subject to taxation when distributed and thus may be eligible for rollover treatment.

Annuities

A commercial *annuity* is a contract that agrees to pay the insured a regular annual income over his or her lifetime or a specified number of years. It is underwritten by an insurance company. When an individual purchases an annuity policy, he or she agrees to pay the insurance company a certain amount of money in exchange for this income.

Taxes on the interest earned on amounts invested in annuities are tax deferred. As with other tax-deferred retirement plans, such deferred earnings are subject to taxation when they are distributed.

SUMMARY

This chapter covered many technical details pertaining to IRAs, qualified plans and other types of retirement plans. Figure 9-11 summarizes the eligibility, contribution limits and distribution aspects of the retirement plans presented in this chapter.

FOOTNOTES

[1]See the following publications for more specific information regarding retirement plans:

- *IRA Basics* and *Qualified Retirement Plans for Businesses*, published by the Institute of Financial Education

- *Individual Retirement Plans Guide* and *Tax-Savings Plans for Self-Employed*, by Commerce Clearing House, Inc.

- *Federal Tax Coordinator 2d*, Volume 12, by The Research Institute of America, Inc.

- *IRS Publication 590* on Individual Retirement Arrangements (IRAs), *IRS Publication 560* on Self-Employed Retirement Plans, and *IRS Publication 575* on Pension and Annuity Income

F I G U R E 9-11

Summary of Eligibility, Contribution Limits and Distribution Aspects of Retirement Plans

Plan	Eligibility	Contribution Limits	Distribution
Contributory IRA*	anyone receiving compensation under age 70½	$2,000 or 100% of compensation, whichever is less	before age 59½, limited availability; after 59½, any amount; minimum distributions must begin by April 1 of the year after reaching age 70½; generally taxed as ordinary income
Spousal IRA	any working spouse for a "non-compensated" spouse under 70½	$2,250 or 100% of compensation, whichever is less (no more than $2,000 contributed to the account of either spouse)	same as contributory IRA
Third-party sponsored IRA	same as contributory or spousal	same as contributory or spousal	same as contributory IRA
Rollover IRA	from an IRA, qualified pension plan, Keogh annuity, retirement bond plan or other qualified retirement savings plan	no dollar limitations; special rules determine eligibility for rollover contribution	same as contributory IRA

*See Figure 9-4 for information on tax deductibility of IRA contributions

F I G U R E 9-11, Continued

Plan	Eligibility	Contribution Limits	Distribution
SEP	age requirement cannot exceed 21	15% of compensation or $30,000 (COLA indexed), whichever is less; employee may contribute an additional $2,000 (IRA)	same as contributory IRA
SARSEP (elective deferrral arrangement)	same as SEP; only available to firms having 25 (or less) eligible employees and 50% or more elect deferrals	$7,000 (COLA indexed); employee deferrals plus employer contributions cannot exceed 15%/$30,000 SEP limit	same as contributory IRA
Defined contribution qualified plan	age requirement cannot exceed 21; generally 1 year of service (2 years permitted if 100% vesting)	the lesser of $30,000 (COLA indexed) or 25% for money purchase or 15% for profit sharing plans	generally not available until death, disability, retirement or termination of employment; loans may be permitted; generally taxable income

F I G U R E 9-11, Continued

Plan	Eligibility	Contribution Limits	Distribution
Defined benefit qualified plan	same as defined contribution	$90,000 (COLA indexed) or 100% of the averaged high-three years of compensation	generally not available until death, retirement, disability or termination of employment; generally taxable income
401(k) salary reduction plan	age requirement cannot exceed 21; 1 year of service (no 2-year service exception)	employee elective deferrals typically matched in a specified way with employer contributions; elective deferrals cannot exceed $7,000 (COLA indexed); total employer contributions (e.g., regular and matching) plus employee elective deferrals cannot exceed the lesser of $30,000 or 25% of compensation	same as defined contribution; also may permit hardship withdrawals

F I G U R E 9-11, Continued

Plan	Eligibility	Contribution Limits	Distribution
Thrift/savings plan	same as defined contribution	a specified mandatory percentage of employee's salary (after-tax); typically matched in a specified way with employer contributions; some plans also allow additional voluntary employee contributions up to specified percentage of salary (also after-tax); total employee and employer contributions cannot exceed 25% of compensation or $30,000 (COLA indexed)	same as defined contribution
Insurance annuity	anyone	no dollar limitations (contributions not deductible)	taxable and non-taxable distributions determined on a prorata basis; possible penalties for cashing out policy prematurely

CHAPTER 10

Decedent Accounts

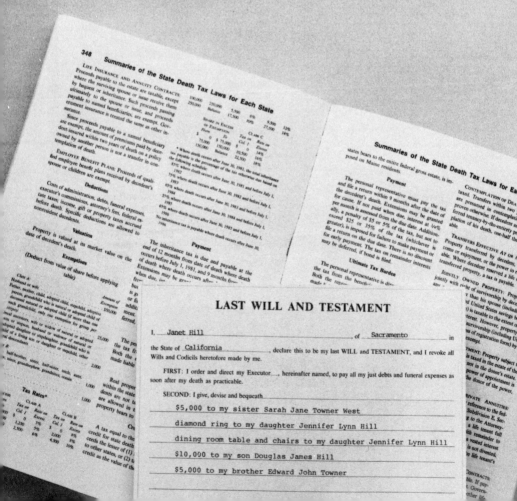

348

Summaries of the State Death Tax Laws for Each State

LIFE INSURANCE AND ANNUITY CONTRACTS: Proceeds payable to the estate are taxable, except where the surviving spouse or issue receive them by bequest or inheritance. Such proceeds passing ultimately to the spouse or issue, and proceeds payable to named beneficiaries, are exempt. Government insurance is treated the same as other insurance.

Since proceeds payable to a named beneficiary are exempt, the amount of premium paid by decedent-insured within two years of death on a policy owned by another person is not a transfer in contemplation of death.

EMPLOYEE BENEFIT PLANS: Proceeds of qualified employee benefit plans received by decedent's spouse or children are exempt.

Deductions

Costs of administration, debts, funeral expenses, executor's commissions, attorney's fees, federal estate taxes, income, gift or property taxes accrued before death. Specific deductions are allowed to nonresident decedents.

Valuation

Property is valued at its market value on the date of decedent's death.

Exemptions

(Deduct from value of share before applying table)

Class A:
Husband or wife

Father, mother, child, adopted child, stepchild, adoptive parent, grandchild who is natural or adopted child of parents, grandchild, only that extension for group per ...

...

Tax Rates*

...

Summaries of the State Death Tax Laws for Ea[ch]

states bears to the entire federal gross estate, is imposed on Maine residents.

Payment

The personal representative must pay the tax and file a return within 9 months after the date of the decedent's death. Extensions may be granted for cause. If not paid when due, interest at ¼% per month is assessed from the due date. Additionally, a penalty of $5 or 5% of the tax, but not to exceed $25 or 35% of the tax (whichever is greater), is imposed for failure to make payment or file a return on the due date. There is no discount for early payment. The tax on remainder interests may be deferred, if bond is filed.

Ultimate Tax Burden

The personal representative is di...
Both the repr...
made...

LAST WILL AND TESTAMENT

I, ___Janet Hill_____, of ___Sacramento_____ in the State of ___California_____, declare this to be my last WILL and TESTAMENT, and I revoke all Wills and Codicils heretofore made by me.

FIRST: I order and direct my Executor___, hereinafter named, to pay all my just debts and funeral expenses as soon after my death as practicable.

SECOND: I give, devise and bequeath_____

$5,000 to my sister Sarah Jane Towner West

diamond ring to my daughter Jennifer Lynn Hill

dining room table and chairs to my daughter Jennifer Lynn Hill

$10,000 to my son Douglas James Hill

$5,000 to my brother Edward John Towner

KEY CONCEPTS

- Dual responsibilities of a financial institution after the death of a depositor;

- Differences between testate and intestate estates;

- Items needed to service decedent accounts on out-of-state estates;

- Items needed for servicing decedent accounts for each form of ownership;

- Authorized recipient of funds of a decedent account for each form of ownership;

- State and federal laws regarding inheritance, estate and gift taxes.

D*ecedent* is the common legal term for a deceased person. When an account holder dies, the account, regardless of its form of ownership, becomes classified as a decedent account. Funds in a decedent account are either withdrawn or transferred to another account by the decedent's legal representative. If an institution handles decedent accounts properly, it may be able to retain the account funds at least temporarily and possibly even for the long term.

This chapter covers the counselor's responsibility to protect the interests of the institution, the surviving account owners and the decedent's creditors and heirs. The chapter also describes how state and federal taxes affect decedent estates and accounts. Then it examines the various items and forms the counselor needs when closing a decedent account or transferring the funds to another account.

THE INSTITUTION'S RESPONSIBILITIES

A depository institution has dual responsibilities upon the death of one of its depositors: to protect the institution and to protect the creditors, heirs and relatives of the decedent, and the surviving tenants of the decedent's account. By protecting the decedent's creditors, heirs and relatives, and the surviving tenants, the institution will most likely be protecting itself as well. The institution's responsibilities begin when it receives notification of an account owner's death, by either newspaper obituary, correspondence or conversation.

Protecting the Institution

Proper handling of decedent accounts helps protect the institution from potential monetary liability. Many states have laws that impose certain tax obligations on persons who receive money as a result of an account holder's death. These laws also require financial institutions to obtain specific tax forms before releasing funds from decedent accounts. Institutions that fail to comply with these requirements ultimately may be responsible for paying the taxes due the state government.

Decedent accounts constitute one of the few areas where counselors must become involved at least to some degree with an account holder's tax situation. Later sections of this chapter explain the various taxes applicable to decedent accounts.

Protecting the Decedent's Creditors, Heirs and Relatives, and the Surviving Tenants

One of the major problems a financial institution faces when handling decedent accounts is making the account funds available only to the proper parties. The "proper parties" are determined by the deposit contract and state law, and can include creditors, heirs, relatives and surviving account tenants. Regardless of the decedent's form of account ownership or whether he or she left a will, some person is always legally responsible for handling the account. The legal representative is designated either by the decedent prior to his or her death or by the state after the death.

DECEDENT ESTATES

A person dies either with a will or without a will. A *will* is a legal document prepared by an individual that explains how to dispose of his or her property or estate after death. A decedent's estate includes all of the person's assets and liabilities left at his or her death.

A person who dies with a will is said to have died *testate,* while a person who dies without a will is said to have died *intestate.* Counselors need to understand the distinction between these two forms of estates, because the nature of the estate determines who handles the account and what forms the institution needs to ensure the proper disbursement of the account funds.

In either case, the distribution of the decedent's property falls under the jurisdiction and supervision of the probate court. The *probate court* has jurisdiction over the probate of wills (the official process of verifying the will's authenticity) and the administration of decedents' estates.

Testate

When a person dies testate (with a will), the estate is distributed according to the terms of his or her will. The deceased person is referred to as the *testator.* By law, any person who has possession of a decedent's will at the time of death must deliver the will to the clerk of the probate court, usually within 30 days.

In every will, the testator appoints a person to execute the terms of the will, called the executor. Any person may be appointed the executor as long as he or she is at least 18 years old, a resident of the United States and legally competent. Frequently, the attorney who drew up the will is named the executor. It is also common for a trust company or financial institution to be appointed executor. One of the executor's responsibilities is to handle the testator's accounts at a financial institution.

The probate court grants the executor a document called letters testamentary. _Letters testamentary_ constitute the executor's formal authority to handle all of the following activities:

- collect all of the decedent's assets, including deposit accounts and investments;

- pay the burial expenses;

- pay any income, estate and inheritance taxes;

- pay all debts, liabilities and expenses related to the administration of the estate;

- distribute the remaining estate in accordance with the terms of the will;

- make a final accounting to the court on completion of the estate's administration.

The executor must provide the financial institution with the letters testamentary prior to making any transaction on the decedent's account. In most cases, the institution retains a copy of the document with the decedent's account records.

Intestate

When a person dies intestate (without a will), the estate is distributed to the heirs in accordance with the laws of the state in which the decedent lived.

The decedent's estate is admitted to probate, at which time the court appoints a competent administrator. An administrator resembles an executor but is appointed by the court following the death rather than by the deceased person prior to death. The administrator handles the decedent's accounts at a financial institution. Ordinarily, the administrator is the spouse or a close relative of the decedent. The order of eligibility for appointment customarily is set by state statute and closely follows the statutes of descent.

The probate court grants the administrator a document called letters of administration. *Letters of administration* constitute the administrator's formal authority to act. This authority resembles that of the executor. After collecting all the assets and paying all expenses, taxes and debts, the administrator must distribute the remainder of the estate to the heirs according to the state law of descent and make a final accounting to the court.

The state law of descent, referred to as *statutes of descent*, describes the persons who inherit the decedent's property and the order in which they inherit it. Spouses, children and grandchildren ordinarily have high priority. When there are no direct descendents, parents and grandparents share the estate. When there are no surviving descendents or ascendents, relatives such as brothers, sisters, cousins, aunts and uncles share the estate.

Financial institutions must obtain the letters of administration from an administrator prior to allowing any transactions on the decedent's account. As with letters testamentary, many institutions require that a copy of the letters of administration be retained with the decedent's account records.

Out-of-State

All financial institutions should establish a policy for handling decedent accounts that involve a decedent who was legally domiciled in another state at the time of death. The *domicile* of a person is his or her true, fixed, permanent home and principal establishment.

Domicile and residence are not necessarily the same. A person may have several residences but only one domicile. For example, assume Tom Schmidt owns homes in Boise, Idaho; San Diego, California; and Key West, Florida. Tom works, votes and is raising his family in Boise and uses the other two homes just for vacations. Therefore, Tom is considered domiciled in Boise. The difficulties involved with this type of decedent account are sometimes complex and pose increased potential liability for the institution.

Sometimes, if the decedent maintained a residence, owned property or conducted business in several states, an estate representative is appointed in each state. Such representatives are termed *ancillary administrators* or *ancillary executors.*

Ordinarily, an institution should not release funds from an account of a deceased depositor who was domiciled in another state if the estate is being probated in the domicile state, unless the following documents are presented:

- certified copies of letters testamentary or letters of administration;

- deposit account passbook, certificate or other evidence of account;

- withdrawal application signed by the executor or administrator;

- affidavit by the executor or the administrator that the decedent was legally domiciled in another state; that no letters have been issued on the petition of any heir, legatee, devisee or creditor of the deceased in the local state; that no petition for letters is pending on the petition of any heir, legatee, devisee or creditor of the deceased in the local state; that no ancillary representative has been appointed and no appointment is pending in the local state; and that creditors of the decedent's estate are located in the local state;

- authenticated copy of an order by the court that issued the letters authorizing the executor or administrator to remove the personal estate from the local state.

Some states also require an inheritance tax waiver from the local state. However, some states require no inheritance tax waiver if the local and domicile states of the decedent have a reciprocal tax agreement. Inheritance tax waivers are explained in the next section.

Because state laws vary considerably, institutions must take great care when dealing with out-of-state executors and administrators.[1] However, some states have created uniform laws.

TAXES THAT AFFECT DECEDENT ACCOUNTS

A complex legal task is determining which assets owned or controlled by the decedent at the time of death must be included in the estate. Although counselors are not responsible for this task, they are involved with helping the authorized persons. Therefore, counselors need to be familiar with estate and inheritance tax concepts and terminology and their applicability to decedent accounts in general. Inheritance, estate and gift taxes differ from the federal or state income taxes with which most people are familiar.

State Inheritance Taxes

An *inheritance tax* is a tax that a state may impose on each beneficiary (inheritor) of the estate. Each beneficiary pays a tax based on the size of the inheritance and his or her relationship to the decedent. The closer the familial relationship, the lower the tax. All states except Nevada levy inheritance taxes. Most states, however, provide for reduced tax rates or exemptions for certain eligible heirs.

Some states require the use of an inheritance tax waiver on a decedent's account.[2] An *inheritance tax waiver* (or consent to transfer property) is a document, signed by the appropriate state taxing official, in which the state releases any claim to the estate assets under consideration (see Figure 10-1 for an example). A separate inheritance tax waiver may be necessary for each financial institution in which the decedent held accounts. However, if the decedent held several accounts at one institution, all of the accounts must be listed on the same waiver. In addition to the account number, the waiver identifies the account balance as of the date of death.

The financial institution's representatives must read this document carefully to note whether full or partial release is allowed. Although the waiver commonly releases the entire balance, sometimes the institution must retain a portion of the account balance pending notification from the state taxing authority. The executor must not be allowed to withdraw or transfer more than the amount indicated on the inheritance tax waiver.

F I G U R E 10-1

Consent to Transfer Property

STATE OF WISCONSIN
CONSENT TO TRANSFER PROPERTY

Submit Both Copies With $5.00
Fee to the Wisconsin Department
of Revenue

Date Issued by Department

Estate of

Date of Death	Decedent's Social Security Number

Address of Decedent at Date of Death (number and street or rural route)

City	State	Zip Code

INSTRUCTIONS: In the space provided below, enter the **description** and **Date of Death value** of the property to be transferred along with the **name** and **relationship** of the person entitled to receive the property.

The Wisconsin Department of Revenue hereby consents to the transfer of the following described **personal** property of the above-named decedent to any surviving joint tenant or to whomever may be entitled to the property by law. **NOTICE**: This consent is **VOID** if any property description is entered below the authorized signature stamp.

RETURN MAILING ADDRESS - Print or type below

Name

Address

City		For Department Use Only
	State Zip Code	HT-206 (R. 12-86)

If the state requires an inheritance tax waiver, the institution must obtain one for its protection. If the institution fails to secure the waiver and the state is therefore unable to collect any taxes due, the institution may be liable for payment of the tax, any interest due on the tax and possibly a penalty for the delay in payment. Counselors who handle decedent accounts thus need to know whether their states require inheritance tax waivers.

Federal Estate Taxes

The *federal estate tax* is an excise tax levied upon the transfer of a person's property at his or her death.[3] The tax is levied on the amount transferred and not on the property itself. The Internal Revenue Code specifies the items that make up the estate.

Several factors interact to reduce estate taxes. As of 1987, the amount of an estate that may pass to others free of estate taxes is $600,000. This amount is derived from the *unified gift and estate tax credit,* an amount authorized under tax codes for use in reducing the tax payable on the gross estate. Estate taxes also may be reduced (up to a certain limit) by a credit for paid state inheritance taxes, thus reducing multiple taxation of the estate. Because of these many variables, one decedent's gross estate may result in thousands of dollars in estate taxes due while another's estate of equal size may have no taxes due.

Tax legislation passed in 1981 favorably affected many individuals' estate planning. Besides reducing tax rates and increasing tax credits, the legislation made several important changes. For example, it removed limits on the *marital deduction,* which is the amount that a spouse may receive free of estate tax. Prior to 1981, this deduction was limited to one-half of the estate. Now the surviving spouse may inherit the entire estate and any estate taxes may be delayed until he or she dies. Then any estate taxes due will be based on the estate of the second deceased spouse (i.e., whatever is left of the original estate).

The 1981 legislation also states that if a husband and wife hold property in joint ownership, only half of the value of the property is counted in the estate for tax purposes. Half is considered as being in the deceased spouse's estate and half in the surviving spouse's estate, regardless of who furnished the funds to acquire the property.

The legislation also repealed the law that presumed that gifts a person had made in the three years prior to death were made in contemplation of death and therefore were subject to estate taxes. Now gifts the decedent made during that time period generally are not considered in computing the estate tax. An exception is gifts of life insurance made within three years of death.

Federal Gift Taxes

Counselors may encounter customers who believe that one way to eliminate estate taxes is to give their property away before death. To some extent, this is true—taxes can be reduced or eliminated in this way. However, the Internal Revenue Code still imposes a *gift tax* on all gifts whose value exceeds a certain amount. Gifts in excess of specified amounts are taxed at the same rate as the estate tax rate.

Tax legislation passed in 1988 considerably changed gift taxes in a favorable way. Individuals now may give up to $100,000 annually to as many people as they wish without incurring any federal gift tax.[4] The maximum gift limit increases to $200,000 if the gift comes jointly from a husband and wife.[5] Amounts paid to an individual for tuition or medical care do not count as part of the $100,000 or $200,000 annual limitation.[6]

PROCEDURES FOR EACH FORM OF ACCOUNT OWNERSHIP

The form of ownership of the decedent's account basically determines the procedures the counselor follows. Each form of ownership requires obtaining certain forms or documents and designates specific individuals as appropriate recipients of the account funds. All forms of ownership require that the account be flagged appropriately upon notification of the owner's death so that unauthorized persons do not make withdrawals.

Single Owner

An individual decedent account is handled by the executor or the administrator, depending on whether the individual died testate or intestate.

Individual Dies Testate

If the holder of an individual account dies testate, the executor handles the account. The counselor's first step prior to transferring or closing the account is to obtain identification from the person who claims to be the executor. This individual must prove that he or she is indeed the person named in the letters testamentary.

After obtaining proper identification of the executor, the counselor should acquire the following documents:

- a copy of the death certificate;

- a certified copy of the letters testamentary;

- an inheritance tax waiver if the state requires it;

- a deposit account passbook, certificate or other evidence of account;

- a withdrawal form signed by the executor.

The copy of the letters testamentary must be certified so that the institution will be assured of a true, unaltered copy. For example, an unauthorized person could improperly obtain the letters testamentary, change the name of the designated executor to his or her own, make photocopies of the document and withdraw funds from the decedent's account. The financial institution must verify the document's authenticity before filing it with the decedent's account records.

The required legal documentation for withdrawal of funds from the decedent's account includes the evidence of account and withdrawal form, signed by the executor. The executor should always be required to sign his or her full name on the withdrawal slip, followed by "executor for the estate of _____." For example, Veronica Loogin, Executor for the Estate of Michael Pagon, should sign the withdrawal slip as follows:

Veronica Loogin, Executor for the Estate of Michael Pagon

The institution should make the funds available in the form of either a check payable to the executor or a transfer to another account (in the fiduciary form of ownership) in the executor's name. In the case of Veronica Loogin above, the check should read, "Pay to the order of Veronica Loogin, Executor for the Estate of Michael Pagon." Or, the new account would be established in the name of "Veronica Loogin, Executor for the Estate of Michael Pagon."

Sometimes an executor presents a certified copy of the Final Account and Distribution of the Estate. This document shows a final accounting of the estate and the distribution of the proceeds to the beneficiaries. This final accounting is approved by a probate court judge. The institution may accept a certified copy of the Final Account and Distribution of the Estate in lieu of a certified copy of the letters testamentary. In this case, it may pay the funds directly to the intended legal recipient or recipients. Checks may be issued to each of these individuals to close the account. Such cases are considered out of the ordinary, however, and the counselor may need to get approval from a supervisor or department manager before taking action.

In situations where co-executors are named and one dies, the institution should obtain a copy of the death certificate and examine a certified copy of the will to determine whether another executor has been named to replace the deceased executor.

Individual Dies Intestate

If the holder of an individual account dies intestate, the administrator handles the account. Like the executor, the administrator must prove his or her identity.

After obtaining proper identification of the administrator, the counselor should obtain the following documents:

- a copy of the death certificate;

- a certified copy of the letters of administration;

- an inheritance tax waiver if the state requires one;

- a deposit account passbook, certificate or other evidence of account;

- a withdrawal application signed by the administrator.

In most states, if the balance in the intestate decedent's account is small, it may be disbursed directly to the heirs. But this is permitted only if:

- the value of the decedent's entire personal estate does not exceed a maximum sum designated by the state;

- no probate is necessary or contemplated; and

- all funeral expenses and other debts have been paid.

Ordinarily, disbursement of funds directly to the heirs is proper only when all applicants are bona fide residents of the state, and they have full knowledge of the facts and a stated number of days (usually 30) have elapsed since the death. The lawful heirs may be paid after they have presented the following documents:

- certified copy of the death certificate;

- affidavit signed by all the heirs setting forth the amount of the estate and the fact that all debts have been paid (see Figure 10-2 for an example);

- inheritance tax waiver (if this is a state requirement);

- deposit account passbook, certificate or other evidence of account;

- withdrawal application signed by all the lawful heirs.

Whether the balance in the account is under or over the statutory figure, the counselor should always exercise caution before paying out to the heirs. The counselor should obtain approval from a department manager and perhaps from the institution's legal counsel before taking action.

Corporation

Since a corporation is an artificial person, it cannot die and therefore cannot be categorized as a true decedent. But natural persons are authorized to control corporation accounts, and their deaths necessitate certain procedures. These procedures are much simpler than those for other forms of ownership.

When notified of the death of an authorized signer on a corporate account, the counselor should flag the account appropriately to prevent unauthorized transactions. Then the corporation must submit a new corporate resolution for the account. Since the corporation can change authorized signers at any time, the institution is obliged to obtain no documentation other than a current resolution.

Joint Tenancy

In a joint tenancy account with right of survivorship, when one joint tenant dies the funds belong to the surviving joint tenant or tenants (see Chapter 6). This is true whether the deceased tenant died testate or intestate.

F I G U R E 10-2

Affidavit for Transfer of Property (under $5,000), Side 1

STATE OF WISCONSIN, CIRCUIT COURT, _____ COUNTY   -PROBATE-

IN THE MATTER OF THE ESTATE OF

_____

_____   **AFFIDAVIT FOR TRANSFER OF PROPERTY (UNDER $5,000)**

_____

File No. _____

Under oath, I state that:

1. _____ , age _____ years, died on _____
   Name   Date

   domiciled in _____ County, Wisconsin, whose post office address was

   _____ .

2. I am an heir, being a _____ of the decedent.
   Relationship

3. The total value of the decedent's **solely owned** property in Wisconsin at the date of death

   was $_____ and did not exceed $5,000.

4. The Property ☐ is ☐ is not marital or deferred marital property.

5. The total estimated value of all property in Wisconsin **in which the decedent had any interest**

   was $_____.

   Note: This amount should include the value of all solely-owned (individual) property, insurance, employee death benefits, transfers in contemplation of death or to take effect at death, life estates, joint property and decedent's interest in marital property held by decedent's surviving spouse.

I ask that the following property be transferred to me [s. 867.03(1)]:

DESCRIPTION OF PROPERTY	BY WHOM HELD	VALUE

Subscribed and sworn to before me

on _____   _____
    Signature

_____   _____
    Name Typed

_____   _____
Notary Public, Wisconsin   Address

My commission expires: _____

PREPARE IN DUPLICATE —s. 867.03 requires transferor to mail a copy of the affidavit to Wisconsin Dept. of Revenue, P.O. Box 8904, Madison, WI 53708

No. PR 1413 AFFIDAVIT FOR TRANSFER OF PROPERTY (UNDER $5,000)
s.867.03, Wisconsin Statutes   5/86

Wisconsin Legal Blank Co. Inc.
Milwaukee, Wis.

F I G U R E 10-2, Continued

Affidavit for Transfer of Property (under $5,000), Side 2

TRANSFER BY AFFIDAVIT (S. 867.03)

(1) When a decedent leaves solely-owned property in this state which does not exceed $5,000 in value, any heir of the decedent, may collect any money due the decedent, receive the property of the decedent if it is not an interest in or lien on real property and have any evidence of interest, obligation to or right of the decedent transferred to the heir upon furnishing the person owing the money, having custody of the property or acting as registrar or transfer agent of the evidences of interest, obligation to or right, with an affidavit in duplicate showing:

    (a) A description of and the value of the property to be transferred.

    (b) The total value of the decedent's property in this state at the date of decedent's death.

(2) Upon the transfer to the heir furnishing the affidavit, and mailing a copy of the affidavit to the Department of Revenue, the transferor is released to the same extent as if the transfer had been made to the personal representative of the estate of the decedent.

(3) This section is additional to the provisions of s. 109.03(3) for payment of decedent's wages by an employer directly to the decedent's dependents.

Ordinarily, the institution may pay the funds in the account upon presentation of:

- a certified copy of the death certificate;

- an inheritance tax waiver if required by the state;

- a deposit account passbook, certificate or other evidence of account;

- a withdrawal application signed by the surviving joint tenant or tenants.

Note that the copy of the death certificate should be certified. Certification assures the institution that the joint tenant is indeed deceased and prevents the surviving tenant or tenants from making unauthorized withdrawals.

Note also that an inheritance tax waiver may be required for decedent accounts held in joint tenancy. This requirement may be confusing to joint owners who believe they owned the account all along and therefore are not inheritors of the funds. While it is true that the surviving owner automatically becomes the sole owner of a joint account and no legal action is necessary to transfer title, the inheritance tax waiver may still be required. Although the right of survivorship guarantees continued ownership, it does not guarantee freedom from taxes.

In the event that all parties to a joint tenancy account die within a short period of time, the funds in the estate belong to the estate of the last tenant to die. Ordinarily, the institution turns these funds over to the executor or administrator after it has received the following documents:

- a certified copy of the death certificate for each deceased joint tenant;

- a certified copy of letters testamentary or letters of administration for the estate of the last deceased;

- inheritance tax waivers for all decedents if the state required them;

- a deposit account passbook, certificate or other evidence of account;

- a withdrawal application signed by the executor or the administrator for the estate of the last deceased.

Out-of-state decedent accounts, of course, may be subject to varying rules, and the counselor should obtain approval from a department manager or the institution's legal counsel before taking action.

Tenancy in Common

Joint tenancy and tenancy in common have significant differences in how the funds are distributed on the death of one tenant. Counselors should remember that tenancy in common does not have a right of survivorship and release of the account funds has similarities to releasing funds from an individual account. When a tenant in common dies, the signatures of all remaining tenants in common and the signature of the decedent's legal representative are required for releasing funds from the account.

Tenant in Common Dies Testate

If a tenant in common dies testate, the counselor may pay out funds in the account after obtaining the following documents:

- a certified copy of the letters testamentary;

- an inheritance tax waiver if required by the state;

- a deposit account passbook, certificate or other evidence of account;

- a withdrawal application signed by all of the remaining tenants in common and the executor.

Again, out-of-state accounts may be subject to varying rules, and the counselor should obtain approval from a department manager or the institution's legal counsel before taking action.

Tenant in Common Dies Intestate

At least two situations and methods for resolution are possible if a tenant in common dies intestate. If the tenant in common dies intestate and the estate is probated, the counselor follows the procedure in the previous section (except that letters of administration are obtained instead of letters testamentary and the administrator signs instead of an executor).

If the tenant in common dies intestate and the balance in the account is under the statutory limit, the counselor must obtain the following documents prior to releasing any funds from the account:

- a certified copy of the death certificate;

- an affidavit signed by all the heirs stating that they are aware of the release of the funds;

- an inheritance tax waiver if the state requires it;

- a deposit account passbook, certificate or other evidence of account;

- a withdrawal application signed by all the heirs and remaining tenants in common.

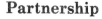

Partnership

When one owner of a partnership account dies, the disposition of his or her ownership interest is handled as specified in the partnership agreement. Upon learning of a partner's death, the institution should flag the account to prevent any further withdrawals. In most cases, the death of one partner dissolves the entire partnership. The legal representative (the executor or administrator) of the deceased partner's estate then handles the account.

Trusts

Procedures for handling decedent trust accounts vary depending on whether the trust is revocable or irrevocable.

Trustee's Death
In the event of a trustee's death, a successor trustee may assume the responsibility for the trust. Usually the trust agreement, whether revocable or irrevocable, provides for a successor trustee who is granted the same powers held by the deceased trustee. Or, the trust agreement may authorize the financial institution to appoint a successor trustee, whereupon the institution should execute a letter of appointment. If the trust agreement contains no such provision, the court may appoint a successor trustee.

Most revocable trust agreements give the successor trustee the same withdrawal privileges as that of the original grantor-trustee except for one significant provision: Only the original trustee can withdraw funds from the trust account, thereby revoking the trust to that extent, and use the funds for any purpose (see Chapter 8). The successor trustee, however, is bound by the terms of the trust and must use any funds withdrawn solely for the benefit of the beneficiary. In effect, the successor trustee becomes the trustee of an irrevocable trust. This means that the beneficiary must benefit from any funds withdrawn from the account. All other terms of the original trust remain in force, and none of the account records are canceled. In this case, the counselor is required to obtain only two items:

- a copy of the successor trustee's appointment;

- a new signature card attached to the original trust agreement.

Whenever possible, the institution should pay funds in the trust account to the successor trustee. However, if a beneficiary is of legal age and is legally competent, he or she may request the funds in the trust account at the time of the trustee's death. If this action agrees with the provisions of the trust, the counselor requests each of the following items prior to disbursement of the funds:

- proper identification of the beneficiary;

- a certified copy of the death certificate;

- an inheritance tax waiver if required by the state;

- a deposit account passbook, certificate or other evidence of account;

- a withdrawal application signed by the beneficiary. (If more than one beneficiary is named, all beneficiaries must identify themselves and sign the withdrawal application.)

No funds should be paid to a minor beneficiary until he or she has attained the age stipulated in the trust agreement. If one of the multiple beneficiaries is a minor, his or her share of the funds may be transferred to another trust account. If the trust terminates on the death of the original trustee, the minor's share of the funds may be transferred to an individual account in the minor's name.

Beneficiary's Death

One of several situations may occur when a beneficiary dies. In the event of a beneficiary's death, the trustee ordinarily may withdraw the funds in the trust account. If the beneficiary dies and the grantor makes no change in the account, the funds may be paid to the estate of the beneficiary when the trustee dies. It is also possible for a beneficiary to die without the trustee's knowledge. Or, after the beneficiary's death, the trustee may neglect to remove the deceased beneficiary's name. In these cases, the beneficiary's estate may already be settled prior to the trustee's death. The legal representatives of both decedents should settle such matters.

If two or more beneficiaries are named in a trust but are not specified as joint tenants, the decedent's heirs receive the pro rata share in the trust. Under most state laws, two or more beneficiaries under one trust hold the trust as tenants in common. Each beneficiary's share, therefore, passes to that beneficiary's heirs.

Like other types of decedent accounts, out-of-state decedent trust accounts are subject to varying rules, and the counselor should obtain approval from a department manager or the institution's legal counsel before taking action.

SUMMARY

Decedent accounts are complex and need to be handled with care. Financial institutions are charged with two responsibilities upon notification of the death of one of its depositors: to protect itself and to protect the decedent's creditors, heirs and relatives, and the surviving tenants of the account.

Decedent accounts may or may not be subject to federal or state taxes such as federal estate tax, inheritance tax and gift tax. Only persons licensed to give tax advice should handle tax questions pertaining to decedent accounts.

Prior to withdrawing or transferring funds from a decedent account, the counselor must obtain certain documentation from the legal representative of the decedent's estate. In most cases the executor, administrator or surviving tenant supplies the counselor with some or all of the following documents: personal identification, letters testamentary or letters of administration, death certificate, inheritance tax waiver (if required by the state), evidence of account and withdrawal application with an authorized signature.

FOOTNOTES

[1] See "Bank Liable for Wrongful Payment to Foreign Executor," *Legal Bulletin*, XXXII (January 1966), pp. 36-38.

[2] The following states require inheritance tax waivers: CA, KY, MA, MS, MT, NE, NJ, NM, NC, WI. Nevada prohibits an inheritance tax in its constitution.

[3] The sections of the federal estate tax law that are most significant for deposit accounts are Internal Revenue Code Sections 2035, 2038 and 2040.

[4] See IRC Sec. 2503(b).

[5] See IRC Sec. 2513(a)(1).

[6] See IRC Sec. 2503(e).

Related Services

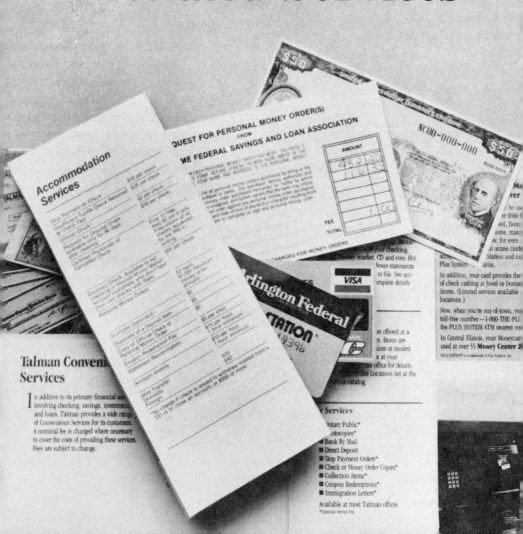

Talman Convenie[nce] Services

In addition to its primary financial ser[vices] involving checking, savings, investment[s] and loans, Talman provides a wide rang[e] of Convenience Services for its customers. A nominal fee is charged where necessary to cover the costs of providing these services. Fees are subject to change.

KEY CONCEPTS

- Benefits of convenience services, credit services, electronic banking services and investment services;

- Features and benefits of money orders, cashier's checks, accommodation checks and certified checks;

- Features and issuing procedures for traveler's checks;

- How and when customers use sight drafts;

- Characteristics of U.S. Savings Bonds;

- Customer benefits of preauthorized payment services and check-cashing services;

- Distinguishing features of credit cards and overdraft credit;

- Customer and institution benefits of electronic banking services;

- Types of direct deposit available to customers and the basic procedure for initiating each type;

- Types of personal and corporate trust services;

- Differences between discount brokerage service and full-service brokerage at a financial institution.

Deposit accounts are a major type of service that depository institutions offer customers. Depository institutions provide depositors with a safe place to keep their money and the potential for a return on their investments. However, depository institutions usually offer a range of related services as well. Services such as direct deposits and check issuing give financial institutions an opportunity to attract new customers and expand their services to current customers.

Many institutions realize the importance of selling their customers on more than one service. Market research has shown that the more services a customer uses at a financial institution, the more likely that customer is to remain with the institution. For this reason, many institutions stress the selling of additional products and services to an existing customer as one of the counselor's responsibilities.

Services related to deposit accounts can be grouped into four categories: convenience services, credit services, electronic banking services and investment services. This chapter expands on these four service categories with examples of the variety of services available at many depository institutions. It briefly defines and describes each service and explains its potential benefits to the customer and the institution.

CONVENIENCE SERVICES

Convenience services are those services that make financial transactions easier or save the customer time and effort. Convenience services may include such items as check issuance, sight drafts, sale and redemption of U.S. Savings Bonds, exchange of foreign currency, preauthorized payments and emergency cash services. Institutions

differ in the convenience services they offer depending on customer and institution needs.

Customers benefit from convenience services primarily through the time and effort they save. For example, a customer can make a deposit to a savings account and purchase a money order to pay a doctor bill at the same time. Without the availability of these convenience services, the customer would have to make several stops to complete his or her necessary financial transactions.

Depository institutions also benefit from offering convenience services. For example, some institutions are able to collect a small fee or service charge from customers to help defray the cost of offering a particular service. In some cases, the income generated by the fee or service charge allows the institution a small profit as well.

Another benefit to the institution is customer goodwill. By offering customers convenience services, the institution may strengthen the depositor-institution relationship. Customers who can conduct the majority of their financial transactions at one institution are more likely to think of that institution as their primary financial services provider. Many institutions find that selling deposit services to current customers is easier and more cost effective than selling them to potential new customers.

⊱Check-Issuing Services

Check-issuing services offered by depository institutions may include money orders, cashier's checks, accommodation checks, certified checks and traveler's checks. Depository institutions may vary in the terms they use for each type of check, but the functions of the checks are similar. Checks issued by depository institutions can be classified into three categories: bank checks, certified checks and traveler's checks.

Bank Checks

A depository institution issues a bank check for a given amount specified by the customer. A bank check may be purchased with cash, a personal check or a withdrawal from a deposit account. Because they are prepaid by the purchaser, bank checks are often accepted as cash. A bank check may be drawn on the institution where purchased or on another depository institution. Types of bank checks include money orders, cashier's checks and accommodation checks.

Money Orders A *money order* is an order purchased from a depository institution, the U.S. Postal Service or a commercial company to pay a sum of money to a party named by the purchaser. People often purchase money orders for making relatively small purchases or paying bills. Some merchants accept a money order more readily than they do a personal check because they know the issuing institution has already collected the money from the customer.

Money orders are usually issued to the customer with no payee specified. Upon receipt of the money order, the customer fills in the payee's name and signs the order. Many institutions advise their customers to fill in the order as soon as possible to avoid the risk associated with losing a blank order.

A carbon copy of the money order is often attached to the original order. The copy shows the date of issuance, the serial number and the amount of the order. Then, if the original order is lost or stolen, the customer can provide the information to the institution from the copy and thus expedite the necessary stop-payment and replacement processes. The issuing institution also keeps a record of the order, usually in the form of another carbon copy.

Frequently money orders carry a small service charge. For example, a $10 money order may cost the customer $10.50—$10 for the money order itself and $.50 for the service charge. Some depository institutions waive the service charge for depositors who meet certain institution requirements, such as maintaining high-balance certificates of deposit.

Here is an example of a situation in which a customer needs a money order. John Engstrom, a passbook savings account customer, comes to the institution to make a deposit. Since he does not have a checking account, he requests a money order for $92.68 to pay his electric bill. The teller collects the money and applicable fee from Mr. Engstrom and issues a money order. Mr. Engstrom fills in the payee blank and signs the order where indicated. He then retains his carbon copy of the order and sends the original to the electric company as payment.

Cashier's Checks   A *cashier's check*, sometimes called a *treasurer's check*, is a check an institution draws on itself, signed by a cashier or other authorized officer and payable to a third party named by the customer. Cashier's checks often are issued for larger amounts than are money orders.

In certain financial transactions, such as the purchase of a home or automobile, the seller may require the customer to use a cashier's check. In the case of mortgage loan closings, many lenders require the purchaser to use either a cashier's check or a certified check. The routineness of this practice attests to the widespread acceptability of the cashier's check as a guaranteed item.

The following example illustrates a circumstance in which a customer may purchase a cashier's check. Mr. Allen is buying a car from Ms. Jones for $2,500. Ms. Jones says that she will not take a personal check for the purchase price. Mr. Allen purchases a cashier's check in the amount of $2,500 and uses it to buy the car.

Accommodation Checks   An *accommodation check* is a check or draft drawn by an institution either on itself or on its account at another institution, signed by an authorized officer and payable to a third party designated by the individual requesting the check. Institutions provide accommodation checks solely for the convenience of their customers.

An accommodation check serves many of the same purposes as a money order. For this reason, some institutions choose to offer only one of these services rather than both.

Here is an example of a situation in which a customer would use an accommodation check. Pete Schneider has a payroll check payable to himself for $800. He wishes to use these funds to pay his $780 bill from Acme Construction. Pete presents his $800 check to the teller. The teller prepares an accommodation check payable to Acme Construction for $780 and gives Pete the check and $20 in cash.

Certified Checks

A *certified check* guarantees that:

- the signature of the drawer is genuine; and
- sufficient funds for paying the check are on deposit.

The financial institution sets aside the certified amount for the express purpose of paying the check and must pay that amount when the payee presents the check for payment. Usually, certified items are personal checks.

To have a check certified, the customer presents the completed draft to the teller. The teller withdraws the draft amount from the customer's account and credits a general ledger account for certification. The teller punches holes in the draft's MICR-encoded account number to ensure that the customer will not be charged twice when the draft returns to the institution. The teller then stamps the check with a certification number. When the check is presented for payment, the institution withdraws the funds from the general ledger account for certification.

Since the institution certifying the draft guarantees payment, stop payment orders generally are not allowed on certified checks. A possible exception occurs when the account owner does not deliver the certified draft to the payee and the payee has no interest in it.

Following is an example of a circumstance in which a customer may request a certified check. John and Gloria Dean are moving to a new home across town. The movers have specified that payment be in the form of a certified or cashier's check for $350. Since the Deans have a checking account at a local institution, John writes a check for $350 payable to the moving company and has the institution certify the check.

Traveler's Checks

A traveler's check is an order, over the signature of the issuing company, to pay on demand the amount shown by the preprinted denomination of the check (see Figure 11-1). A traveler's check differs from a personal check in that it is not drawn on the signer's own account. The

F I G U R E 11-1

Traveler's Check

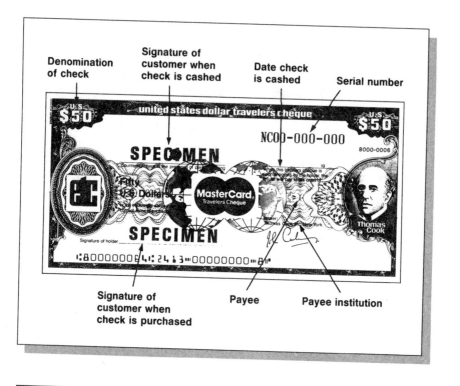

Denomination of check — Signature of customer when check is cashed — Date check is cashed — Serial number — Signature of customer when check is purchased — Payee — Payee institution

check may be drawn on the institution where purchased or at another institution.

Traveler's checks have been sold since 1891 as a means of protection against loss or theft of cash. Today, checks are available from many issuers, including American Express, Visa, MasterCard, Barclay's, Republic and Thomas Cook.

Two reasons why many people prefer traveler's checks over cash are acceptability and safety. Because the checks are prepaid and thus never returned for insufficient funds, many merchants around the world readily accept them as cash. Also, traveler's checks, unlike cash, are insured and replaceable if lost or stolen.

For the convenience of the purchaser, traveler's checks are available in a variety of denominations and currencies set by the issuer. Travelers taking extended vacations may prefer to get their checks in larger denominations, such as fifties or hundreds, rather than being burdened with a large supply of smaller-denomination checks. People traveling abroad may choose to buy traveler's checks in the currency of their destination country to avoid the need to exchange currencies upon arrival.

When a customer purchases traveler's checks, the issuing institution records the sale, including the purchaser's name, the denominations and serial numbers of checks purchased, and the method of payment. The institution gives the customer a copy of this record and recommends retaining it in a safe place separate from the traveler's checks. (If they are kept together and the checks are lost or stolen, the record also will be gone.) At the time of the sale, the customer receives instructions on obtaining a refund or replacement checks in the event of loss or theft.

Sometimes the customer is required to sign each check at the time of purchase. If the issuing institution does not require immediate signing, it usually advises the customer to sign the checks at his or her earliest convenience. Some traveler's check companies require that the checks be signed to validate the checks' insurance feature.

Sight Drafts

A *sight draft*, also called a *customer draft*, is a customer's order to a financial institution holding his or her

Move money bet. Financial institutions

a way to close an through the mail

funds to pay all or part of them to another institution for credit to the customer's account at that institution (see Figure 11-2). Customers find sight drafts helpful when they want to transfer funds from one institution to another for the purpose of opening or adding to an account and are unable to make the withdrawal in person. The main benefit of a sight draft is convenience.

Here is an illustration of how a customer may benefit from a sight draft. Jennifer Jones recently moved from California and wants to transfer her funds from a bank in California to a bank in New Jersey. If she processes the transaction without a sight draft, it will be a three-step procedure:

- She will mail a withdrawal request to her institution in California.

- The California institution will mail her a check for the balance of her account.

- She will go to her new bank, endorse the check and open or add to her account.

However, a sight draft condenses this process into two steps:

- Jennifer will go to the institution in New Jersey and instruct it to transfer the funds from the institution in California. The new institution will prepare a sight draft for her signature and send it to the California institution with instructions to withdraw the funds.

- The California institution will withdraw the funds and send a check for the balance to the new institution. The new institution will deposit the funds into Jennifer's account there.

F I G U R E 11-2

Sight Draft

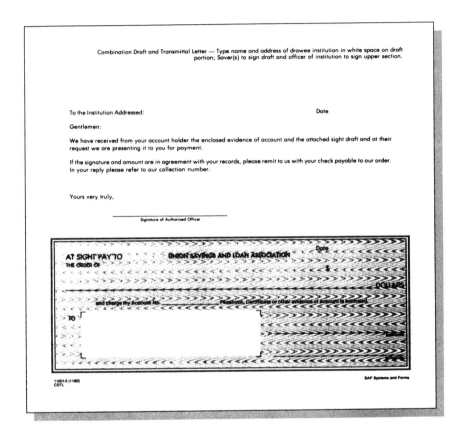

Combination Draft and Transmittal Letter — Type name and address of drawee institution in white space on draft portion; Saver(s) to sign draft and officer of institution to sign upper section.

To the Institution Addressed: Date

Gentlemen:

We have received from your account holder the enclosed evidence of account and the attached sight draft and at their request we are presenting it to you for payment.

If the signature and amount are in agreement with your records, please remit to us with your check payable to our order. In your reply please refer to our collection number.

Yours very truly,

_____
Signature of Authorized Officer

AT SIGHT PAY TO
THE ORDER OF

UNION SAVINGS AND LOAN ASSOCIATION   Date

$

DOLLARS

and charge my Account No.   Passbook, Certificate or other evidence of account is enclosed

TO

11001-5 (11/82)
CDTL

SAF Systems and Forms

Following are additional benefits to the customer of using a sight draft:

- A sight draft reduces the number of days of lost interest, because the funds are sent directly to the receiving institution.

- The customer can make the request to transfer funds prior to a long-term certificate's maturity, with instructions to close the account on the maturity date. Then the customer can instruct the new institution to open the account as soon as it receives the funds.

Sight drafts also benefit the institution that prepares them. A customer may decide it is more worthwhile to do business with an institution that provides such a convenient method of withdrawing and depositing funds.

Savings Bonds

U.S. Savings Bonds are interest-bearing certificates of debt issued by the United States Treasury and offering the investor a minimum guaranteed return. Also, they are backed by the full faith and credit of the U.S. government.

Some of the features common to all types of savings bonds are that they are:

- registered;

- nontransferable;

- redeemable at specified redemption values;

- variable as to time of maturity; and

- fully taxable by the federal government, although interest can be tax deferred.

Registered means that the federal government records the owner's name. In this way, the owner can get replacement Savings Bonds at no charge if the originals are lost, stolen, mutilated or destroyed. The owner applies to the Bureau of Public Debt for replacement of lost or stolen bonds.

Nontransferable means that ownership of the bond may not be transferred or assigned to another person. Bonds may be issued in the name of one person; in the names of two persons as co-owners; or in the name of one person as owner, with a second person as a beneficiary. When issuing a bond to co-owners, the institution uses the word "OR" to designate the type of ownership. The letters "P.O.D." ("payable on death") designate the beneficiary of a bond in the beneficiary form of ownership.

Redeemable at specified redemption values means that the U.S. Treasury specifies:

- the minimum length of time the bond must be held before redemption; and

- the redemption value of each bond depending on its denomination and issue date.

Variable as to time of maturity means that like bonds are issued with the same duration to maturity, but they may be redeemed at the discretion of the bondholder after a minimum of six months.

Fully taxable means that the owner must report any income realized from a U.S. Savings Bond for federal income tax purposes. However, interest that accrues on a savings bond is not taxed until the bond is cashed, disposed of or reaches maturity. Savings Bonds are not subject to state or local income taxes.

Two types of Savings Bonds the Treasury currently issues are Series EE and Series HH bonds (which replaced

Series E and Series H bonds, respectively, in 1980). The major difference between these two types of bonds is the way interest is paid. *Series EE bonds* are appreciation-type securities, meaning that interest earned on them is not actually paid to the owner until he or she cashes them in. *Series HH bonds* are current-income securities; they pay the owner interest every six months.

Individuals can order a Series EE bond through many depository institutions. A Series EE bond is issued at discount and sold in denominations ranging from $50 to $10,000 (see Figure 11-3). *Issued at discount* means that the purchaser pays less than face value for the bond. In the case of Series EE bonds, the purchaser pays 50% of the bond's face value. Figure 11-4 illustrates a standard application form for a Series EE bond.

Series EE bonds pay a variable rate of interest based on the average yield of five-year Treasury securities. Bonds issued since November 1, 1986, have a guaranteed minimum return of 6% if held at least five years. If the owner cashes the bond during the first five years after the issue date, the bond will pay a lower rate of interest.

Series EE bonds are a popular instrument for deferring income taxes, because interest earned on these bonds is not taxable to the owner until he or she redeems the bonds. By holding the bond for an extended period of time, investors may be able to decrease their tax burden. Note that the maximum allowable annual purchase of Series EE bonds for an individual is $30,000 ($15,000 purchase price).

A depository institution may act as an agent to redeem Series E and EE savings bonds. Institutions cannot charge a service fee or commission for redeeming bonds, but many still offer the service for the convenience of their customers. However, a depository institution may

F I G U R E 11-3

Series EE Bonds

Denomination	$50	$100	$200	$500	$1,000	$5,000	$10,000
Issue Price	$25	$50	$100	$250	$ 500	$2,500	$ 5,000

F I G U R E 11-4

Order for Series EE Bonds, Side 1

PD F 5263
Dept. of the Treasury
Bur. of the Public Debt
(Rev. May 1990)

ORDER FOR SERIES EE U.S. SAVINGS BONDS

OMB No. 1535-0084
Expires 9-30-91

PLEASE FOLLOW THE INSTRUCTIONS ON THE BACK WHEN COMPLETING THIS PURCHASE ORDER.

1. **OWNER OR FIRST-NAMED COOWNER (Bonds registered to)**

   Name

   Soc. Sec. No. ___ — ___ — ___

2. **BONDS TO BE DELIVERED "CARE OF"** (Do not complete this section unless name is different from the owner or first-named coowner in section 1 above.)

   Mail to:

3. **ADDRESS WHERE BONDS ARE TO BE DELIVERED**

   (NUMBER AND STREET OR RURAL ROUTE)

   (CITY OR TOWN)   (STATE)   (ZIP CODE)

4. **COOWNER OR BENEFICIARY** Coownership will be assumed if neither or if both blocks are checked (See #4 on back) The following person is to be named as   □ coowner   □ beneficiary:

   Name

5. **BONDS ORDERED**

Denom.	Quantity	Issue Price	Total Issue Price	FOR AGENT USE ONLY
$ 50		X $ 25.00	= $	
$ 75		X $ 37.50	= $	
$ 100		X $ 50.00	= $	
$ 200		X $ 100.00	= $	
$ 500		X $ 250.00	= $	
$ 1,000		X $ 500.00	= $	
$ 5,000		X $ 2,500.00	= $	
$ 10,000		X $ 5,000.00	= $	
TOTAL ISSUE PRICE OF PURCHASE			$	AFFIXED AGENT STAMP CERTIFIES THAT TOTAL AMOUNT OF PURCHASE IS CORRECT

6. **DATE PURCHASE ORDER AND PAYMENT PRESENTED TO AGENT**

   (MO.)   (DAY)   (YR.)

7. **SIGNATURE**

   PURCHASER'S SIGNATURE

   PURCHASER'S NAME, IF OTHER THAN OWNER OR FIRST-NAMED COOWNER (Please print)   ( )   DAYTIME TELEPHONE NUMBER

   STREET ADDRESS (If not shown above)   CITY   STATE   ZIP CODE

   The estimated average burden associated with this collection of information is 10 minutes per respondent or recordkeeper and varies from 10 to 30 minutes per response, depending on individual circumstances. Comments concerning the accuracy of this burden estimate and suggestions for reducing this burden should be directed to Bureau of the Public Debt, Forms Management Officer, Washington, DC 20239-1300 or the Office of Management and Budget, Paperwork Reduction Project (1535-0084), Washington, DC 20503

   AGENT COPY

F I G U R E 11-4, Continued

Order for Series EE Bonds, Side 2

INSTRUCTIONS FOR COMPLETING THE PURCHASE ORDER

1. **OWNER OR FIRST-NAMED COOWNER (Bonds registered to)** Clearly PRINT in block letters the full name and social security account number of the owner or first-named coowner. If this is a gift bond purchase, use the owner's name and social security number (if available). If the owner's social security number is unavailable, use the purchaser's S.S.N. See example below.

   Name ┌J┐┌O┐┌H┐┌N┐┌ ┐┌T┐┌ ┐┌S┐┌M┐┌I┐┌T┐┌H┐...

   Soc. Sec. No. ┌1┐┌2┐┌3┐ - ┌4┐┌5┐ - ┌6┐┌7┐┌8┐┌9┐

   Generally, only residents of the United States, its territories and possessions may be named on Series EE savings bonds. Bonds may be registered as follows:

   (a) Individuals in their own right - The bonds may be issued in the names of individuals (whether adults or minors) in single ownership, coownership, or beneficiary (P.O.D.) forms of registration.

   (b) Others - Bonds are also available in other forms of registration. If the form of registration or the address information cannot be completed as a result of the constraints of this form, please use Form PD 4882. Trust forms of registration must be submitted on Form PD 4882.

2. **BONDS TO BE DELIVERED "CARE OF".** After "Mail to:" print the name to whom the bonds are to be delivered if different from the owner or first-named coowner shown in 1. above. If the same as in 1. above, leave blank.

3. **ADDRESS WHERE BONDS ARE TO BE DELIVERED.** In all cases, print the address where the bonds are to be delivered.

4. **COOWNER OR BENEFICIARY.** If you wish to name a coowner or beneficiary on the bonds, check the appropriate box to indicate the form of registration desired and print the person's name.

   If you name a coowner: The bonds may be cashed by either coowner. The name of a living coowner cannot be eliminated without the written consent of that coowner.

   If you name a beneficiary: The bonds may not be cashed by the beneficiary during the lifetime of the owner. The name of a beneficiary can be eliminated without the beneficiary's consent.

5. **BONDS ORDERED.** Indicate next to the appropriate denomination the number of bonds being purchased; the total price involved for each denomination (no. of bonds X issue price); and the total amount of purchase. If you fail to indicate the denomination preferred, issue will be made with the fewest number of pieces which equal the total amount of purchase.

6. **DATE PURCHASE ORDER AND PAYMENT PRESENTED TO AGENT.** Indicate the date on which the purchase order and payment is presented (received) and accepted by the bank or other financial institution authorized to act as an agent of the Treasury Department.

7. **SIGNATURE.** Please sign this purchase order and print your name and address if it does not appear in the registration of the bonds. In order to promptly resolve any problems connected with this purchase order, also please provide a telephone number where you ordinarily may be reached Monday through Friday, from 9 a.m. to 5 p.m.

NOTE: Upon completion, submit purchase order and total amount of purchase to a financial institution authorized to receive savings bond orders. ALLOW ABOUT THREE WEEKS FOR PROCESSING

NOTICE UNDER THE PRIVACY AND PAPERWORK REDUCTION ACTS. The collection of the information, including social security number you are requested to provide on this form is authorized by 31 U.S.C. Ch. 31 and the regulations in 31 CFR Ch.11, Subch. B., relating to the public debt.

The purpose for requesting the information is to enable the Bureau of the Public Debt and its agents to issue savings bonds, to process transactions, to make payments, and identify owners and their accounts. The Bureau and its agents will use the information for these purposes. Furnishing the information is voluntary; however, without the information Treasury may be unable to issue a savings bond or to conduct other transactions.

Information obtained concerning securities holdings and transactions is considered confidential under Treasury regulations (see, e.g., 31 CFR, Part 323) and under the Privacy Act and is provided only to owners of securities or their authorized representatives and is not disclosed to others unless otherwise authorized by law.

F I G U R E 11-5

Series HH Bonds

Denomination	Semi-annual Interest Checks
$ 500	$ 15.00
$ 1,000	$ 30.00
$ 5,000	$150.00
$10,000	$300.00

limit the dollar amount of bond redemptions for individual customers according to institution policy.

Series HH bonds differ from Series EE bonds in several ways. Series HH bonds are issued at par (face) value and sold in denominations of $500 to $10,000. Interest on Series HH bonds issued on or after November 1, 1986, is paid in the form of a semiannual check at a rate of 6% per annum (see Figure 11-5).

Series HH bonds are available through Federal Reserve banks and from the Bureau of Public Debt and may be purchased only through the exchange of Series E/EE bonds and savings notes. By purchasing HH bonds, investors retain the tax advantage obtained from the E/EE bonds. This is possible because the customers use the interest accrued from the E/EE bonds to purchase HH bonds. Since they do not actually receive the original interest, taxation is deferred until they cash in the HH bonds.

Although depository institutions do not issue HH bonds, their employees need to know the basics of how they function. For example, a customer may come to a financial institution to redeem Series HH bonds in order to purchase a certificate of deposit. In this case, the counselor needs to know how to send the bonds in to the Federal Reserve Bank for collection. Counselors may also receive inquiries from customers about where to purchase HH bonds or about their method of paying interest.

Foreign Currency

Foreign currency includes all money other than U.S. dollars and coins. Some depository institutions will accept foreign currency from their customers and exchange it for U.S. dollars. The procedure for exchange of foreign currency may differ among institutions. In cases where the depository institution exchanges the currency through a third party, such as a correspondent bank, the customer may not receive credit for the funds until the institution is credited for the transaction. Depending on institution costs and procedures, institutions may charge for the exchange of foreign currency.

Preauthorized Payment Services

Preauthorized payment services allow customers to authorize their financial institutions to debit recurring payments from accounts. *Transmatic* ® is the trade name of a franchised, preauthorized payment system for financial institutions developed by SAF Systems and Forms. The system allows customers to bypass writing monthly checks for items such as loan payments, insurance premiums and other fixed-amount recurring bills. It also permits the bypassing of in-person deposits of payments received from other parties, such as tenants and employees.

A Transmatic® check is a preauthorized check in the amount the customer has authorized the institution to draw on his or her checking or NOW account. The date on which the Transmatic® check is drawn can be left to the discretion of the customer. For more efficient preparation of these checks, some depository institutions limit the customer's options to two or three specific dates, such as the 1st, 10th or 15th days of the month.

Some of the circumstances in which customers find the Transmatic® system useful include:

- payments on loans (mortgages, car loans, personal loans);

- deposits to deposit accounts;

- collection and deposit of tenants' rent checks; and

- payment of insurance premiums (life, health, auto, home).

The primary benefits to customers using the Transmatic® system are the saving of time and the reduction of paperwork. Customers save time by not having to write a check each month for recurring expenses. Customers also reduce their monthly paperwork because recurring payments are made from their deposit accounts automatically.

Institutions benefit from Transmatic® through the timely collection of loan payments and the goodwill the service creates. An institution that collects a loan payment from a customer's account at another financial institution on a designated day of the month benefits by knowing it will collect the payment on time. The goodwill generated by offering the service strengthens customer loyalty to the institution.

The counselor's procedure for initiating preauthorized payments has four easy steps:

1. The customer signs an authorization form that permits the checking or NOW account institution to honor preauthorized checks drawn on his or her account by another depository institution. The counselor indicates the payee and the amount of the check on the authorization form.

2. The counselor sends the completed authorization form, along with a transmittal letter from the institution, to the institution that holds the checking or NOW account. The initiating institution may send an indemnification agreement to the institution that holds the checking or NOW account. The indemnification agreement guarantees the checking or NOW account institution against any loss due to the Transmatic® transaction.

3. On the agreed-upon date, the initiating institution prepares a check (either manually or on the computer system) payable to itself. The preauthorized check contains all of the essential elements found on a normal check with the exception of the account holder's signature (see Figure 11-6). In place of the signature, the check carries language to the effect that "this payment has been authorized by your depositor and the above-

F I G U R E 11-6

Transmatic® Check

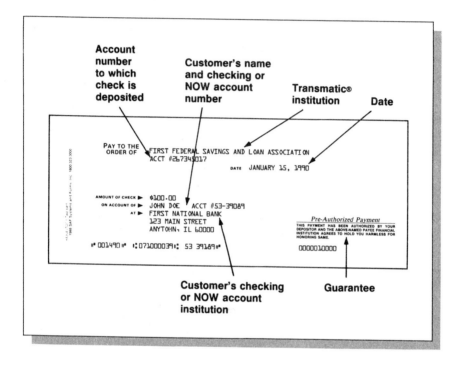

named payee financial institution agrees to hold
you harmless for honoring same."

4. The check is credited to the appropriate account
or accounts. Once endorsed, the Transmatic®
check clears the normal check clearing system
and is eventually paid by the bank on which it

is drawn. Then the institution either returns the check to the customer with his or her cancelled checks or retains it for safekeeping.

Prestige® Emergency Cash

Some depository institutions offer services that allow customers to cash personal checks or withdraw cash from their deposit accounts when they are out of town. One example of this type of service is Prestige® Emergency Cash (PEC). The Prestige® system was designed for savings institutions by SAF Systems and Forms to fill a need for interstate cash availability for travelers.

Deposit account holders benefit from PEC by having access to emergency cash when traveling out of town. Depository institutions benefit by addressing a potential customer need and thereby strengthening the business relationship with their customers.

The Prestige® card, shown in Figure 11-7, may be made of plastic or paper. It is similar in size and appearance to the typical credit card and carries the customer's name and account number on its face. To minimize the danger of unauthorized use, the card contains no sample signature.

When issuing a Prestige® card, the institution gives the customer several pieces of important information. One item is a directory or a toll-free 800 telephone number to help the customer locate participating institutions.

The maximum PEC amount is $200, whether obtained by cashing a personal check or by withdrawing from a deposit account. Only personal checks can be cashed. Payroll checks, traveler's checks, third-party checks (unless drawn on the institution cashing the check) and government checks are not acceptable.

F I G U R E 11-7

Prestige® Emergency Cash Card

Although all of the above restrictions are standard PEC limitations, they may be waived by mutual agreement of both the home and disbursing institutions. (The home institution is the one at which the customer holds the account; the disbursing institution is the out-of-town institution at which the customer cashes the check.)

CREDIT SERVICES

Two credit services that may be available at depository institutions are credit cards and overdraft credit. While other forms of credit are available to the consumer, credit cards and overdraft credit are the types most closely related to deposit accounts. This section explores these two services in detail.

A depository institution's primary reasons for providing credit services to its customers are to:

- help protect existing customer relationships; and

- make the institution more competitive in its efforts to attract new customers.

Credit Cards

A *credit card* is a plastic card the cardholder can use to make purchases or obtain cash advances utilizing a line of credit made available to him or her by the issuing financial institution. The two major cards financial institutions issue are Visa and MasterCard. An institution may choose to offer either one or both of these cards.

A credit card program available at a depository institution may be either secured or unsecured. A *secured credit card program* requires the customer to pledge a deposit account balance to obtain the card. An *unsecured credit card program* does not require the customer to have a deposit relationship with the card issuer. To the merchant accepting the credit card for a purchase, there is no difference between secured and unsecured credit cards.

One benefit to the customer of a secured credit card is a lower rate of interest charged by the issuing institution. Some institutions will lower the interest rate charged to customers to offset the deposit account balance required to obtain the card. Institutions offering secured credit cards may also choose to waive the annual fee.

The major benefit to depository institutions of offering secured credit cards is protection against credit card loan losses. If the customer defaults on the credit card loan, the institution has a source of funds in the pledged account.

Unsecured credit cards benefit customers by not requiring them to pledge their deposit accounts in order to obtain credit. Because the issuing institution lacks the security of a pledged account, unsecured credit cards usually have more stringent underwriting requirements. If customers fail to make payments on credit advanced to them, the institution may have a more difficult time recovering its losses.

However, unsecured credit cards benefit institutions because of their wide consumer appeal. Consumers often prefer an unsecured credit card service because it:

- offers a convenient way to pay for purchases by converting individual purchase transactions into a monthly bill;

- allows them to obtain small loans conveniently; and

- lets them stretch out payments for purchases.

An institution that issues secured or unsecured credit cards can set the features of the program. Average credit lines, annual interest rates, annual fees and availability of a grace period prior to the accrual of interest charges may differ from one depository institution to another. An issuing institution may also decide to offer additional services to cardholders. Some examples are cash advances, rebates, travel and accident insurance, and credit card registration services.

A depository institution may provide credit card services in one of the following ways:

- acting as a card issuer;

- acting as an agent;

- acting as a participating agent.

If the institution is a card issuer, it makes the credit decisions, funds the credit and incurs the profit or loss on the service. Start-up costs for a card issuer are significant, and usually only large institutions choose this alternative. It is profitable only if the institution has a very large volume of credit card accounts.

If the institution acts as an agent, it solicits customer applications on behalf of the card issuer. The agent may receive a solicitation fee and be able to have its name appear on the card. However, the actual credit decisions, funding, and profit or loss on the account are the responsibility of the card issuer.

If the institution acts as a participating agent, it funds a portion of the outstanding loans generated by its customers and shares in the profit or loss on its accounts. Whether or not the card issuer shares in the credit decisions varies from institution to institution.

Overdraft Credit

Overdraft credit services are of two types: overdraft protection and overdraft revolving credit.

Overdraft protection safeguards the customer from the expense and embarrassment of drawing a check on insufficient funds. It provides funds from another source to cover a check that would overdraw the account. The source of such funds can be any of the following:

- an automatic transfer from another deposit account;

- a deposit account loan against an associated deposit account;

- an unsecured loan, such as a credit card account.

Some characteristics of overdraft protection are:

- It is designed primarily to support the checking account service.

- The size of the credit line is usually relatively small.

- The loan is apt to be handled such that a subsequent deposit will wipe out the loan.

Overdraft revolving credit provides customers with instant access to a credit line via overdrafts on their checking accounts. In this system, funds are transferred from the loan account (the credit line) to the checking account to cover the overdraft.

Unlike with overdraft protection, the amount transferred to cover the overdraft is likely to be a multiple of a round number such as $50. The institution sends the customer a separate loan statement every month requesting that he or she make a minimum specified payment. Deposits to the checking account are usually not applied to the outstanding loan balance unless the customer is behind in the loan payments.

Following are examples of how overdraft protection and overdraft revolving credit can benefit customers of depository institutions:

- Irene Flaster writes a check for $695 to purchase a new sofa. Irene has $625 in her checking account, so the check triggers a potential overdraft. Because she has overdraft protection at her institution, Irene is protected from the embarrassment of an insufficient-funds check. The institution advances her the additional $70 to cover the check and charges her a nominal interest charge. Two days later, Irene makes a $1,000 deposit, of which $70 plus interest is used to pay off the loan.

- Hubert Allen's home urgently needs plumbing repairs. Hubert doesn't have the funds to pay for the repairs this month, but he has overdraft revolving credit at his institution. He writes a check to his plumber, and the needed funds are automatically transferred to his account in $50 increments. The following month, Hubert pays off his loan along with the interest charged.

ELECTRONIC BANKING SERVICES

Electronic banking services are those services available through depository institutions that utilize computer and electronic technology instead of checks and other paper transactions. Also called *electronic funds transfer system*, electronic banking allows consumers to access deposit accounts electronically to pay bills, make deposits and withdrawals, transfer funds between accounts, and other transactions.

In 1978, the federal government passed the Electronic Fund Transfer (EFT) Act. This act provided a framework for establishing the rights, liabilities and responsibilities of participants in electronic funds transfer systems. It also set specific guidelines for institutions offering EFT services and delineated consumers' rights.

Electronic banking services offer benefits to both the customer and the institution. The customer enjoys greater convenience, speed and accuracy when conducting transactions. The institution benefits through an improved depositor-institution relationship and the potential cost savings associated with electronic transactions.

A common element in many electronic banking services is the use of the *automated clearinghouse (ACH)*. The ACH is an organization formed by financial institutions that uses a computer-based facility to settle automatic payment and deposit transactions in given geographical areas. In short, ACH settles electronic payments. An example of an ACH transaction is the automatic payment of an insurance premium from a customer's checking account to the insurance company account.

The major advantages of the ACH system are:

- It permits clearing of items electronically, usually in one day.

- It makes funds available sooner.

- It eliminates the need to handle paper checks.

Examples of electronic banking services available at many depository institutions are debit cards, internal transfers of funds, direct deposit, pay-by-phone services, wire transfers and home banking. The remainder of this section explores each of these services individually.

Debit Cards

A *debit card* is a plastic card designed to give a customer access to funds in his or her deposit account to obtain cash, purchase goods and services, or transfer funds from one account to another. Debit cards resemble credit cards, but there are differences. The major difference is that when a customer uses a debit card, funds are deducted from his or her account either immediately or within a few days.

Many institutions encourage counselors to sign customers up for debit cards when opening deposit accounts. This practice often makes the customer perceive additional value in opening the account and enhances the relationship between the institution and the customer.

Used primarily in *automated teller machines (ATMs)* and point-of-sale (POS) terminals, debit cards are gaining in consumer popularity as new technology continues to increase the cards' capabilities. An ATM is similar to a cash dispenser in purpose and operation. In addition to withdrawal functions, an ATM may provide a full range of other functions, including deposits of funds and transfers. A POS terminal allows a merchant to access the funds in a depositor's account, with the customer's authorization, to pay for goods and services.

Some depository institutions offer Visa or MasterCard debit cards. Such a card has the universal acceptability of a major credit card and debits the purchase price directly from the customer's account.

The major benefits to customers of using debit cards are convenience and accessibility to funds. Debit cards allow customers to transact business on their accounts without having to visit their financial institutions. Many debit cards give customers 24-hour access to their funds on deposit.

Depository institutions that offer debit cards benefit through increased customer satisfaction and potential reductions in operating costs. By processing routine transactions such as deposits and withdrawals electronically, an institution often can save money on transaction costs. A routine transaction using a debit card can be processed quickly, inexpensively and accurately, and free up a teller to process other transactions.

Because debit cards work in electronic systems, institutions must comply with specific laws and regulations designed to protect customers. Regulation E applies to any deposit account that allows the account holder to make transactions through an electronic terminal, telephone, computer or magnetic tape. The major provisions of Regulation E include:

- required disclosure of terms and conditions to the account holder;

- definitions of account holder's liability for unauthorized transactions;

- procedure for handling errors on EFT transactions;

- requirement that customers receive documentation of transactions;

- other stipulations and definitions beneficial to customers.

Internal Transfers

Internal transfers are those transactions authorized by a customer in which funds are transferred from one account to another within the same institution.

Three types of internal transfers are automatic loan payments, interest transfers and systematic savings. Automatic loan payments are similar to Transmatic® payments except that funds are debited from deposit accounts within the institution. Interest transfers are regular transfers of interest earned on certificates of deposit that are deposited into another deposit account within the institution. Systematic savings is a savings plan in which customers designate specific amounts to be withdrawn from their savings or checking accounts and deposited into other accounts on a regular basis.

The primary benefit to customers of internal transfers is convenience. By having their loan payments and deposits made automatically on a designated day of the month, customers are assured of timely payments toward their obligations. Also, customers who wish to obtain additional cash flow from their certificates of deposit may choose to have their interest transferred each month to their savings accounts, where it will be readily available and earn additional interest.

Internal transfers benefit institutions in several ways. They allow institutions to offer a needed service that is relatively inexpensive to administer. They ensure that institutions will receive loan payments on time. By permitting transfer of interest from certificates to savings accounts, institutions can realize cost savings: Automatic transferring of interest to another account at the institution is cheaper than issuing an interest check, and the funds may remain on deposit with the institution for a longer time.

Direct Deposit

Direct deposit is a preauthorized system that automatically deposits funds into customers' deposit accounts. The funds may be from customers' employers, the government or other financial institutions. Although direct deposit normally is done electronically, sometimes it involves handling physical checks.

With *payroll direct deposit*, an employer automatically credits an employee's deposit account. Before each payday, the employer arranges for the transfer of funds from the company account to the employee's deposit account. On payday, the employee receives a confirmation of the deposit to the account rather than an actual paycheck. An employee may be able to specify that a portion of the deposit go into a savings account and the remainder into a checking account.

When the funds come from the government, they are called simply direct deposit. Anyone who receives any of the following monthly payments may have the Treasury Department deliver his or her funds directly to a financial institution:

- Social Security;

- Supplemental Security Income;

- Railroad Retirement;

- Civil Service Retirement;

- Veterans Administration Compensation and Pension;

- Air Force Active Duty and Retirement;

- Navy Retirement;

- Army Retirement;

- Marine Corps Active Duty;

- Federal Salary.

With *dividend check direct deposit*, the funds come from a financial institution. Some customers prefer to obtain monthly or quarterly interest checks from their certificate accounts at one institution and deposit the funds to a checking or deposit account at another institution. Customers can also have stock dividend checks and company retirement benefit checks deposited to their accounts automatically.

Procedures for initiating direct deposit vary depending on the source of the funds being deposited. Direct deposit of government payments is initiated by the customer through the receiving financial institution. Payroll direct deposit and dividend check direct deposit are initiated by the customer through the issuing company or institution.

To initiate direct deposit of government payments, the customer brings proof of payment (either a check or an award letter from the issuing agency) to the financial institution for processing. The counselor completes the appropriate form (see Figure 11-8) and gives a copy to the customer. The form is mailed to the Department of the Treasury for processing, and the initial funds are transferred directly to the institution, usually within three to six weeks. Upon receiving the initial payment, some institutions mail a receipt to the customer acknowledging the deposit to the proper account.

To initiate direct deposit of payroll or dividend checks, the customer contacts the issuer of the payment. The issuer may ask the customer for certain information, such as the ABA routing number of the receiving institution and the customer's account number. Once the issuer receives this information, it usually completes the direct deposit process.

Direct deposit benefits customers by ensuring that their recurring deposits will go to their deposit accounts on a timely basis. Further, timely deposits may allow customers to earn additional interest. Finally, deposits made electronically, through ACH, make the funds immediately available to customers; a direct deposit in the form of a check may or may not be immediately available, depending on the procedures of the receiving institution.

Direct deposit benefits institutions because it ensures a regular flow of funds into customers' deposit accounts.

F I G U R E 11-8

Authorization for Direct Deposit of Recurring Federal Payments

Standard Form 1199A
(Rev. June 1987)
Prescribed By
Treasury Department
Treasury Dept. Cir. 1076

DIRECT DEPOSIT SIGN-UP FORM

OMB No. 1510-0007
Expiration Date 1/31/90

DIRECTIONS

- To sign up for Direct Deposit, the payee is to read the back of this form and fill in the information requested in Sections 1 and 2. Then take or mail this form to the financial institution. The financial institution will verify the information in Sections 1 and 2, and will complete Section 3. The completed form will be returned to the Government agency identified below.

- A separate form must be completed for each type of payment to be sent by Direct Deposit.

- The claim number and type of payment are printed on Government checks. (See the sample check on the back of this form.) This information is also stated on beneficiary/annuitant award letters and other documents from the Government agency.

- Payees must keep the Government agency informed of any address changes in order to receive important information about benefits and to remain qualified for payments.

SECTION 1 (TO BE COMPLETED BY PAYEE)

A NAME OF PAYEE (last, first, middle initial)

ADDRESS (street, route, P.O. Box, APO/FPO)

CITY   STATE   ZIP CODE

TELEPHONE NUMBER
AREA CODE

B NAME OF PERSON(S) ENTITLED TO PAYMENT

C CLAIM OR PAYROLL ID NUMBER

Prefix   Suffix

D TYPE OF DEPOSITOR ACCOUNT   CHECKING   SAVINGS

E DEPOSITOR ACCOUNT NUMBER

F TYPE OF PAYMENT (Check only one)
☐ Social Security
☐ Supplemental Security Income
☐ Railroad Retirement
☐ Civil Service Retirement (OPM)
☐ VA Compensation or Pension
☐ Fed Salary/Mil. Civilian Pay
☐ Mil. Active
☐ Mil. Retire
☐ Mil. Survivor
☐ Other _____ (specify)

G THIS BOX FOR ALLOTMENT OF PAYMENT ONLY (if applicable)
TYPE   AMOUNT

PAYEE/JOINT PAYEE CERTIFICATION

I certify that I am entitled to the payment identified above, and that I have read and understood the back of this form. In signing this form, I authorize my payment to be sent to the financial institution named below to be deposited to the designated account.

SIGNATURE   DATE

SIGNATURE   DATE

JOINT ACCOUNT HOLDERS' CERTIFICATION (optional)

I certify that I have read and understood the back of this form, including the SPECIAL NOTICE TO JOINT ACCOUNT HOLDERS.

SIGNATURE   DATE

SIGNATURE   DATE

SECTION 2 (TO BE COMPLETED BY PAYEE OR FINANCIAL INSTITUTION)

GOVERNMENT AGENCY NAME

GOVERNMENT AGENCY ADDRESS

SECTION 3 (TO BE COMPLETED BY FINANCIAL INSTITUTION)

NAME AND ADDRESS OF FINANCIAL INSTITUTION

ROUTING NUMBER   CHECK DIGIT

DEPOSITOR ACCOUNT TITLE

FINANCIAL INSTITUTION CERTIFICATION

I confirm the identity of the above-named payee(s) and the account number and title. As representative of the above-named financial institution, I certify that the financial institution agrees to receive and deposit the payment identified above in accordance with 31 CFR Parts 240, 209, and 210.

PRINT OR TYPE REPRESENTATIVE'S NAME   SIGNATURE OF REPRESENTATIVE   TELEPHONE NUMBER   DATE

Financial institutions should refer to the GREEN BOOK for further instructions.
THE FINANCIAL INSTITUTION SHOULD MAIL THE COMPLETED FORM TO THE GOVERNMENT AGENCY IDENTIFIED ABOVE.

1199-204

11714 10/87

GOVERNMENT AGENCY COPY

SAF Systems and Forms, Inc.
CHICAGO, IL 1-800-323-3000

Direct deposit also strengthens the relationship between the customer and the institution.

Following are examples of how customers may use direct deposit:

- Isabel Parks has started a new job at Smith Furniture Company. One company benefit is a payroll direct deposit plan. Isabel obtains a form from her employer and fills in the appropriate information with help from her financial institution. Once completed, the form goes back to her employer for processing.

- John Walker retired last year and is now receiving a monthly Social Security check. He decides to sign up for direct deposit. John takes the check to his institution and completes the appropriate form. The counselor gives John a copy of the signed and completed form for his records and tells him that the procedure will be completed within three to six weeks. The counselor also tells John that it is the institution's policy to send written confirmation of the receipt of the first deposit in addition to his statement.

Pay-by-Phone Services

Pay-by-phone services allow customers to pay authorized bills, such as utility bills, by calling a designated phone number and requesting that funds be debited from their deposit accounts and credited to the merchant.

Pay-by-phone services were introduced in 1973. Relatively few financial institutions currently offer pay-by-phone services, but many experts in electronic funds transfer services predict increased availability with wider consumer acceptance in the years to come.

Depository institutions that offer their customers pay-by-phone services do so internally or through outside agencies. Some institutions that offer these services internally have found that high operating costs and insufficient customer transaction volumes limit their profitability. Because of this, many institutions now use outside agencies to handle pay-by-phone services.

Benefits to customers of pay-by-phone services are primarily time and cost savings. A customer who uses a telephone bill payment service saves the time it would take to write checks as well as the cost of checks, stamps and envelopes. However, the cost savings to the customer may be somewhat offset if the institution charges a fee for using the service.

The primary benefits to institutions of offering a telephone bill payment service are the possible fee income generated and increased customer loyalty from those who use the service.

Wire Transfers

A *wire transfer* is an electronic transfer of funds from one financial institution to another. Initiated by the customer from the sending institution, a wire transfer is a quick, safe way to transfer funds between institutions.

A wire transfer eliminates the physical handling of cash or checks. A wire transfer sent by a financial institution in the morning or early afternoon often reaches the receiving institution on the same day. Because no one actually handles the cash, a wire transfer incurs little chance of loss or theft.

To send a wire transfer, a customer authorizes the institution to wire funds to the appropriate person at the receiving institution. The sending institution gathers the details of the amount and destination of the funds and perhaps charges a fee for the transaction. It then sends the funds electronically through the Federal Reserve System to the receiving institution. Upon receipt of the funds, the receiving institution notifies the customer that the funds have arrived.

Wire transfers benefit customers by ensuring speed and safety. The funds usually reach their destination on the same day, unlike funds transferred by mail or hand delivery. The speed feature can also save the customer money. With large sums, it is important that the customer make transfers expediently so as not to lose interest on the funds. Customers with large deposit accounts particularly appreciate the ability to transfer funds between financial institutions easily and conveniently.

Institutions benefit from wire transfer services through fee income and the ability to provide increased customer service. Some institutions charge a fee for both incoming and outgoing wire transfers.

Home Banking

Home banking services allow customers to conduct financial transactions on their deposit accounts via computers, telephones or cables from their homes. Home banking services are relatively new to depository institutions and are not yet available at many. Many experts, however, predict that home banking is the future for financial institutions.

Although both institutions and consumers may gain considerable benefits from home banking, it is too early to tell whether these services will become standard fare for customers of depository institutions. Some questions that remain to be answered include:

- What level of service will people want, and at what price?

- What will be customers' primary reason for subscribing—access to accounts, bill paying, video home shopping, video entertainment or education?

- Will home banking systems expand to offer a broader range of types of equipment and a larger number of designated terminals?

- Will institutions' computers be able to handle home banking? (Consider that most home banking transactions will occur over a short time span; the majority of transactions will probably take place in the evening hours and be concentrated around the beginning of each month.)

- Will institutions be able to price their service profitably yet retain consumer demand for it?

- Can financial institutions afford not to offer home banking if their competition does?

INVESTMENT SERVICES

Many investors are interested in more sophisticated investments than the basic deposit accounts offered at depository institutions. Some financial institutions cater to investment needs by offering their customers brokerage and trust services.

Brokerage Services

A *brokerage service* at a financial institution allows customers to buy and sell securities and may or may not give investment advice. *Securities* is a general term referring to any note, stock, bond, mortgage, coupon, warrant, right, option, share or similar instrument. A *broker* is a person registered with the Securities and Exchange Commission (SEC) to effect transactions in securities for other people's accounts. In other words, a broker acts as an intermediary by buying and selling securities for customers. In exchange for this service, a broker receives a fee called a *commission*.

A financial institution may choose to offer either a full-service or a discount brokerage service. While both full-service and discount brokers deal with securities, they function very differently in a number of ways. *Full service* means that a broker or a registered representative provides investment advice to customers. A *discount broker* does not give investment advice but acts merely as an application taker. Because full-service brokers offer customers investment advice, their commissions are higher than those of discount brokers.

An institution may enter the brokerage business in one of three ways:

- work with a discount brokerage firm;

- form a joint service corporation;

- buy out an existing brokerage company and operate it as a subsidiary.

The last two options allow an institution to offer either full-service or discount services.

When an financial institution works with a discount brokerage firm, it merely accepts customer orders for execution and dispenses no investment advice. The brokerage service area must be completely separate and distinguishable from all other business areas of the institution. Also, all institution books and records must be kept separately from those of the brokerage company.

When an institution forms a joint service corporation, it positions itself between discount and full-service operations by offering limited investment advice. Examples of joint service corporations are firms such as Invest and ShareAmerica. These programs typically assist the institution through every step from initial setup to handling customer orders. They may also provide training, advertising and promotional support. Commissions earned in joint service corporation operations are shared between the financial institution and the joint corporation.

An institution that merges with, or acquires, an existing brokerage company obtains complete control over the brokerage services provided to its customers. The institution must form a subsidiary to accommodate the brokerage service.

The benefits to customers of using a depository institution's brokerage services are varied. Many customers like the convenience of being able to accomplish complex financial transactions at the same institution where they hold their deposit accounts. The reduced commissions charged by discount brokerage services are another benefit for some customers.

Financial institutions choose to offer brokerage services for a variety of reasons:

- to earn a profit;

- to more fully satisfy customers' investment needs;

- to meet competitors that already offer brokerage services;

- to beat the competition, if an institution is the first in its market area to offer such services;

- to protect its existing relationships with good (profitable) customers from the onslaught of cash management account products;

- to convert brokerage-only investors into broader depository institution customers.

Trust Services

Trust services available at depository institutions include the right to act in any fiduciary capacity permitted under the laws of the state in which the institution operates. Currently not all depository institutions offer trust services.

Many customers like the convenience of using depository institution trust services over those of trust companies or other corporations. Customers may establish trusts to:

- provide for the transfer of assets upon their death;

- protect their assets;

- obtain access to funds in the event of incapacity;

- reduce taxes;

- obtain professional asset management.

Trust services can be categorized as either personal or corporate. In many trust departments, the personal trust business predominates. Personal trust services available at financial institutions may include:

- acting as trustee or agent under testamentary trusts (wills and Totten trusts), living trusts (such as IRA and other types), land trusts, insurance trusts and other, similar trust arrangements;

- managing securities portfolios;

- serving as financial estate planner;

- managing real property;

- serving as guardian or custodian for property;

- acting as custodian for securities;

- providing investment advice.

Corporate trust services available may include:

- acting as trustee or agent for escrow funds;

- serving as custodian for property;

- managing securities portfolios;

- administering trust indentures (an indenture is a document that states the terms under which a security is issued);

- acting as a stock transfer agent;

- managing endowments;

- acting as trustee or agent for employee benefit trusts (SEP, Keogh, other pension plans, profit sharing, etc.);

- serving as a trustee or agent for a secondary market securities issuer.

Customers of financial institutions benefit from trust services through the convenience of being able to handle complex financial matters at the same institutions where they hold their deposit accounts. Customers may also incur reduced trust management costs, although this is not always the case.

Institutions benefit from trust services through increased fee income and customer loyalty. Fees charged for handling both personal and corporate trust services depend on the type and complexity of the account and the dollar amount of the assets involved.

SUMMARY

Depository institutions are in business to provide service to their customers. A broad range of services they offer are deposit account related. These services can be further categorized into convenience services, credit services, electronic banking services and investment services.

Financial institutions benefit in many ways from offering services related to deposit accounts. Two major benefits are increased customer loyalty and fee income. Customers profit from the convenience and the savings in time and money that these services provide.

Convenience services available include check-issuing services, sight drafts, U.S. Savings Bonds, exchange of foreign currency, preauthorized payment services and check-cashing services. Some institutions offer depositors reduced fees for convenience services in exchange for maintaining a specified minimum balance.

Credit services available include credit cards and overdraft credit. Credit cards may be either secured or unsecured, and terms of the credit agreement vary among institutions. Overdraft credit may be either a form of overdraft protection or a line of credit used in conjunction with a checking or NOW account.

Electronic banking services are gaining popularity with customers of financial institutions. Types of electronic banking services currently available include debit and ATM cards, internal fund transfers, direct deposit, pay-by-phone services, wire transfers and home banking.

Many institutions also offer their customers investment services. Two types of services frequently available are brokerage services and trust services. Brokerage services may include either full-service or discount brokers. A financial institution may choose to offer a brokerage service by working with an outside discount broker, forming a joint service corporation or buying out an existing brokerage company. Some institutions offer customers a wide range of trust services, including personal and corporate trust services.

A   **accommodation check**   A check or draft drawn by an institution either on itself or on its account with another institution, signed by an authorized officer and payable to a third party named by the customer making the withdrawal; also called a bank check.

accounts-in-trust statutes   The state laws that protect a financial institution from liability in paying out funds to a beneficiary under a Totten (tentative) trust. Such statutes do not determine ownership, but only protect the institution in making such a payment where no other claim has been made to the account.

accounts-in-two-names statutes   The state statutes that protect a financial institution from liability in paying out funds to one or more of the surviving joint tenants after the death of a joint tenant.

ACH   *See* automated clearinghouse.

administrator   A person who is appointed by the court to dispose of the estate of a person who died without a will.

ancillary administrator   An estate representative appointed by the court in a state other than the decedent's domicile state. An ancillary administrator is appointed if the decedent maintained an out-of-state residence, or owned property or conducted business interests out-of-state.

ancillary executor   An estate representative appointed in a will to administer the disposition of an estate in a state other than the decedent's domicile state. The named ancillary executor would handle the disposition of the decedent's out-of-state residences, properties and/or businesses.

annual yield   *See* effective yield.

annuity 1. A fixed interest or dividend payment made at periodic intervals to an investor. 2. A type of investment offered by life insurance companies.

artificial person A legal entity, such as a corporation, having the powers, rights and privileges of an individual.

ATM *See* automated teller machine.

attorney in fact Any person appointed and authorized by another to act as an agent under a power of attorney agreement.

automated clearinghouse (ACH) An organization formed by financial institutions using a computer-based facility to settle automatic payment and deposit transactions among financial institutions in a given geographic area.

automated teller machine (ATM) A device that is similar to a cash dispenser in purpose and operation. However, an ATM performs a full range of transactions, usually including deposits of funds and transfers.

B **backup withholding** The IRS's requirement that the institution withhold a portion of the interest earned on a deposit account from a customer due to certain circumstances, such as failing to provide a tax identification number or underreporting interest or dividend income.

bank check A check issued by a depository institution for a specific amount specified by the customer and purchased with cash, or check or a withdrawal from an account at the institution.

beneficial interest The right to use or benefit from money or property, as opposed to legal title.

beneficial ownership   The right to use or benefit from property. Also called the equitable interest.

beneficiary   The person designated to receive the benefits accruing from the funds in a trust account or an insurance policy.

blended interest rate   An interest rate structure such that only the balance of a deposit account that is above the designated amount earns a higher rate and the balance below earns a lower rate.

broker   An agent who negotiates contracts of purchase and sale (of real estate, commodities, securities or other services or products). A full-service broker provides the customer with investment advice; a discount broker is an application taker only and provides no investment advice.

brokerage service   An organization that allows customers to buy and sell securities and may or may not give investment advice.

C   **cashier's check**   A check drawn by a bank on itself, signed by a cashier or other authorized bank officer and payable to a third party named by the customer.

certificate of deposit   A type of deposit account typically with a fixed minimum term and a minimum initial deposit; interest rates may be either fixed or variable; also called certificate or CD. Called share certificates at credit unions.

certified check   A check that guarantees that (1) the signature of the drawer is genuine and (2) sufficient funds are on deposit for its payment. The amount certified is set aside by the financial institution for the express purpose of paying the check, and the financial institution is obligated to pay the check when payment is requested.

charter A legal authorization to conduct business. It may be granted by the state or federal government.

check A type of draft; the Uniform Commercial Code defines it as "a draft drawn on a bank and payable on demand."

check hold *See* uncollected funds.

check safekeeping *See* check truncation.

check truncation The process of microfilming customers' paid checks; the microfilm is the official record of the transaction and is retained by the financial institution. Canceled checks are stored rather than being returned to the customer. Also called check safekeeping.

clearinghouse An organization of financial institutions established to exchange and settle checks drawn on each other. *See also* automated clearinghouse.

club account An account in which a customer makes a certain number of periodic deposits over a specified time interval. At the end of this time period, the institution usually closes the account and distributes the funds in a lump sum to the customer.

commercial bank A privately owned and operated financial institution chartered by a state or federal agency for the purposes of facilitating commerce, providing a safe repository for deposited funds, facilitating the transfer of those funds by check and extending credit.

commission The fee a broker receives for buying or selling securities for a customer.

common law The body of law developed in England primarily from judicial decisions based on custom and precedent, unwritten in statute or code, and constituting the basis of the English legal system and of the system in all of the United States except Louisiana.

community property A form of ownership by husband and wife, recognized in certain states, which includes all property that was (1) gained or earned by either spouse during the marriage, (2) not owned individually at the time of marriage, and (3) not acquired by either spouse during marriage by inheritance, will or gift.

compensation The salaries, wages, professional fees and other amounts received for services rendered. Examples of compensation include commissions, tips, bonuses and income earned from self-employment in which personal services are rendered.

competence The quality or condition of being legally able to act in a particular way.

compound interest Interest that accrues when earnings for a specified period are added to principal; thus interest for the following period is computed on the principal plus accumulated interest.

conservator A legally appointed guardian for an incompetent person.

constructive distribution The type of distribution that results in the total IRA balance being considered by the IRS to be distributed as a result of a prohibited transaction. *See* prohibited transactions.

contingent beneficiary The person(s) designated to receive IRA death benefits in the case where the primary beneficiary predeceases the grantor.

contract   A binding agreement between two or more parties that is enforceable by law.

contributory IRA   A type of Individual Retirement Account established by individuals who set aside all or a portion of their yearly compensation; also called a regular or individual IRA.

conveyance   **1.** The transfer of title to property from one person to another. **2.** An instrument or document by which title is transferred, such as a deed, will, check or cash.

corporate resolution   A legal document, drawn up by a corporation's board and certified with the corporate seal, that authorizes and empowers specific corporate officers to take specific actions regarding the corporation's business. A corporate resolution also appears on the corporation signature card.

corporation   **1.** A form of business organization legally binding a group of individuals to act as one entity, carrying on one or more related enterprises and having the powers, rights and privileges of an individual; the corporation continues to exist regardless of changes in its membership or ownership. **2.** An artificial person; a legal entity created by law and organized under state or federal authority.

correspondent bank   A financial institution that provides one or more services for another institution in return for the maintenance of deposit balances and/or fees. Typical services are check handling for out-of-area checks, trust services and technical services.

co-trustee   One of two or more trustees of the same trust.

credit card   A plastic card that can be used by the holder to make purchases or obtain cash advances using a line of credit made available by the card-issuing financial institution.

credit union   A mutually owned and operated depository institution that provides its members with deposit accounts and loans. Distinguished from other depository institutions by the "common bond" requirement for membership: a member must share a specified trait with the other members.

custodial gift   A gift to a minor child from an adult who retains control over the gift, or grants such control to another adult, until the child reaches the age of majority and legally can accept responsibility for the gift.

custodian   A fiduciary having control and possession (custody) of something that belongs to someone else; the custodian is responsible for its care and preservation.

customer draft   *See* sight draft.

D   **daily compounding**   A frequency of calculating interest whereby interest is added to the principal each day and then earns interest itself.

debit card   A plastic card designed to give a customer access to funds in his or her deposit account to obtain cash, purchase goods and services or transfer funds from one account to another.

decedent   A deceased person, ordinarily used with respect to one who has died recently. A deposit account held in the name of an executor or administrator of a deceased person's estate is called a decedent estate account.

defined benefit plan   A plan where the employer makes contributions among the plan participants' accounts according to a formula that reflects both the retirement income needs of employees and their years of service to the company. The annual contribution is the amount needed from year to year to accumulate plan assets sufficient to pay each participant's projected retirement benefit.

defined contribution plan   A qualified plan where the employer makes contributions among the plan participants' accounts according to an allocation formula. Each participant's account balance at retirement age will determine the retirement benefit.

Depository Institutions Act of 1982   A major federal law, also known as the Garn-St Germain Act, that touched on a range of activities for commercial banks, thrifts and credit unions. Major provisions included expanded lending powers for depository institutions, new investment authorities, noncash capital assistance for qualified financial institutions, and a requirement that federal financial regulators develop a "money market" account for banks and thrifts.

Depository Institutions Deregulation and Monetary Control Act of 1980   A major federal law affecting all depository institutions. Among the important provisions of the law were an orderly phase-out of regulated maximum interest rates on accounts in depository institutions; an increase on federal insurance for individually owned savings accounts; and nationwide authorization of NOW accounts. The law expanded the influence of the Federal Reserve System on all financial institutions by changing reserve requirements on certain accounts and expanding access to certain Federal Reserve Services to all depository institutions. Provisions specifically affecting federal savings associations included increased authorization to make consumer loans and authorization to engage in credit card operations.

direct deposit A preauthorized system in which customers' government benefits are automatically deposited to their checking or deposit accounts. Persons who receive any of the following monthly payments may instruct the Treasury Department to deliver their checks directly to a financial institution: Social Security, Supplemental Security Income, Railroad Retirement, Veterans Administration Compensation and Pension, Air Force Active Duty and Retirement, Navy Retirement, Army Retirement, Marine Corps Active Duty and/or Federal Salary. *See also* dividend check direct deposit and payroll check direct deposit.

direct transfer The moving of IRA funds from one IRA trustee directly to another IRA trustee, with no check being made payable to the IRA participant. This form of transfer is not subject to any time or frequency restrictions.

disclosure statement **1.** In reference to IRAs, a nontechnical explanation of the terms and conditions of the IRA trust account agreement. This form must be provided to all IRA participants. **2.** In general, the information required by government regulations to be given a borrower prior to consummation of a loan.

discount broker *See* broker.

disintermediation The process by which individuals build up their holdings of market instruments, such as U.S. government and agency issues, stocks and bonds, and slow down their additions to deposit accounts at financial institutions.

distributions   The withdrawals from retirement plans. IRA distributions may be either actual or constructive. An actual distribution is one in which the participant receives payment of the funds. A constructive distribution is any one of several circumstances in which IRA law deems that the participant has received a distribution, even though the participant has not received payment of any IRA funds.

diversification   The balancing of funds among various types of investments.

dividend   The return on investment that shareholders at credit receive.

dividend check direct deposit   A preauthorized system where customers' interest checks are automatically deposited to their checking or deposit accounts.

domicile   An individual's true, fixed and permanent home and principal establishment and to which, whenever he or she is absent, he or she has the intention of returning. The term is not synonymous with residence; a person may have several residences but only one domicile.

donor   *See* grantor.

draft   An instrument on which one party orders another party to pay money to a third party.

durable power of attorney   Expands the legal power of attorney in that it survives the disability or incompetency of the principal, unless a court directs otherwise.

E   **earnings distribution date**   The date on which interest is credited to the account or otherwise made available to the owner.

effective yield The actual return expected on an investment after any compounding.

electronic banking services The services available through depository institutions that utilize computer and electronic technology instead of checks and other paper transactions.

electronic funds transfer system (EFTS) A system whereby financial information is transferred from the deposit account of the payer to the deposit account of the payee. The payment message may be executed immediately, as in a purchase transaction at the retail point-of-sale terminal, or it may be executed on a batch basis, as in the daily distribution of transactions by the automated clearinghouse to member financial institutions.

employer IRA *See* third-party sponsored IRA.

equitable interest *See* beneficial ownership.

estate **1.** The ownership rights that a person has to lands or other property; the term also denotes the property itself. **2.** All of an individual's assets and liabilities left at his or her death.

evidence of account Written agreement on a deposit account with transactions confirmed by issuance of a receipt or advice. Traditionally, passbooks and certificates.

excess contribution An amount greater than the IRA participant's annual allowable contribution. An excess contribution is subject to a 6% penalty imposed on the participant by the Internal Revenue Service. An excess contribution is not deductible for the participant.

exculpatory clause A clause in a contract that relieves one party from liability in certain circumstances.

executor/executrix   An individual appointed in a will and approved by a probate court to administer the disposition of an estate according to directions in the will.

F **federal estate tax**   An excise tax levied upon the transfer of a person's property at his or her death.

fiduciary   A person or corporation with the responsibility of holding or controlling property for another.

financial intermediary   An institution that accepts money from individuals and uses those funds to make loans and other investments in its own name.

full service broker   *See* broker.

fully taxable   A characteristic of ownership, e.g., a U.S. Savings Bond, in which any income or gain realized must be reported by the owner for federal income tax purposes.

G **Garn-St Germain Act**   *See* Depository Institutions Act of 1982.

general partner   A partner who shares equally, or as contractually agreed on, with the other general partners in the partnership's profits and losses.

gift language   The language found in a joint tenancy deposit contract that clarifies the fact that all funds placed in the account are owned by all the joint tenants together; a deposit by any one tenant is considered a gift to the other tenants.

gift tax   A tax on gifts whose value exceeds a certain amount.

grace period A time period within which a depositor can withdraw funds from a certificate without penalty.

grantor The owner of the money or property who makes a settlement or creates a trust of property; also called a settlor or donor.

guardian A type of fiduciary who is legally vested with the power, and the duty, of personally managing the property and rights of another who, because of age, disability, degree of understanding or self-control, or some other misfortune, is considered incapable of handling his or her own affairs.

H **hold** A notation made on an account record to show that a specific amount of money temporarily is withheld from the balance that is available to the owner or to show that the account requires special handling.

home banking services A system that allows customers to conduct financial transactions on their deposit accounts via computers, telephones or cables from their homes.

I **incompetence** A legal term meaning that a person is underage or of unsound mind and legally is not permitted to act in certain ways.

individual account A type of account owned and controlled by one natural person as distinguished from ownership by a corporation or other legal entity.

Individual Retirement Account (IRA) A tax-deferred, trusteed deposit account into which certain eligible individuals contribute funds for retirement up to annual contribution limits. Approved vehicles for IRAs include deposit accounts and certificates at financial institutions, insurance annuities, mutual fund offerings and certain self-managed securities accounts at stock brokerage firms.

inheritance tax   A tax imposed on each inheritor (beneficiary) of an estate. Each beneficiary pays a tax based on (1) the size of the inheritance and (2) the beneficiary's relationship to the decedent.

inheritance tax waiver   A release signed by the appropriate state taxing official in which the state relinquishes any claim to the assets of the estate, or a portion thereof, under consideration.

intermediation   The investment process by which savers and investors place funds in financial institutions in the form of deposit accounts, and the financial institutions in turn use the funds to make loans and other market investments.

internal transfers   The transactions authorized by a customer in which funds are transferred from one account to another within the same institution.

intestate   **1.** Not having made a will. **2.** Leaving no will at death.

IRA   *See* Individual Retirement Account.

irrevocable trust   A trust where the grantor does not reserve the right to change or annul the trust agreement.

issued at discount   A selling price that is less than the face value. Series EE Bonds are issued at discount.

J **joint tenancy** A form of ownership by two or more parties who share equal rights in and control of property, with the survivor or survivors continuing to hold all such rights on the death of one or more of the tenants.

K **Keogh plan** A tax-deferred, trusteed savings plan that allows self-employed individuals, or those who own their own unincorporated businesses, to accumulate funds for retirement. Employers who establish a Keogh plan for themselves must also make contributions for their qualified employees.

L **leeway period** The period of time during which IRAs may be established or IRA and Keogh contributions made, applying to the preceding tax year. The leeway period for contributory IRAs other than rollovers is the period of time between January 1 and April 15.

legal guardian A person appointed by the court to manage any substantial property of a minor.

letters of administration The administrator's formal authority to dispose of the estate of a person who died without a will.

letters testamentary The executor's formal authority to execute a will and dispose of the decedent's estate.

limited partner A partner who is restricted in the amount of profits he or she can take from a partnership. A limited partner cannot lose more than his or her individual investment in the business and has limited power to act on behalf of the partnership.

liquidity   The ability to convert an investment to cash without significant financial loss at a particular point in time.

local check   A check written on a bank within the same Federal Reserve check processing region as the depository institution.

M **magnetic ink character recognition (MICR)**   The electronic reading of machine-readable characters printed in magnetic ink, such as those appearing on checks. Routing and transit numbers on a check typically are MICR-encoded.

majority   The age, provided by state law, when a child becomes an adult. In most states, a child reaches majority at the age of 18; a few states set the age of majority at 19 or 21.

marital deduction   The amount that may be given to a spouse free of estate tax.

maturity date   The date on which the account holder may redeem the certificate for the principal balance plus interest.

members   The group of savers and borrowers in a mutual financial institution who elect directors, amend the bylaws, approve any basic corporate change of policy or organization, and in general possess most of the rights of ownership that stockholders have in a stock corporation.

MICR   *See* magnetic ink character recognition.

minor   A person who has not yet attained the age of majority as provided by state law. *See also* majority.

MMDA *See* money market deposit account.

money market deposit account (MMDA) A deposit account offered by financial institutions that is designed to be directly equivalent to, and competitive with, money market mutual funds. The account has some limitations on the monthly number of certain transactions.

money market mutual fund A mutual fund that invests in short term obligations, such as commercial paper or Treasury bills.

money order An order, purchased from a financial institution, the U.S. Postal Service or a commercial company, to pay a sum of money specified by the purchaser to a party named by the purchaser.

money purchase pension plan A type of qualified defined contribution plan. A plan where a specified percentage of an employee's annual salary, up to allowable limits, is contributed.

mutual institution A financial institution that issues no capital stock, but is owned and controlled solely by its members. Members do not share in profits.

mutuality The equality of status and opportunity among members.

N **natural guardian** A parent of a minor.

natural person An individual person, in contrast to an artificial person such as a corporation or other legal entity.

negotiable An instrument capable of being transferred from one person to another by being delivered with or without endorsement so that the title passes to the transferee.

nonlocal check   A check written on a bank outside the Federal Reserve check processing region of the depository institution.

nontransferable   A characteristic of ownership of certain items, e.g., deposit accounts, stocks, bonds, etc., that does not allow the owner to transfer or assign his or her ownership rights to another person without first changing ownership on the records of the issuer.

NOW account   A deposit account from which the account holder can withdraw funds by writing a negotiable order of withdrawal (NOW) payable to a third party. Interest may be paid on a NOW account.

NOW draft   A negotiable instrument written on a NOW account to make third-party payments.

O   **overdraft protection**   A line of credit on which customers can write checks for an amount over and above the balance in their checking accounts.

overdraft revolving credit   A consumer credit service that provides the customer access to a credit line on which customers can write checks for an amount over and above the balance in their checking accounts. Funds are transferred from the credit account to the checking account, usually in multiples of some round number such as $50.

owner-employee   A sole proprietor or one who owns more than a 10% interest in his or her business.

ownership The complete ownership of property is made up of two elements: (1) the legal title and (2) the right to use or benefit from the property, called the beneficial ownership.

P **partnership** A form of business organization in which two or more persons join in a commercial or business enterprise, sharing profits and risks as they have contractually agreed. No stock is issued, and the partnership exists only as long as all partners stay in the business; a change of partner necessitates the formation of a new partnership.

partnership agreement A legal document that establishes ownership of the business. The agreement contains the purpose of the business, powers and authority of each of the partners, how profits and losses are shared, and the distribution of assets upon termination of the partnership.

pay-by-phone service A service that allows customers to pay authorized bills by calling a designated phone number and requesting that funds be debited from their deposit account and credited to the merchant.

payroll direct deposit A preauthorized system whereby customers' paychecks are deposited automatically into their checking or deposit accounts.

penalty A charge imposed for a total or partial withdrawal from a certificate prior to the end of the contractual term.

personal identification number (PIN) A secret number or code used by an account holder to authorize a transaction or obtain information regarding his or her account. The PIN may be used in conjunction with a plastic card to ensure that the person activating an automatic device with a plastic card is the individual to whom the card was issued.

PIN   *See* personal identification number.

pledge   The delivering of goods or personal property for use as security or collateral on a loan or a promise. Deposit accounts may be pledged as collateral for a loan.

P.O.D. account   A type of account opened in the name of an individual, with instructions to "pay on death" to another named individual. P.O.D. accounts are permitted in few states; the state statute authorizing this type of account should be cited on the deposit contract.

power of attorney   **1.** A document that authorizes one person to act legally in place of another person under specified conditions for specified purposes. **2.** The official capacity of a person named in the power of attorney document.

preauthorized payment (PAP) service   An agreement signed by the customer that permits an institution to withdraw or deposit funds to a specific account on a recurring basis.

Prestige® Emergency Cash (PEC)   A spin-off of the Transmatic® System. A service that gives customers the ability to cash personal checks or withdraw cash from their savings accounts while they are out of town.

primary beneficiary   The person(s) designated to receive benefits from an IRA in the case of the death of the grantor.

probate court   The court that has jurisdiction over the probate of wills and the administration of decedents' estates. The *probation* of a will is the official process of proving its authenticity.

profit-sharing plan A type of qualified defined contribution plan whereby contributions are contingent upon a company's profits or retained earnings.

prohibited transactions The actions involving an IRA that the IRS considers will result in a constructive distribution. Prohibited transactions include actions involving an IRA with borrowing money; selling, leasing or exchanging property; or receiving unreasonable compensation for managing it. *See also* constructive distribution.

proxy 1. The authority or power to act for another. 2. A document giving such authority. 3. The person authorized to act for another.

prudent man rule A rule that implies that fiduciaries should make only those investments which a prudent, common-sensed, practical business person would make with his or her own funds, having regard for both the safety and stability of the principal and a reasonable income return.

Q **qualified retirement plan** An employee benefit plan that qualifies for special tax treatment under Internal Revenue Code Section 401(a).

R **redeemable at specified redemption values** A characteristic of a U.S. Savings Bond set by the Treasury as to the minimum length of time the bond must be held before redemption and the redemption values of a particular bond depending on its denomination and issue date.

registered   An ownership in which the owner's name is recorded by the issuer, i.e., a savings bond is registered in the name of the owner by the federal government.

registered representative (RR)   A broker-employee who handles customers' orders. Individuals are required to complete rigid courses and examinations to qualify as registered representatives.

regular IRA   *See* contributory IRA.

regular savings account   A form of deposit account with no legal limits or requirements as to amount, duration, or times of additions or withdrawals. Called a share account at credit unions.

Regulation D   A requirement of the Federal Reserve System that depository institutions maintain reserves against their transaction accounts and nonpersonal time deposits with original maturities of less than four years.

relationship banking   The selling of additional products and services that enhance the value of the initial account.

representative payee   A type of fiduciary who is appointed by the federal government to handle certain federal benefit payments on behalf of another.

required reserve   A specified amount of cash in a financial institution's own vault or claims on cash on deposit with other financial institutions, the minimum amount of which is prescribed by the institution's regulatory agency or agencies. The purpose of requiring a minimum amount of reserves is to maintain the ability to pay liabilities, e.g., customers' cash withdrawals, in cash.

revocable trust A trust that allows the original owners of the funds to change the terms of the trust agreement to adapt to possible changes in intention.

right of survivorship A distinguishing feature of joint tenancy and tenancy by the entirety: when one tenant dies, the surviving tenant or tenants continue to own the entire estate. Without the right of survivorship, the deceased tenant's interest in the estate would pass to his or her heirs.

rollover IRA A type of IRA that allows employees who receive a lump-sum distribution upon leaving an employer, or upon termination of an employer's qualified plan, to deposit all or any portion of the funds in an IRA. Only amounts not previously declared as income may be put into a rollover IRA. The portion of eligible distribution that is put into such an account enjoys the same tax-deferral status as a regular contributory IRA.

rule against perpetuities A rule that prevents the locking up of trust funds beyond a reasonable length of time. The exact length of time varies with state laws.

rules of the account class The account specifications, such as duration, term, early withdrawal penalty and interest rate, that are established by an institution's board of directors and included in the deposit account contract. Rules of the class are established for each account classification, such as regular savings, NOW accounts, certificates of deposit and so on.

S **salary reduction plan** A tax-deferred savings plan that allows employees to contribute, usually through payroll deductions, up to a specified percentage of their salaries into one or more employer-selected plans. Employees' contributions are made with pretax dollars which are not reported for income tax purposes. Employers usually also will match the employees' contributions in a specified way. Also called Section 401(k) plan.

SARSEPS   The tax-deferred salary reduction arrangements for employees of small firms (25 employees or less). Employees can elect to defer some of their income from taxation by making voluntary pre-tax contributions under the employer's SEP.

savings association   A financial intermediary that accepts savings from the public and invests those savings mainly in residential mortgage loans; always a corporation, it may be either a mutual or a capital stock institution and may be either state-chartered or federally chartered. Also called a savings and loan association, cooperative bank, homestead society, or building and loan association.

savings bank   A type of financial intermediary organized in the 1800s to encourage thrift and provide a safe and profitable place for industrial workers to save. They may be mutually or stock owned and be state or federal chartered.

savings institution   A classification of financial intermediary that includes savings associations and savings banks. *See also* thrift institution.

SEC   *See* Securities and Exchange Commission.

Section 401(k) plan   *See* salary reduction plan.

secured credit card program   A consumer credit service where the customer is required to pledge a deposit account balance to acquire a credit card.

securities A general term referring to any note, stock, bond, mortgage, coupon, warrant, right, option, share or other similar instrument.

Securities and Exchange Commission (SEC) A federal agency that administers the Securities Exchange Act of 1934 and has broad regulatory responsibilities over the securities markets, the self-regulatory organizations within the securities industry and persons conducting a business in securities.

Securities Exchange Act of 1934 The act that provides for the regulation of securities brokers and dealers and securities trading generally.

SEP *See* Simplified Employee Pension Plan.

Series EE Bond An interest-bearing certificate of debt issued at discount by the United States Treasury and sold in denominations of $50, $75, $100, $200, $500, $1,000, $5,000 and $10,000. The bonds are redeemable at face value upon maturity. Replaced Series E Bonds in 1980.

Series HH Bond An interest-bearing certificate of debt issued at par (face) value and sold in denominations of $500, $1,000, $5,000 and $10,000 on which interest is paid semiannually by Treasury check. Replaced Series H Bonds in 1980.

settlor *See* grantor.

share account Name for a deposit account held at a credit union.

share holder Name for a depositor at a credit union.

sight draft A customer's order to a financial institution holding his or her funds to pay all or part of them to another institution in which the customer holds an account; also called a customer draft.

signature card   A form, executed by an account holder, establishing the form of account ownership and setting forth some of the basic terms of the account and provisions of the deposit contract.

simple interest   Interest paid on the principal balance only.

Simplified Employee Pension Plan (SEP)   A plan used by an employer to make contributions toward an employee's retirement income. The employer makes contributions, up to annual contribution limits, directly to an IRA set up by an employee with a savings institution, insurance company or other qualified financial institution. Also called Section 408(k).

smart card   A plastic card with an embedded microcomputer chip that contains programmable functions and a memory. It also has a magnetic stripe, permitting its use in ATMs.

spousal IRA   A type of contributory IRA that enables a working spouse to establish and contribute to an IRA for his or her nonworking spouse. Spousal IRAs are available to spouses who file joint federal income tax returns.

statutes of descent   The state laws that describe the persons who inherit a decedent's property and also the order in which they inherit. Spouses, children and grandchildren ordinarily have higher priority.

stock   A certificate in evidence of a shareholder's proportionate ownership of a corporation. The owner may have voting rights and rights to any dividends declared by the board of directors.

stockholder   A person who owns part of a corporation as represented by the shares held.

stock institution   A financial institution organized as a capital stock corporation, with investors providing operating capital by purchasing an ownership interest in the institution, represented by shares of stock.

stop order   *See* suspension order.

stop payment order   An order by the customer instructing the financial institution to refuse payment of a specified draft or check.

successor trustee   The person designated by a trust agreement or by a court to be trustee under a trust in the event the original trustee dies, resigns, is removed or becomes incompetent.

survivorship   *See* right of survivorship.

suspension order   A written instruction from an account owner to an institution to refuse or restrict all payments of withdrawals from his or her deposit account. A suspension order may be imposed by any one account owner, but signatures of all account owners are required to release the suspension order.

T   **tax identification number**   The number used to identify an individual or entity for federal income tax purposes.

tenancy by the entirety   A form of ownership by husband and wife, recognized in certain states, in which the rights of the deceased spouse automatically pass to the surviving spouse.

tenancy in common A form of ownership in which two or more parties own property, but in which each owns a separate pro rata interest; when one owner dies, that owner's share passes to his or her heirs, not to the remaining owner(s). In tenancy in common account ownership, signatures of all owners are necessary for withdrawal.

tentative trust *See* Totten trust.

testate 1. To make a will. 2. Having left a will at death.

testator A deceased person who has left a will.

third-party sponsored IRA A trust created by an employer for the exclusive benefit of his or her employees or their beneficiaries, or by an association of employees for the exclusive benefit of its members or their beneficiaries, and treated as an Individual Retirement Account. Also called Section 408(c) IRA.

thrift institution A classification of financial intermediary that includes savings associations and savings banks. *See* savings institutions.

thrift/savings plan A type of qualified defined contribution plan. With this plan, employees contribute, usually through payroll deductions, a specified mandatory percentage of their salaries to qualify for specified matched employer contributions. The plans may also provide for receiving unmatched voluntary employee contributions up to 10% of the employee's salary. All employee contributions are made with after-tax dollars which are nondeductible.

tiered interest rate An interest rate structure in which the entire account balance earns a higher rate once it reaches the designated level.

TIN *See* tax identification number.

Totten trust   A revocable trust account established without a written trust agreement.

trade name   An assumed name under which a business operates.

Transmatic®   The trade name of a franchised, preauthorized payment system for savings institutions that was developed and is offered by SAF Systems and Forms.

traveler's check   An order, over the signature of the issuing company, to pay on demand the amount shown by the denomination of the check. Traveler's checks may be cashed almost anywhere in the world and are insured against loss, theft and destruction.

treasurer's check   *See* cashier's check.

trust   A completed transfer of ownership of property by the owner (grantor) to another (the trustee) for the immediate or eventual benefit of a third person (the beneficiary).

trust agreement   A written agreement under which a grantor transfers legal ownership of property to another person or entity (the trustee) for the benefit of a third person (the beneficiary) subject to the various terms and provisions of a trust.

trustee   The legal title holder and controller of funds in a trust account established for the benefit of another according to a trust agreement.

U   **uncollected funds**   Funds that have been deposited in an account or cashed against an account by a check that has not yet been cleared through the check collection process and paid by the drawee bank. Financial institutions typically place a temporary hold on their customers' uncollected funds, making those funds unavailable for withdrawal until the time period of the hold expires.

unified gift and estate tax credit   An amount used under the federal tax codes to reduce the tax payable on the gross estate.

Uniform Transfers to Minors Act   An act that sets forth provisions for giving a minor an intangible gift (e.g., bank accounts, stocks or bonds) that results in income shifting with an adult serving as custodian. The custodian has direct control over the gift and can sell and reinvest proceeds from the gift for the minor with the minor recognizing any gain and/or annual income that results. The minor's income from the gift cannot be combined with the custodian's property. In some states, the Uniform Gifts to Minors Act accomplishes these same purposes.

unincorporated joint venture   A group of two or more persons joined together informally to carry out a single business objective; when the joint venture has accomplished its objective, it is disbanded.

unity of interest   One of the four requirements of a valid joint tenancy. The unity of interest requires that all joint tenants have the same legal claim and ownership rights to the property. *See also* joint tenancy.

unity of possession   One of the four requirements of a valid joint tenancy. The unity of possession requires that all joint tenants have an undivided share of the whole estate rather than a pro rata share in the estate. *See also* joint tenancy.

unity of time   One of the four requirements of a valid joint tenancy. The unity of time requires that all joint tenants come into ownership at the same time. *See also* joint tenancy.

unity of title   One of the four requirements of a valid joint tenancy. The unity of title requires that all joint tenants receive title by the same conveyance or means. *See also* joint tenancy.

unsecured credit card program   A traditional consumer credit service where the customer is not required to have a deposit relationship with the credit card issuer.

U.S. Savings Bonds   An interest-bearing certificate of debt issued by the United States Treasury. It is non-transferable, noncallable, registered, redeemable at specified redemption values, variable as to time of maturity and fully taxable. *See also* Series HH Bonds and Series EE Bonds.

V **variable as to time of maturity**   A characteristic of U.S. Savings Bonds that allows its redemption at the bondholder's will after a minimum length of time.

vest   To give a person a legally fixed immediate right of present or future enjoyment of ownership.

voluntary association   A body of persons acting together, without charter, but upon the methods and forms used by incorporated bodies in pursuit of some common enterprise.

W **will**   A legal document prepared by an individual that explains how to dispose of his or her property after death.

wire transfer   An electronic transfer of funds from one financial institution to another.